Taking sides in social research

In the past it was generally taken for granted that the goal of social research was the production of objective knowledge, and that this required a commitment to value neutrality. In more recent times, however, both these ideals have come to be challenged, and it is often argued that all research is inevitably political in its assumptions and effects.

In a major contribution to the debate, Martyn Hammersley assesses recent versions of this argument, and also those to be found in the classic and still influential works of C. Wright Mills, Howard S. Becker and Alvin Gouldner. He concludes that the case for partisanship is not convincing, and that an intelligent and sceptical commitment to the principles of objectivity and value neutrality must remain an essential feature of social research.

Martyn Hammersley is Professor in Educational and Social Research at the Open University.

D1386969

01949

Taking sides in social research

Essays on partisanship and bias

Martyn Hammersley

London and New York

First published 2000
by Routledge
2 Park Square, Milton Park, Abingdon, Oxon, OX14 4RN

Simultaneously published in the USA and Canada
by Routledge
270 Madison Ave, New York NY 10016

Transferred to Digital Printing 2006

Routledge is an imprint of the Taylor & Francis Group.

© 2000 Martyn Hammersley

Typeset in Goudy by Taylor & Francis Books Ltd

All rights reserved. No part of this book may be reprinted or reproduced
or utilised in any form or by any electronic, mechanical, or other means,
now known or hereafter invented, including photocopying and recording,
or in any information storage or retrieval system, without permission in
writing from the publishers.

British Library Cataloguing in Publication Data
A catalogue record for this book is available from the British Library.

Library of Congress Cataloging in Publication Data
Hammersley, Martyn.
Taking sides in social research: essays in partisanship and bias/
Martyn Hammersley.
Includes bibliographical references and index.
1. Social sciences–Research. 2. Social sciences–Methodology.
3. Values. I. Title.
H62.H2338   1999
300'.7' 2–dc21   99-31251

ISBN 0–415–20286–8 (hbk)
ISBN 0–415–20287–6 (pbk)

Publisher's Note

The publisher has gone to great lengths to ensure the quality of this
reprint but points out that some imperfections in the
original may be apparent.

Printed and bound by CPI Antony Rowe, Eastbourne

This book is dedicated to
the memory of Peter Foster,
colleague and friend.

Contents

Acknowledgements

My family have borne some of the costs of this book. My love and thanks go to them.

An earlier version of Chapter 1 was given at the University of Plymouth in November 1995, and at the London Institute of Education in June 1996. This was published in D. Scott (ed.) *Values and Educational Research*, Bedford Way Papers No. 9, London Institute of Education, 1999. Chapter 6 is based on a paper presented at the University of Southampton in March 1996, and at the Fourth International Sociological Association Conference on Social Science Methodology, University of Essex, July 1996. I am obliged to those who participated in the discussions on these occasions for their questions and comments. In addition, I am very grateful to Howie Becker for taking the time to comment on Chapter 3, and to Barry Cooper and Max Travers for their responses to an earlier version of Chapter 6. Permission to reprint the latter from *Sociological Research Online* is also acknowledged.

A long-term debt is owed to Roger Gomm, not just for allowing me to include a jointly written paper in this volume, but more importantly for discussions over many years of the issues dealt with throughout the book. Peter Foster was the other participant in those discussions, and he wrote detailed comments on most of the chapters. Indeed, my interest in the whole topic stems from him. I wish he were still with us, not least so that we could continue our discussions into the future – but most of all for his family.

Introduction

In the second half of the twentieth century, much social research moved away from treating natural science as a model, or at least from 'positivist' interpretations of it. Where, in the first half of the century, debate had been about whether or not social research could follow the scientific path (and about what it would mean to do so), by the end there were influential voices among social researchers denying not just the possibility but even the desirability of this project.[1]

One of the key assumptions of the earlier view was that science could produce objective knowledge: accounts that correspond to how the world is. And it was widely believed that this necessitated commitment on the part of scientists to the ideal of value neutrality. It was assumed that by taking the production of knowledge as their sole immediate goal, and seeking to avoid deviation from rational pursuit of that goal, social scientists could minimise error in their findings. This required their maintaining independence from pressures deriving from other goals and interests. Moreover, it was argued that the production of knowledge, or at least of value-relevant knowledge, was sufficient in itself as a worthwhile goal; indeed, that its pursuit warranted public patronage.

Of course, there were always some who rejected various aspects of this position, and especially commitment to value neutrality. But, in recent decades, the balance of opinion has swung to the point where few would defend that principle. At first, despite this, there remained almost universal attachment to the goal of producing objective knowledge. Later, with the growing influence of 'critical' approaches, of relativism, and of postmodernism, even commitment to objectivity has come to be challenged or fundamentally reinterpreted. There have been increasing claims, especially among qualitative researchers, that

---

1 Some also deny that natural scientists themselves operate in the distinctive way they are usually assumed to do. Much of the sociology of scientific knowledge carries this message. See, for example, Woolgar 1988.

enquiry cannot but be partisan; and that it should not pretend to be otherwise. What is required, it is insisted, is that research be explicitly partisan – in the service of social transformation, equality, democracy, social justice, etc. (see, for example, Ben-Tovim *et al.* 1986; Lather 1986a and b; Gitlin *et al.* 1989; Roman and Apple 1989; Troyna and Carrington 1989; Oliver 1992; Back and Solomos 1993; Humphries and Truman 1994; Siraj-Blatchford 1994; Troyna 1995; Griffiths 1998; Moore *et al.* 1998).

These developments are the background to the essays in this book; the aim is to identify and assess the arguments that motivate currently influential notions of researcher partisanship. This is not a straightforward task, however. It is rare today to find the case against value neutrality spelled out in any detail; for the most part, that principle is simply assumed to be discredited. Similarly, partisanship is frequently presented as if it needed little supporting argument; indeed, it is discussed in ways that cover over controversial issues. An influential example is the manner in which Patti Lather begins her article, 'Issues of validity in openly ideological research'. She declares: 'Once we recognise that just as there is no neutral education there is no neutral research, we no longer need apologize for unabashedly ideological research and its open commitment to using research to criticize and change the status quo' (Lather 1986a: 67). She takes this as a *starting point* – something to be 'recognised' – rather than as requiring detailed argument to back it up. And she is not unusual in this attitude.[2]

One reason why there may be little felt need to engage with arguments for value neutrality is that their rejection is in line with an instrumentalist view of knowledge whose influence has spread virtually all the way across both theoretical and political spectra. Knowledge and enquiry are valued today primarily for their contribution to practical activities of one kind or another: political, professional, or commercial. Positions that are very different in orientation nevertheless share this instrumentalism: it is to be found not only in the literature on political partisanship but also among those who are committed to maximising the contribution of research to national economic performance and who commend 'Mode 2' research (Gibbons *et al.* 1994).[3] In other words, there is a general rejection of the idea that social research should be concerned simply with producing value-relevant, objective knowledge. The emphasis, instead, is on the need for research to serve, perhaps even to be integrated into, other

---

2 One of the few voices to have challenged this, in an edited collection dedicated to partisan research, is Daphne Patai. She comments: 'In fact, putting scholarship at the explicit service of politics carries many (and rather obvious) risks, and should not be greeted with the facile assumption that *of course* it is what "we" should do' (Patai 1994: 68 and *passim*; see also Patai and Koertge 1994). Unfortunately, her critique seems to have been largely ignored.

3 See the discussion of 'the communication environment of the social sciences' in Fenton *et al.* 1998: ch. 3. Gibbons *et al.* (1994) deny that Mode 2 work is replacing or ought to replace Mode 1 work, but this is strongly implied by their discussion. In effect, 'Mode 2' is simply a new brand name for applied research, on the occasion of its 'relaunch'.

kinds of practice, whether these are concerned with improving economic productivity or with challenging the political status quo.[4]

Another reason why older arguments about value neutrality and objectivity are no longer taken seriously is that they are believed to have been undercut by developments in the philosophy and sociology of science. Thus, it is by now widely accepted that researchers cannot avoid making assumptions (both factual and evaluative) about the world: assumptions that have not been independently tested. And it is argued that these shape every aspect of their work in fundamental ways. Very often, it is concluded from this that researchers setting out from different positions will necessarily reach different conclusions. On this basis, the very possibility of objective knowledge is denied.[5]

This is just one aspect of an emphasis on how research is itself part of the social world it studies: that it does not operate outside that world, in some pure realm of autonomy. And the lesson drawn from this is that researchers must carry out their work in clear consciousness of its socially situated character. It is on this basis that advocates of researcher partisanship demand that the assumptions underlying research be made explicit, so that control can be exercised over them in terms of ethical and political (not just methodological) criteria. It is also argued that researchers must be aware of the effects that their work has on the world, and seek to bring these under ethical and political control as well. Moreover, in the context of the oppositional politics to which most advocates of partisanship are committed, this translates into the argument that research either supports the status quo or challenges it; and the belief that it must be explicitly directed towards bringing about change. This, in turn, often leads to the conclusion that the task of research goes beyond producing accounts of how and why things are as they are to making clear what is wrong and what must be done to remedy it. Indeed, the fact of reflexivity is often seen as implying that the role of the researcher properly includes collaboration in the political activity necessary to bring about social change.

Behind most notions of researcher partisanship, then, is a commitment to the unity of theory and practice. Sometimes this is based on assumptions that are close to Marxism or Frankfurt critical theory (see, for example, Kemmis 1988). In other versions, it seems to be combined with elements of postmodernism (see, for instance, Gitlin *et al.* 1989). Thus, the findings of research are to be assessed not simply, or perhaps even at all, in terms of the criterion of traditionally understood

---

4 'Critical' research is an interesting test case here. Its name implies the need for independence, but what is meant in practice is independence from the dominant ideology. And, very often, this is taken to imply commitment to an oppositional ideology: socialism, feminism, anti-racism, etc. In this respect the 'critical' approach is simply a mirror image of the view which demands that research should service the state. In both cases, enquiry is subordinated to political goals. See Chapter 5.

5 As a number of writers have pointed out, this conclusion does not follow from the premises; see, for example, Phillips 1990.

validity, but rather in terms of their political assumptions, implications and/or consequences (see Lather 1986a; Gitlin and Russell 1994).

In support of the dismissal of value neutrality, and advocacy of partisanship, appeal is often made to a small number of classic sources: not just to Marx, and Marxist writers (notably Gramsci), but also to C. Wright Mills' book, *The Sociological Imagination*; Alvin Gouldner's article, 'Anti-minotaur: The myth of a value free sociology'; Howard Becker's 'Whose side are we on?'; and Gouldner's 'The sociologist as partisan'. In the terms of Latour's discussion of citation practices in science (Latour 1987), these sources are treated as black boxes: as having established that partisanship is unavoidable, and that the principle of value neutrality can only be an ideology with which political commitments are disguised, consciously or unconsciously. Yet the arguments in these sources are open to serious question, and are sometimes even cited in ways that distort their meaning. Thus, Becker's article, 'Whose side are we on?', is routinely misinterpreted as advocating active partisanship, in the sense of a commitment on the part of the researcher to serve the interests of 'the underdog'.[6] And, while Mills is often appealed to as a model of what we might call the 'engaged' social scientist, what that model entails and the criticisms that have been made of it are rarely given attention. Similarly, though Gouldner's work is widely appealed to, little attention has been given to his notion of 'objective partisanship', and to the problems associated with it.

This tendency in the recent literature for much of the argument underlying rejection of value neutrality, and in support of partisanship, to be taken for granted means that anyone seeking to assess that literature is faced with the initial task of trying to clarify the reasons why these positions are adopted. Moreover, what one finds when doing this is that the assumptions involved are diverse and sometimes in conflict.

Different models of researcher partisanship

Variation in conceptions of researcher partisanship can be sketched in terms of two main dimensions. First, while any conception of partisan research requires that concerns other than truth direct the process of enquiry, some views treat those concerns as additional (and closely related) to the goal of producing knowledge. Indeed, they may even see truth and justice as indivisible. This assumption is characteristic of some strands of the Enlightenment, which hold that 'nature has linked together in an unbreakable chain truth, happiness and virtue' (Condorcet 1955: 193). By contrast, there are approaches that treat other values as *supplanting* the commitment to truth, the latter being dismissed as spurious on sceptical grounds or reinterpreted in relativistic terms (so that

---

6 For a few examples of this dominant interpretation, see Finch 1985: 120; Silverman 1985: 178; Denzin 1989: 23; Punch 1994: 89 and 94; Mac an Ghaill 1991: 116; and Troyna 1995: 397.

there can be conflicting 'truths'). There is, then, a fairly fundamental distinction between those versions of partisan research which retain a commitment to
objectivity, to the possibility of knowledge that is valid from all points of view,
and those that do not. And there is further variation to be found under each of
these headings, as Figure 1.1 shows.

Those who reject the possibility of objective knowledge argue that research
should realise other values in the way it is pursued and/or through the impact
of its findings. Often, one of the values emphasised in this context is diversity
of perspectives. It is argued that this diversity should be celebrated, for
example by 'giving voice' to the marginalised. Moreover, in these terms,
research of more traditional kinds may be treated as intrinsically unethical,
since it sets up validity criteria whose application discriminates against the
views of those who do not accept these criteria. Along these lines, Romm
argues that 'knowledge-construction activities should be linked to cultivating
forms of relationship which do not unfairly authorise particular ways of
accounting at the expense of others' (Romm 1997: 1.2). Here, the aim of
research seems to be to facilitate people expressing themselves in their own

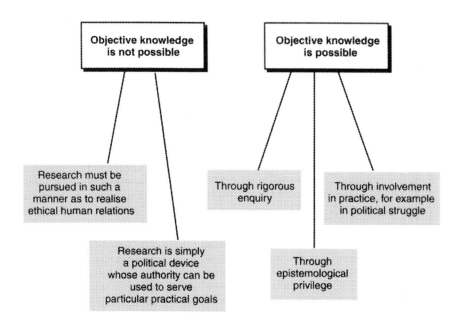

Figure 1.1 Epistemological bases for researcher partisanship

terms, especially those whose voices are not usually heard.[7] Other advocates of partisanship adopt a more 'Machiavellian' approach, treating research and knowledge as political weapons.[8]

For those advocates of researcher partisanship who retain the possibility of objective knowledge, there are at least three ways in which this can be justified. One is similar to that employed by more traditional views of research: involving appeal to some notion of rigorous enquiry. Within the history of Marxism, undoubtedly the most influential tradition espousing researcher partisanship, a range of conceptions of enquiry is to be found, from the more philosophical (often, but not always, modelled on the work of Hegel), through those that appeal to positivist, conventionalist or realist interpretations of natural science, to those informed by structuralism. However, also present in Marx's work, and emphasised by some Marxists, is the idea that the working class is in an epistemologically privileged position to understand capitalist society and how it can and should be transformed (see Lubasz 1969 and McCarthy 1978). This has come to be called 'standpoint epistemology', and has been further developed by feminists; though, of course, with women now occupying the epistemologically privileged position (see Hartsock 1983; Harding 1987). Finally, emphasis may be placed on the role of practical activity, including political struggle, in generating knowledge. This can be found in the literature on 'critical action research' (Carr and Kemmis 1986) and in some feminist views of social enquiry (Mies 1983 and 1991).

It is important to note that those approaches that see objective knowledge as being produced by conventional forms of enquiry usually treat partisanship as an *effect* of such enquiry. It is believed that precisely through being rigorous and objective, and thereby producing sound knowledge, researchers inevitably serve the cause of progress, and thereby the interests of those groups who are currently disadvantaged. By contrast, approaches that adopt the idea of epistemological privilege, or emphasise the role of practical political struggle in generating knowledge, imply that an explicit and conscious partisanship must be built into the research process itself. Thus, it is sometimes argued that feminist research should be characterised by 'conscious partiality' (Mies 1983: 122) or 'strong objectivity' (Harding 1992). Here, paradoxically, the adoption of the perspective and/or the interests of a particular group (for example, women) is seen as essential if objectivity is to be achieved. Any other position is viewed as equally partisan, but as lacking objectivity because it implicates research in ideology.

It is rare to find much clarity among recent advocates of researcher partisanship about which of these various positions is being adopted. Typically, they

---

7   Tierney 1994 takes a similar view. For criticism of Romm's position, see Hammersley and Gomm 1997a.

8   Back and Solomos 1993 come close to this position; see the discussion later in this Introduction. See also Jayaratne's 1983 defence of quantitative method from a feminist point of view.

combine advocacy of partisanship with explicit or implicit commitment to traditional notions of validity, but do not explain how these are to be put together without contradiction. And, sometimes, this is compounded by appeals to relativistic and sceptical ideas about the very possibility of objective knowledge. An example is Siraj-Blatchford, who insists not only on the importance of researchers adopting a '"committed" perspective' (modelled on that of Gramsci), but also on their being 'rigorous and self-critical in terms of the validity and representativeness of their data' (Siraj-Blatchford 1994: 16, 10). However, she does not explain how concepts like validity and representativeness can be sustained within a partisan approach. Similarly, she expresses agreement with Polanyi and Merton that researchers must be committed to 'finding truth through dialogue' (Siraj-Blatchford 1994: 33). Yet, a few pages later, she declares that organic intellectuals 'have a dual role to play: to provide social groups with "homogeneity" and an awareness of their economic, social and political position, and also to assimilate and defeat ideologically the traditional intellectuals' (Siraj-Blatchford 1994: 42). The obvious conflict between engaging in dialogue to discover the truth and setting out to defeat ideological opponents is not commented upon, and seems likely to be intractable.[9] Later still, Siraj-Blatchford claims that 'it is possible to accept the substance of the post modern critique without embracing post modernism as an historical project in itself' (Siraj-Blatchford 1994: 44). Putting aside whether there is a single substance (or can be any 'substance') to postmodernism, and what kind of 'historical project' it could amount to, there is the question of how postmodernism can be combined with a Gramscian position. After all, a central theme of much postmodernist writing is critique of the fundamental assumptions of Marxism and critical theory.[10]

As I have indicated, Siraj-Blatchford is not alone in failing to address the difficult issues involved in the notion of researcher partisanship, and in putting together apparently contradictory ideas. Indeed, there are those who seem explicitly to justify such syncretism. Examples include Stanley and Wise's acceptance of contradiction (Stanley and Wise 1983: 178), and Denzin and Lincoln's notion of the researcher as bricoleur (Denzin and Lincoln 1994; see Hammersley 1999a). Moreover, this is a tendency that is reinforced by some elements of postmodernism, notably its emphasis on playfulness and irony, and its recommendation of non-conventional forms of academic writing such as dialogue and collage.

A second dimension of possible variation among advocates of researcher

---

9 A similar tension can be found in Gillborn 1995; see Hammersley 1998e.
10 Lather's work displays a similar mixture. She moves from an early reliance on Gramsci and other 'critical' writers to a more postmodernist position in later work, while yet somehow retaining a commitment to 'emancipation'. In the same way, Michelle Fine assumes that postmodernism can be combined with a commitment to 'social change' (Fine 1994: 30). Of course, some of the post-structuralist and postmodernist sources on which Lather and others draw also display this ambiguity. See Habermas 1987 and Dews 1987 for powerful critiques.

partisanship is over whether it involves commitment to values, on the one hand, or to the service of some particular category of person, group or organisation, on the other. Figure 1.2 outlines the main possibilities here.

There is a similar vagueness about the position taken on this second dimension among contemporary advocates of researcher partisanship. Thus, Roman and Apple define the task of research as 'to participate in emancipatory and democratizing social transformation, not simply the "neutral" collection, analysis, and reportage of data' (Roman and Apple 1989: 41). However, they do not explicate any of the contestable terms involved in this sentence: 'emancipatory', 'democratizing', 'social transformation', '"neutral"'. Nor do they explain exactly what form participation by researchers in the task of social transformation is to take, or address the problems likely to be associated with this. It is as if the experience of twentieth-century intellectuals in their relations with political parties and movements had been erased from collective memory.

While, on the one hand, there is sometimes an emphasis on the need for independent intellectual judgement in terms of values rather than the subordination of intellectual work to the interests of any particular group (see, for example, Troyna and Carrington 1989), there is also often denial that the researcher has a 'privileged speaking position' (Back and Solomos 1993). Yet the problems with each of these views are not addressed. By contrast, this issue has been a central topic of debate in French discussions of the role of the intellectual. Initially, the contrast here was between, on the one hand, the intellectual as witness to universal values in a world that (perhaps inevitably) tends to ignore them (see, for example, Benda 1927), and, on the other, the idea of engagement, of siding with particular political tendencies or organisations in order to bring about social change (see Schalk 1979). At the same time, there was also conflict between those who, like Sartre, refused to join the Communist Party – insisting on their independence – and those who became

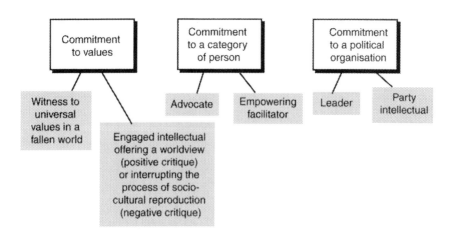

Figure 1.2 Forms of commitment involved in partisanship

party intellectuals. Later, both these models of engagement were rejected, sometimes in favour of what is referred to as the 'specific intellectual', whose task is to put his or her knowledge and skills at the service of groups engaged in local resistance against powerful structures, and/or more generally to subvert the claims of knowledge/power (see Foucault and Deleuze 1972; Foucault 1977; Kristeva 1977; Lyotard 1993). However, there has also been a revival in France of a more modest and conventional conception of the public role of the intellectual, as political commentator (see Aron 1983).[11] While some contemporary Anglo-American advocates of researcher partisanship have appealed to French models, they have not addressed these differences and the debates stemming from them (Young 1973; Barone 1994; Ball 1995).

Rather than seeking to produce a coherent position, many of the advocates of partisanship seem to be more concerned with distancing themselves from views that are open to challenge. A case in point is an article by Back and Solomos on the dilemmas of anti-racist research (Back and Solomos 1993).[12] They begin by rejecting a value-neutral approach, with the comment that it is 'politically naive and methodologically problematic' (Back and Solomos 1993: 182). But they also criticise the work of Ben-Tovim *et al.*, who have argued that research should be an integral part of anti-racist struggle. The charge is that these latter authors do not address important tensions and dilemmas involved in what they recommend, that they claim a 'privileged speaking position', and that they assume that 'the forces of progress are, if not homogeneous, unifiable' (Back and Solomos 1993: 184). Yet, while this discussion makes clear what Back and Solomos reject, the nature of their own position remains obscure.

In the main body of their article, these authors discuss some important dilemmas that they faced in the course of their research on 'race' in local government and politics in Birmingham. One of these dilemmas concerned the effect of the interviewer challenging what he judged to be racist comment on the part of white informants. The authors report that 'this so radically transformed the interactional context in which the interview was taking place that the interview could not continue' (Back and Solomos 1993: 188). They also describe how they adopted a 'profoundly inconsistent' ethical stance, making 'arbitrary decisions about how much access we would allow our informants to the research material and our findings' (Back and Solomos 1993: 189). What this amounted to, it seems, was that black informants were given much more access than white. They also note the problem that, though rejecting the notion of value neutrality, they were sometimes forced to rely on it when presenting their findings publicly (Back and Solomos 1993: 194). They conclude that:

> it is difficult to sustain one ethical position in all contexts. This begs
> the question of the utility of establishing or advocating unitary speaking

---

11 For a history of the idea of the intellectual in twentieth-century France, see Jennings 1997.
12 The results of this research are reported in Solomos and Back 1995.

positions. In the course of doing research it is sometimes necessary to defend spurious speaking/hearing positions. While we see no easy way for research on racism that is not in some way political, we have also found it strategically appropriate to adopt other speaking positions in an attempt to pre-empt accusations of partiality and invalidity.

(Back and Solomos 1993: 196)

In short, 'the necessities of political struggle' demand a 'flexible' approach (Back and Solomos 1993: 197).[13]

What we have here is a justification for inconsistency, on grounds of political expediency. The authors are clearly committed to 'an anti-racist project that can effect change through research' (Back and Solomos 1993: 197). But what they do not tell us is how political and research goals can be reconciled within this. The closest they come to addressing this problem is the comment that:

[while] we are rejecting a 'value free' perspective we still have to show why our account ... is a plausible explanation of processes and events. While we recognize that accounts provided by research are partial, this does not absolve us of the need to provide an analysis which is persuasive.

(Back and Solomos 1993: 196)

However, by using the terms 'plausible' and 'persuasive', in place of 'valid', they seem to imply that what is required is simply that research findings be convincing enough to have the correct political effect. At the same time, these authors expect lay people to treat their research as objective. They complain that when they made 'a political intervention' by sending a copy of an article to those involved in the events described, it was interpreted 'in an extremely selective fashion' (Back and Solomos 1993: 195). In other words, the participants judged it according to its political usefulness for their own purposes. In response to this, Back and Solomos wrote a letter to one of their critics in which they accuse him of 'misunderstanding ... the nature of academic research' (Back and Solomos 1993: 194). Yet it is difficult to see what the complaint could be here, other than that he failed to be deceived by their appeal to value neutrality.

More than most writers, Back and Solomos recognise the dilemmas involved in partisan research, but the only solution they offer involves strategic deception – use of the authority of research to serve political goals. In many ways, this is the opposite of the position adopted by Romm, outlined earlier. But, at a deeper level, these contrasting positions share in common a denial that research is, or ought to be, concerned primarily with the production of knowledge. The contrast between them arises, to a large extent, from differences in the assumed character of the people being studied. Romm presupposes that they will be

---

13 This echoes Gouldner's argument for the strategic use of value neutrality, despite rejecting it in principle; see Gouldner 1965: 14.

people who should be 'given voice'. By contrast, Back and Solomos are dealing with local politicians and officials, whom they regard as part of the power structure that is responsible for racism.[14] In other words, the contrast between the two positions arises from judgements about the moral or political character of those being studied.

Both the dimensions I have discussed raise fundamental and difficult problems, then. And, as the case of Back and Solomos has shown, these are closely related. The first involves epistemological and methodological issues. It is rare for advocates of partisanship to admit, as Gitlin *et al.* do, that their concern is primarily with whose interests are being served (Gitlin *et al.* 1989: 245). But, even here, no explanation is given for how research could be sustained on this basis; after all, its public justification as an activity seems to depend on the assumption that it is committed primarily to the pursuit of knowledge, and therefore to the avoidance of bias. Nor do we find, in the literature on researcher partisanship, explicit value arguments about what goals research ought to serve. Instead, 'whose side to be on' is treated as a foregone conclusion, as if the world were made up of 'goodies' and 'baddies'. Furthermore, what emerges clearly from some accounts, including that of Back and Solomos, is that partisan research is parasitic on what it criticises; in much the same way that, in theoretical terms, scepticism and relativism are parasitic on what they purportedly reject (Hammersley 1998b:19). If more conventional forms of enquiry did not exist, partisan research could not survive.

The issue of the practical role implied by researcher partisanship is also rarely discussed in depth: we are hardly ever told what sort of 'engagement' is legitimate, and why. And it should be noted that most contemporary advocates of partisanship work in universities. As a result, important questions arise about how political engagement of different kinds relates to the proper role of the university academic, a role whose character is far from uncontentious, and which is currently undergoing considerable change.

Given the lack of clarity in the literature on researcher partisanship, my aims in this book are twofold. First, to identify the range of arguments that can be put forward in its favour, and to correct some common misinterpretations of them. Secondly, to subject those arguments to close scrutiny, with a view to reaching a conclusion about the position social researchers ought to take on this issue. The various chapters approach this task from different, though complementary, directions.

An outline of the chapters

The first chapter seeks to clarify what is meant by 'value neutrality', on the one hand, and by 'partisanship', on the other. It then examines two rationales for

---

14 Their research was complicated by the fact that there were some black people in local government. who were themselves victims of racism.

partisanship, classifying these as Enlightenment and post-Enlightenment in character. The first has long been influential within sociology, and within the social sciences generally. It assumes that there is a close relationship, perhaps even amounting to identity, between the pursuit of knowledge and pursuit of the good society. Some Enlightenment thinkers believed that scientific investigation and the knowledge it produces offered a basis for establishing a rational society that would achieve, or at least approximate, human ideals. And some twentieth-century social researchers have inherited the idea that research necessarily contributes to social progress, and that policy-making and practice of all kinds must be founded on it. One recent manifestation is the notion of evidence-based practice. However, other versions treat research as essentially oppositional in character, for example as properly in alliance (overtly or covertly) with those on the margins who have the capacity to create a new type of society that is in the interests of all. The post-Enlightenment rationale, by contrast, rejects the assumption that research is always progressive in character; indeed it often abandons both the belief that knowledge can be anything other than personal expression or social product, and the very idea that there can be socio-political progress. From this point of view, research cannot avoid being partisan because it cannot represent *everyone's* interests. And the conclusion drawn is that researchers must be conscious of, and perhaps explicit about, the cause that their work is designed to serve. I argue that both these rationales are unconvincing. Post-Enlightenment arguments undermine the Enlightenment rationale all too effectively, but are themselves internally contradictory; and they also undercut the very activity of research (and, for that matter, politics too). I point out that Weber's advocacy of the principle of value neutrality drew on post-Enlightenment ideas and provides a justification for research that is far more subtle than most of his critics allow. There are aspects of Weber's position that should not be accepted – for example, the notion that there are ultimate values to which commitment is necessarily irrational. Nevertheless, following Weber, I argue that researchers should be committed primarily to the pursuit of knowledge, and therefore should be as neutral as they can towards other values and interests in their work, in an attempt to maximise the chances of producing sound knowledge of the social world.

C. Wright Mills's book, *The Sociological Imagination*, continues to be influential in shaping ideas about the purpose and character of sociological work. In Chapter 2 I try to clarify Mills' views about the role of the social scientist by comparing them with two of the main sources on which he drew: with Marx and Marxism, on the one hand, using the positions of Gramsci and Althusser as benchmarks; and with Weber, on the other. I suggest that his position is open to serious criticism from both directions, but especially from a Weberian point of view. Drawing on the now quite considerable secondary literature, I argue that while the content of Mills' views and his writing style are close to the Marxist model, his conception of the role of ideas in society is in important respects liberal, owing more to the views of pragmatists like James and Dewey. And, as a result, it suffers from widely recognised weaknesses. Similarly, I suggest that, despite superficial similarities, his opposition to bureaucracy, his commitment to democracy, and his view of the role of the sociologist depart in very significant ways from those of Weber. Mills seems to have ignored the post-Enlightenment elements of Weber's position and to have adopted an Enlightenment view of the task of sociology, treating it as capable of bringing about radical progressive social change, both within the United States and worldwide. My conclusion is that Mills does not provide a convincing case for the role of the politically committed sociologist.

Becker's article, 'Whose side are we on?', is another source that is still frequently cited, thirty years after it originally appeared. And it is usually treated as a classic argument for sociological partisanship, as advocating research designed to serve the interests of underdogs. In Chapter 3 I examine this article in detail, and identify some ambiguities within it. I argue that Becker's central point was that sociologists cannot avoid being interpreted as siding with one party or another in the situations they study. He suggests that this is almost inevitable if they do their work properly: taking account of the perspectives of the diverse groups of people involved, rather than simply relying on official views. However, Becker also insists on the need for researchers to apply scholarly standards in judging evidence, so as to minimise bias, and on the primacy of knowledge production as sociology's goal. Thus, he does not argue that sociologists should set out to be partisan: to produce findings that serve the interests of a particular group or even that seek to realise values other than truth. At the same time, he *does* assume that the pursuit of knowledge will serve the interests of oppositional groups rather than those of the powerful, on the grounds that the latter's position necessarily depends on controlling information and public image. So, paradoxically, he sees research as contributing to the achievement of Leftist political goals precisely by concentrating exclusively on the task of pursuing the truth for its own sake.

The fourth chapter examines Gouldner's influential critique of the principle of value neutrality and his argument for a partisan, or committed, sociology. The form as well as the content of the critique are examined, and its foundation in the sociological analysis of myth and ideology investigated. I show that his argument is undermined by an ambiguity: about whether it is an empirical analysis of value neutrality as an occupational ideology, or a methodological argument about the role of that principle as a guide in sociological work. Of course, Gouldner would probably not have accepted this distinction, but I argue that it is unavoidable; and that his failure to respect it negates the force of his views. Rather than revealing defects in the case for value neutrality, Gouldner's critique displays instead the weaknesses of the kind of sociological analysis he applies. In the second half of the paper, I examine his criticism of Becker and his responses to the reception of *The Coming Crisis in American Sociology*, using these as a basis for clarifying the kind of partisan sociology that he recommended. I argue that he misinterprets Becker's position, and also that his own justification for partisanship is open to serious question. It assumes a highly implausible picture of the relationship between sociological research and politics, and also obscures some fundamental questions about the nature of the good society.

Chapter 5 is concerned with explicating and assessing some more recent arguments in favour of partisanship, which occurred in the field of research on racism in education. It is not surprising to find such arguments in this context. Racism is at odds with the very idea of education, on most interpretations. So the conclusion is sometimes drawn that educational research ought to be anti-racist in its goals; with value neutrality being seen as, at best, the toleration of racism, at worst as a form of racism itself. In this chapter I examine a dispute that arose about the extent of racism among teachers in English schools, trying to specify exactly what is at issue between the two sides, while acknowledging the difficulty in doing so, given my own commitment to one of them. I argue that the dispute is not simply a disagreement about matters of empirical fact, or even about the weight of evidence that is necessary before conclusions can be reached regarding the prevalence of racism. Rather, in many ways, the dispute involves a clash between two different conceptions of social research: between what can be called 'critical' and 'analytic' approaches. These conflict with one another at the most fundamental level: about the purpose of research. I argue that while these two approaches are not incommensurable, in the relativist sense, they do involve a near intractable opposition. Nevertheless, I identify two areas where there may be some scope for reasonable discussion between the protagonists; though I argue that the critical approach is, by its very nature, resistant to such discussion.

The final chapter, written with Roger Gomm, addresses the issue of bias; which is, of course, at the heart of the arguments against partisanship. However, the term 'bias' is by no means straightforward in meaning. Sometimes, it is used to refer to the adoption of a particular perspective, from which some things become salient and others merge into the background. It is more usual, though, for it to refer to systematic error of some kind; in particular to systematic error deriving from a conscious or unconscious tendency on the part of researchers to produce and interpret data in a way that inclines towards erroneous conclusions, conclusions which are in line with their political or practical commitments. Of course, the use of 'bias' to refer to systematic error depends on other concepts, such as 'truth' and 'objectivity', whose justification and role have also been questioned. In particular, it seems to rely on discredited foundationalist assumptions of an epistemological kind. Moreover, the various radical epistemological positions that some social scientists have adopted as an alternative, such as relativism and standpoint epistemology, either deny the validity of this concept of bias – explicitly or implicitly – or transform it entirely. In this chapter, we argue that while it is true that abandonment of a foundationalist conception of science has important implications for the meaning of 'bias' and its associated concepts, they are defensible; indeed, that they form an essential framework for research as a social practice. In this context, we examine error as a matter of collegial accountability, and define 'bias' as referring to one of several potential forms of error. We conclude by pointing to what we see as the growing threat of bias in the present state of social research, not least as a result of researcher partisanship.[15]

Social research has long been in recurrent crisis, and many of the issues central to that crisis have not changed. Thus, debates about objectivity, value neutrality, and the proper relationship between research and various forms of practice (especially politics) have a long history. Unfortunately, the attention given to these issues does not seem to have led to more sophisticated understanding of the problems involved, or of the different positions that can be taken towards these. Instead, much the same points have been repeated, and often in increasingly corrupt forms; they have become little more than slogans. While my aim in these essays is to elaborate a particular position on the issue of partisanship, I have also tried to present the arguments involved in some detail, both those to be found in what are now treated as classic sources and those implicated in contemporary debates. I hope that even readers who are not convinced by the position I adopt will nevertheless find the book useful in clarifying what is at stake.

15 This chapter was previously published in *Sociological Research Online*, and attracted some critical comment: see Romm 1997 and Temple 1997; see also Hammersley and Gomm 1997a and b.

1   Taking sides in research

An assessment of the rationales for partisanship

It is increasingly common to find the argument presented that researchers should explicitly align themselves with some particular group or category of actor, carrying out research in such a way as to serve that group's interests. Among the most explicit declarations of partisanship, currently, are: feminists who define the goal of their work as to promote the emancipation of women (Mies 1991); anti-racist researchers who see their task as to participate in the struggle against white racism (Back and Solomos 1993); and disability researchers who formulate their goal as empowering the disabled to emancipate themselves from the conditions imposed on them by able-bodied society (Oliver 1992; Zarb 1992).

However, arguments that research should be partisan are by no means restricted to such overtly political forms. For example, there are frequent calls for social research in particular substantive areas to serve the needs of the professionals who work in them. Hence, it is sometimes argued that, first and foremost, educational research ought to contribute to the process of education, and this is interpreted as being achieved by inquiry that is structured so as to facilitate the work of teachers or of educational managers. Indeed, very often it is proposed that educational practitioners themselves should carry out research, not outside academics, so as to *ensure* that inquiry makes a direct contribution to practice (Stenhouse 1975; Gitlin *et al.* 1989; Bassey 1995; Hargreaves 1996).

Another type of call for partisanship is involved in demands that research be dedicated to meeting the economic and social requirements of national societies. For example, it has in recent years become the declared aim of the Economic and Social Research Council that the research it funds should serve the needs of users, helping 'the government, businesses and the public to understand and improve the UK's economic performance and social well-being' (ESRC Annual Report 1993/4: back cover). Here, it seems, research is required to be partisan in a nationalistic sense.

All this advocacy of partisanship, albeit of diverse kinds, represents an important change over the past twenty years or so. As I noted in the Introduction, great emphasis was previously given to the role of objectivity in enquiry, and very often this was taken to imply neutrality towards values other than truth. Today, however, there are very few defenders of the principle of value neutrality, and even the concept of objectivity has been challenged in some quarters (see, for example, Eisner 1992 and Harding 1992).

However, it is difficult to gauge the significance of this shift: to know if, or how far, it implies a change in views about actual research practice. One of the reasons for this is that there is a considerable lack of clarity in the way that such words as 'partisanship' and 'value neutrality' are used, and in the arguments that can be read as promoting or rejecting what they stand for. In short, it is often not easy to identify what statements about the goals and practice of social research actually imply in concrete terms. What we have are general declarations about 'whose side' research should be on, or whose needs it should serve, but not always any clear indication of how, or how far, such commitments ought to shape the research process.

A first requirement, then, is clarification of what 'value neutrality' and 'partisanship' could mean. What is at issue here is the proper nature of the relationship between research and values, the latter being interpreted in a wide sense to refer to any type of goal, interest or preference.

The meanings of 'value neutrality' and 'partisanship'

The term 'value neutrality' or 'value freedom' is sometimes used to refer to the view that research can be and should be free from the influence of *all* values. This interpretation is generally adopted by critics of value neutrality, rather than by those who advocate it. And, indeed, it is self-contradictory, because in pursuing knowledge researchers must necessarily treat truth as a value. Most defenders of value neutrality have drawn a distinction between truth and other values, often labelling the latter as 'practical' because they lie outside the 'theoretical' realm of research. And some have argued on this basis that research should take no account of practical values: it should be solely concerned with the pursuit of knowledge for its own sake. However, most defenders of value neutrality believe that practical values can and should play an important role in the selection of problems for investigation, and in operating as ethical constraints on *how* knowledge is pursued.

There are other areas of ambiguity as well. One concerns the nature of the claims made under the heading of value neutrality. Some take these to be factual in character, so that those who adhere to value neutrality are interpreted as assuming that research can be, and often is, unaffected by practical values. Most advocates of value neutrality, however, treat it as a principle that should guide their behaviour, recognising that commitment to this principle does not guarantee the elimination of bias deriving from practical commitments. In short, they see value neutrality as an ideal not as a fact.

Another source of ambiguity concerns not the effects of practical values on the pursuit of research but rather the *implications* of research findings and the *consequences* of their publication, as evaluated in terms of practical values. Some critics of the principle of value neutrality argue against it on the grounds that all research has implications and consequences that are relevant to practical values, and therefore cannot be value neutral. Indeed, they may go beyond this to claim that the character of those implications and consequences is determined by the orientation of the researcher (conscious or unconscious) and/or by the institutional and cultural framework within which the research was carried out.[1] Most defenders of value neutrality, however, would draw a distinction between the factual conclusions of research, on the one hand, and evaluations of its implications and consequences, on the other; they would not see any logical relation between the two. For this and other reasons, they may also deny that researchers have primary responsibility for the implications and consequences of their research, outside of narrowly defined ethical limits.

A final source of ambiguity concerns what commitment to the principle of value neutrality implies about researchers. Some interpretations suggest that it requires them to be completely apolitical in their personal orientations. Others propose only that researchers should strive to minimise the effects of their non-research commitments on their work. Yet others argue that such commitments play a legitimate role in research, and that it is only their capacity to produce bias that must be controlled. Despite these differences, though, most advocates of value neutrality agree that researchers must not seek to promote practical values through research.[2]

The most influential presentation of the case for the principle of value neutrality, and also one of the most sophisticated, is that of Max Weber (Weber 1949; Bruun 1972). For him value neutrality is an ideal: research should be primarily concerned with the pursuit of knowledge, so that the value of truth must have primacy as a goal for the researcher (as researcher) over all other values. He also argues against the expression of practical value judgements in academic contexts. At the same time, he believed that research should be value *relevant*. This means that the phenomena studied must be selected, indeed conceptualised, on the basis of their relevance to practical values. He also argued that researchers could produce evaluations of and prescriptions for policy, albeit of a conditional kind: conditional on acceptance of the ultimate practical values presupposed. Finally, he certainly did not believe that social scientists should renounce political commitments; quite the reverse. While Weber emphasises that ultimate values are multiple and in conflict, and that science cannot and

---

1 This argument can be framed in terms of epistemology, of functionalist sociology, or of psychoanalytic psychology; though each has faced criticism. The analogy between this argument and certain kinds of explanation of crime in terms of the character or circumstances of the offender (for instance, that bad behaviour must have been produced by bad conditions) is striking; see Matza 1969. For a discussion of the argument that research is necessarily political, see Hammersley 1995a: ch. 6.

2 I will not discuss the role of values in research ethics here. On this see Hammersley and Atkinson 1995: ch. 10. In my view, ethical considerations cannot be framed in terms of serving one 'side' or another; but then neither do I believe that politics should be reduced to this, except in very extreme situations.

should not pretend to validate choices amongst them, he nevertheless regarded value relevance as an essential feature of social research.[3]

In summary, then, the term 'value neutrality' has been used to refer to a number of different positions. Moreover, there is potential overlap between some of these, including that of Weber, and interpretations of research as partisan. While, for Weber, research must be value neutral in the sense of pursuing the truth, it can be partisan in the limited respect that problems must be selected for investigation – and explanations, theoretical evaluations and prescriptions constructed – so as to be of direct relevance to particular practical values, and thereby perhaps to the interests of specific groups or categories of actor. Despite this, the term 'partisanship' is probably better reserved for views that allow a larger and non-conditional role for practical values within research. Here, the goal that governs the research process would be a practical one, rather than (as with Weber) solely the production of practically relevant knowledge. This implies that decisions about how the research is carried out, what is reported and how, etc. need to take account of the interests of the group or party being served, not just considerations of validity and relevance. Indeed, in effect, the task may be to put forward the strongest possible case for (or against) some policy, in line with those interests. Thus, on this definition, partisanship requires not only that researchers be explicit about their political commitments, but also that they should act directly upon them. As a result, there is no restriction placed on evaluation and prescription in research reports. Indeed, policy recommendations become the main products of research, and researchers are often seen as responsible for the implementation of these recommendations (alone or in collaboration with others), and presumably also for their consequences.[4]

In the remainder of the chapter I want to examine the arguments for partisanship in research, in the sense outlined above. Two approaches will be identified that, for convenience, I will refer to as the Enlightenment and post-Enlightenment rationales. These two rationales are not always clearly distinguished by those who argue for partisanship; even though, as we shall see, they conflict in important respects.

The Enlightenment view

> There is a trinity against which the gates of hell will never prevail: the true, which brings forth the good; and from both of these the beautiful.
>
> (Diderot; quoted in Allen 1993:41)

---

3 For discussion and criticism of value neutrality, and further references, see Foss 1978 and Proctor 1991.

4 Elsewhere, I have distinguished between academic and practical research; see Hammersley 1999b. It is perhaps worth stressing that practical research is not necessarily partisan in the sense outlined here. It simply involves stress on the need for findings to have direct practical relevance.

The term 'Enlightenment' is, of course, problematic. As Gay (1963) points out, our image of the Enlightenment is to a considerable degree the image of it projected by the Romantics and other critics, and much of our sense of unity in the views of the *philosophes* is a product of that image. In this paper, I will use the term 'Enlightenment view' to refer to a specific idea that was influential in the eighteenth century, and that was shared by many but not all of those usually thought of as Enlightenment thinkers. This is the notion that the value of truth is strongly interrelated with other progressive values, such as freedom, equality and social welfare.[5] A great deal is often built on this idea. It may be taken to imply that, fundamentally, there are just two sides in politics: the progressive and the reactionary. And the justification for taking sides – and for which side to take – is built into the very language used. How could one be against progress or human emancipation? It is for this reason that we find social researchers advocating, or declaring that research is to contribute to, 'social change'; as if such change could only be in one direction. According to this view, then, research (properly conceived and executed) is by definition a progressive force in the world, in that it serves the goals of human improvement or emancipation. There is assumed to be a close link between the universalism of knowledge (that it is true for everyone) and universal human interests. At the same time, like progressive politics, research is partisan in the sense that it supports those who are working for the universal good and opposes those who are not: in short, it serves the party of humanity. This stance is what Gouldner (1973a: ch. 2) and Pateman (1981: 2) refer to as 'objective partisanship'. The Enlightenment view implies that were intellectuals not to be partisan in this sense they would be engaged in the production of ideology, creating myths that protect particular, and therefore reactionary, interests. And this would be a betrayal of their commitment to truth.

Intrinsic to this position is the idea that science, or reason more generally, can produce conclusive knowledge about all matters relevant to bringing about desirable social change, both factual and valuational. For this reason, value commitment is not regarded as endangering the objectivity of research (that is, its capacity to discover the truth), so long as the values pursued are genuine ones (because of the close affinities among, if not ultimate equivalence of, such values). And, given the assumption that there are only two sides in politics, it is concluded that ideology can only come from one direction. Initially, it was seen as deriving from the traditional authorities of the past (the Church and 'unenlightened' rulers), and as being dispelled by the rational thinking of the moderns. Subsequently, particular groups within the modern world came to be regarded as constituting the source of ideology. For example in the case of Marx, in the context of capitalism, it was the bourgeoisie.

---

5 This idea was not novel to the eighteenth century; it is also to be found in medieval and ancient philosophy. However, the influential form it takes today derives primarily from the Enlightenment period.

On this Enlightenment view, then, research ought to be explicitly and consciously directed towards social improvement, emancipation, etc. Along with this, it may be argued that theoretical frameworks should be selected at least partly on value grounds, and the validity of hypotheses judged not just in terms of the evidence but also on the basis of their practical implications and consequences.[6] For example, in his classic article, 'Decolonializing applied social sciences', Rodolfo Stavenhagen argues that macro theories about national societies should be selected and evaluated according to the values of those who use them, and how adequate they prove to be in political terms. He claims that 'in the long run any theory of society ... will be validated by its utility as an instrument of action in the hands of organized social groups' (Stavenhagen 1971: 335). And the organised social groups he has in mind are those who are engaged in 'progressive' political change.

The distinctive feature of the Enlightenment perspective, then, is that it presents partisanship of a certain kind as serving universal interests, and therefore as consonant with pursuit of that other universal value, truth. There are, however, several ways in which this universalisation or objectification of the value of partisanship has been attempted; and several different parties supposedly representing universal interests, which research should therefore serve if it is to be enlightening.

One of the most influential versions of this position is, of course, Marxism; which was for a long time the main example of explicitly partisan inquiry in the social sciences. As Lichtheim notes, according to Marx:

> History is kept going by class struggles, and the proletarian class interest is viewed as the form in which, under modern conditions, Reason affirms itself as the organising principle of society. What appears to the empirical sociologist as the assertion of a sectional group interest is regarded by Marx as the (partly conscious) mechanism of a process whereby 'prehistory' is overcome, and mankind is 'brought to itself'.
>
> (Lichtheim 1966: 3)

What is distinctive about Marxism, compared with many earlier Enlightenment views, then, is that it presents a philosophy of history, a transformation of Hegel's *Phenomenology of Mind*, in which progressive values are immanent in the historical process. Like Hegel, Marx saw history as culminating (at least potentially) in the realisation of true, that is ideal, human nature. Thus, he put forward a picture of history as the dialectical overcoming of humanity's alienation from its own nature. He saw human beings' estrangement from *external*

---

6 This does not necessarily follow from adoption of the Enlightenment view. Instead, the latter may motivate a single-minded pursuit of knowledge, in the belief that this necessarily has progressive political consequences. This seems to be Howard Becker's position in 'Whose side are we on?' (Becker 1967); see Chapter 3.

nature as having been superseded through development of the forces of production, but this had occurred only at the expense of increased alienation of people
from one another, that is of alienation from *true human nature*. He argued that
this process had reached its most intense form in Western capitalism, where the
material resources necessary for human liberation from nature are available but
the relations of production represent the most extreme level of social alienation. Thus, he believed that capitalism contained all the preconditions for the
self-realisation of humanity. It perfected the forces of production that provided
the material base for such self-realisation. Equally important, from a subjective
point of view, the extreme social alienation of the working class under capitalism supplied them with a perspective for understanding its nature and a
motive for bringing about radical change, to a communist society.[7]

For these reasons, Marx saw the Western proletariat as the universal class
whose victory over the bourgeoisie would herald *human* emancipation. It had
privileged access to the knowledge that would abolish alienation, and was in a
position to act on it. Partisanship in favour of the working class was thus
universalised, being presented as service to humanity as a whole. Indeed, Marx
assumed that knowledge about the world is intimately related to the dialectical
process by which society develops. As Maurice Merleau-Ponty comments in his
book, *The Adventures of the Dialectic* [summarising Lukács interpreting Marx]:
'The "historical mission of the proletariat", which is the absolute negation of
class, the institution of a classless society, is at the same time a philosophical
mission of the advent of truth' (Merleau-Ponty 1973: 45–6). And the converse
was also taken to be the case: that the pursuit of knowledge must be guided by
the project of achieving a classless society. For Marx, as for Hegel, the proper
task of philosophy or science was to serve History, conceived as the process in
and by which humanity realised (in both senses of that term) its true character.

Much research that is not explicitly Marxist has been influenced by this kind
of philosophy of history. Thus, the 'critical' tradition, which has generated critical sociology, critical ethnography, critical discourse analysis and critical
orientations in many other areas often relies on it, albeit implicitly (see
Hammersley 1992a: ch. 6). It has also influenced some versions of feminist
research, notably those promoting 'standpoint epistemology' (Smith 1974; Flax
1983; Hartsock 1983; Harding 1986 and 1987).

However, in recent times the adoption of this type of philosophy of history
has waned in many fields, even among Marxists. In part, what has happened is
its transformation into a more limited and ahistorical form, which I will call

---

7 As should be clear, in my view there is no sharp distinction to be drawn between the early and
the late Marx; see Avineri 1968. However, Enlightenment views of the role of knowledge can
also be found among those who draw such a distinction and base their Marxism exclusively on
the later Marx: 'In principle, true ideas always serve the people; false ideas always serve the
enemies of the people' (Althusser 1971: 24, cited in Collier 1979: 67). This echoes Lenin's
'Marxism is all-powerful because it is true', which was the epigraph of the Althusserian journal,
Cahiers marxistes-léninistes: see Reader 1995: 33.

'radical egalitarianism'. This is a view that appears to govern the thinking of many of those who see research as necessarily, or as properly, value-committed. Here a model of oppression is adopted that points to disparities in power between different categories of person (men and women, whites and blacks, able-bodied and disabled, etc.). And the abolition of these inequalities is presented as in the interests of everyone, equality being the proper state of humanity. Moreover, since from this point of view oppression can only be overcome by subordinate groups acting on their own behalf (rather than by members of the dominant group 'liberating' them), the duty of the researcher is to serve subordinate and marginalised groups (see, for example, Griffiths 1998).

Alongside Marxism, and developments out of it like radical egalitarianism, there has been a competing tradition that also provides a basis for partisanship, albeit with a rather different political complexion. It too derives from the Enlightenment. I will refer to it as French positivism, since it is exemplified in the work of Saint-Simon, Comte and Durkheim; though it came to be very influential in and through twentieth-century American sociology.[8] It involves a more linear conception of social development than Marxism, focusing on the shift from traditional to modern societies. Once again, though, this position assumes that there is an intrinsic compatibility between social research and the values of the modern world. Science and rational understanding are seen both as products of social development and as important means for furthering it. Thus, Comte regarded sociology as the pinnacle of the sciences and as providing the basis for a new, scientifically validated type of social formation. In a more modest way, Durkheim saw sociological research as playing an essential role in diagnosing the ills of transitional societies and in facilitating their transformation into a fully modern mode of social organisation (Lukes 1973; Bryant 1985).

While there is no equivalent to the standpoint epistemology of Marxism within this positivist version of the Enlightenment view, there are particular categories of actor who are treated as the key audience for the knowledge produced by social research. Where for Marxists this audience was the working class, for the positivists, generally speaking, it is politicians, administrators and professionals of various kinds. Here too, though, the assumption is that scientific analysis can understand the nature of the rational society, and how it is to be achieved; so its products must be made available to those with the power to bring about change.[9]

In practice, the difference between Marxist and positivist views of the relationship between research and practice is less sharp than is sometimes supposed,

8 An example is Coleman's view of the proper relationship between research and practice in modern societies; see Coleman 1972.
9 There is a parallel here with the relationship between some eighteenth-century philosophers and enlightened despots; though, of course, most twentieth-century positivists have taken for granted some kind of democratic polity.

and the two traditions have often been drawn on simultaneously. Thus, Engels' construction of Marxism was influenced by positivism, as was that of some later Marxists (see Kolakowski 1978: ch. XVI). And, with Lenin and the emergence of the Soviet Union, great emphasis came to be placed in orthodox Marxism on the role of the Communist Party, and subsequently on that of the socialist state, in determining the interests of the working class. As a result, social research was seen as properly partisan if it served the goals of party and state officials, that is of those in power.

We can also see the combined influence of positivism and Marxism in much British sociology of the 1950s and early 1960s. At this time there were attempts to separate Marx's sociology from his philosophy and politics (see, for example, Bottomore and Rubel 1956: ch. 1; Dahrendorf 1959: 27–32). And the scientific sociology that was being developed on the basis of the work of the founders of the discipline – Marx, Durkheim and Weber – was often viewed as capable of playing a key role in advising social democratic governments. Glass's argument for sociologically trained policy-makers and administrators is significant here, as is the role that Halsey and others played in advising the Labour Government of the mid-1960s, notably in relation to education policy (Glass 1950; Kogan 1971).

We can also find an integration of positivism and Marxism, of a rather different kind, in the work of Alvin Gouldner. While his political commitments were very much of the radical Left, and were informed by Marxism, his stance draws on positivism as well; not least in seeing the discipline of sociology as playing a central role in transforming society. This is summed up in the title of one of his books, *For Sociology*, which was a response to Althusser's *Pour Marx* (Althusser 1969). Gouldner believed that sociologists should be partisan in the Enlightenment sense, in that through pursuing their work they simultaneously contribute to transforming the world in the direction of how it ought to be. He writes:

> social theory must determine, evaluate, critique the conditions that enable it to organize itself; in *enacting* these conditions it tests and appraises the worth of the theory it has established. In establishing and testing these conditions for itself social theory also acts universalistically, on behalf of the rest of the world. For the quest for rational discourse is not a sectarian need of social theorists alone but a world need.
>
> (Gouldner 1973a: 93)

Here it seems almost as if sociologists have become the revolutionary class.

I have looked at two fairly elaborate Enlightenment-based rationales for partisan research, Marxism and French positivism, plus some variations on each. However, the link from partisanship to universalism can be provided in less theoretically elaborated ways. For example, the view that social research ought to serve the professions is often supported by appeal (usually implicit) to the idea that those occupations are based on an altruistic service orientation:

that they work in everyone's interests.[10] Similarly, the belief that social research should service the state may be legitimated by the notion that liberal social democratic governments work to represent the public interest. And the idea that research ought to meet national economic needs can be supported by a model of international society as a non-zero sum game in which economic competition among nations increases the welfare of *all* of them.[11]

From all these Enlightenment points of view, then, there is a harmony between social inquiry and social improvement, defined in various ways. Research is seen as a precondition for progress and the contribution that it makes in this respect constitutes its major if not its sole justification. Equally, it is assumed that a commitment to the social good cannot *distort* inquiries into truth; indeed, it may be taken to enhance them. So, there is no need for neutrality in this respect. Distortion can only be produced by the influence of the wrong values, these being seen as ideological representations of particularistic interests.

This Enlightenment view is not an easy one to defend today, in any of its forms. Its basic assumptions have been subjected to a great deal of telling criticism from the late eighteenth century onwards. Romanticism questioned the contribution of reason to human life, reviving recognition of the value of myth and feeling. The historicists emphasised the diversity of cultures, and proclaimed their intrinsic validity. Indeed, the possibility was raised that Reason is simply the expression of modern Western culture and therefore itself partial and particularistic. Nietzsche denied the harmony of values and questioned the practical value of knowledge, insisting for example on the 'disadvantages of the study of history' (Nietzsche 1874). Increasingly, it came to be recognised that there are competing value perspectives, and that reason does not offer any guaranteed resolution of the conflicts among them (Berlin 1990). Similarly, the capacity of reason to produce even factual knowledge whose validity is absolute began to be widely questioned, as was the assumption that rationality is actually the most important determinant of human action. At the end of the nineteenth century and in the first decades of the twentieth century there was growing recognition of the role of the irrational in human behaviour (Hughes 1959). And the experience of the West in the twentieth century provided prima-facie evidence, at the very least, against any intrinsic harmony of values, and in particular against the idea that the pursuit of knowledge always promotes the good. The most significant events here were the use of science and technology by both sides in the First World War and, in the Second World War, by the Nazis in concentration camps, and by the Allies in developing and using the atom bomb.

These changing attitudes towards reason and science led to increasing

---

10 This assumption was characteristic of much early sociological work in the field; see, for example, Carr-Saunders and Wilson 1933 and Marshall 1963.

11 For evidence of the origins of this in free-trade theory, see Johnson 1968.

criticism of Enlightenment progressivism, of the kind represented by French positivism. And Marxism also attracted criticism, initially for creating the political disorder out of which fascism rose to power, later for the vices of 'actually existing socialism' in Eastern Europe. In addition, the philosophies of history or meta-narratives on which both traditions relied were increasingly dismissed as non-scientific, as recklessly over-reaching what it is possible for science to validate.[12] Nor have their empirical predictions fared well against subsequent events. Contrary to Marx, the development of advanced capitalist societies did not lead to the growth and immiseration of the Western working class or to the emergence of revolutionary consciousness on their part.[13] In a rather similar way, and not without irony, the predictions of some American sociologists in the 1950s that all modern societies were converging towards a common model involving the end of ideological politics was undermined by the civil and student unrest of the 1960s, and the subsequent emergence of black power, feminist and environmentalist movements.[14]

A further development in the 1970s and 1980s was that criticism of such philosophies of history became widespread not just on the Right but also on the Left, where they had previously been most influential. Particularly significant in this respect has been the work of structuralists, post-structuralists and post-modernists. They have subjected Enlightenment meta-narratives, especially Marxism, to moral and political as well as to intellectual criticism, arguing that such totalising perspectives are themselves oppressive. In part, their critique reflects the fact that, in the twentieth century, nation-states have increasingly appealed to Enlightenment values to legitimate themselves. And, of course, the reality of twentieth-century politics has fallen a long way short of its ideals. On the evidence of the terrors perpetrated by regimes that claimed to embody Enlightenment values, many post-structuralists and postmodernists argued that teleological meta-narratives simply operate as weapons by which some groups dominate others; in other words that they are themselves essentially totalitarian.[15] Also influential was recognition of the way in which these ideas served (or at least could be used to serve) the political and commercial interests of the West against the Third World.

In these ways, the ideas that support the Enlightenment position have

---

12 It is perhaps important to note that twentieth-century logical positivism played an important role in this critique.

13 There is, of course, some debate about the precise nature of Marx's theory, and therefore about the validity of the predictions he makes; as well as about how much leeway one should allow for the effects of historical contingency. But the Marxist idea that the proletariat represents the universal class, which has the potential to bring about human emancipation, seems to have been abandoned by many Marxists and critical theorists in the twentieth century. On the concept of the revolutionary proletariat, see Lubasz 1969 and McCarthy 1978.

14 See Shils 1955; Bell 1960; Lipset 1960: ch. 13. For an assessment of the end of ideology thesis, see MacIntyre 1971: ch. 1. See Goldthorpe 1964 on the 'convergence thesis' generally.

15 This is a view that had already been developed in a different form by Adorno and Horkheimer; see Jay 1973: ch. 8.

become discredited. And the other, less elaborate, rationales for universalising partisanship have not fared much better. Radical egalitarianism has been challenged by a resurgent neo-liberal Right that has emphasised the costs of pursuing equality, for personal autonomy and general welfare. There are also problems arising from the fact that radical egalitarianism assumes that there is a consensus about what forms of inequality are inequitable.[16] As a result, even on the Left, many have come to value difference as much as equality.

Also problematic is the idea that the professions are altruistic in motivation and in how they function in society. This idea was subjected to sharp sociological analysis long ago, as well as to political criticism from both Left and Right. It was pointed out that, at least to some extent, professionalism operates as an ideology by which occupations compete with one another for status, and that it disguises the way they serve powerful interests (see Becker 1970: ch. 6; Johnson 1972). Thus, professionals are often concerned with maintaining or expanding their own domains, or with furthering their interests in some other respect, not solely with serving their clients. And in doing this, it was sometimes suggested, they play a wider role in social reproduction, thereby sustaining inequality. Meanwhile, from the Right, professionalism was criticised as a restrictive practice that distorted the operation of the market and thereby interfered with the maximisation of consumer satisfaction. In my view, it is difficult to deny that there is *some* truth in both of these criticisms. Furthermore, as with radical egalitarianism, there is the ever-present danger that pursuit of one value, however altruistically, will have negative consequences for others.

The idea that the state serves the public interest, and the notion that universal interests are promoted by economic competition amongst nation-states, have also been questioned. Marxist and other analyses of the role of the state in capitalist societies have highlighted its partisanship in favour of particular interests (Miliband 1969). Liberals, too, increasingly see the state as necessarily committed to certain substantive ideals; even when it is only concerned with counterbalancing powerful groups and keeping the peace, rather than with promoting some broader conception of the common good.[17] And the application of neo-classical economics to international relations seems even less appropriate than it is to national and local markets. It represents a neglect of the political factors operating in that field.[18]

I suggest, then, that what I have called the Enlightenment view is no longer intellectually credible, even though its influence remains widespread. However, many of those who have rejected it have nevertheless retained the belief that social inquiry should be value-committed and partisan. They have done this on the basis of what I will call post-Enlightenment philosophy.

---

16 For a discussion of the complexities surrounding judgements of equality and inequality, see Hammersley 1997.

17 See Larmore 1987, Galston 1991, and Douglass *et al.* 1988.

18 See the arguments, from different positions, of Kennedy 1993 and Huntingdon 1996.

The post-Enlightenment view

> For a philosopher to say, 'the good and the beautiful are one', is infamy; if he
> goes on to add, 'also the true', one ought to thrash him.
>
> (Nietzsche; quoted in Allen 1993: 41)

Like its predecessor, the post-Enlightenment view also presents research as
necessarily involving practical values, and therefore recommends that it should
be explicitly directed towards serving political goals. Advocates of this position
very often portray the principle of value neutrality as simply an ideological
device that obscures the value commitments of researchers, the effects of these
on their work, and the social functions which that work performs. For them, it
is not a matter of value-neutral versus value-committed research; the only
significant contrast is between research that makes its value commitments and
their role explicit, and that which does not; or that which is directed towards
serving some political cause and that which does not recognise the political
cause it serves.

Those adopting the post-Enlightenment view also very often share with proponents of some versions of Enlightenment philosophy a conception of partisanship
as involving opposition or resistance to the status quo. However, there is no explicit
reliance here on a historicist meta-narrative to justify this opposition. As I
noted, such meta-narratives have come to be rejected as cognitively indefensible
and/or as totalitarian, often in reaction against the use of rationalism as a justification for state power and for Western imperialism. Nor is there explicit
reliance on a concept of science or reason as giving access to the truth by pene-
trating the dominant ideology. In the context of the post-Enlightenment view,
social critique becomes epistemological critique: the claims of the powerful to
represent truth, progress, etc. are rejected not on the grounds that they have
distorted these ideals but because no knowledge is possible of what is true or
good in universalistic terms. Rationality, in this sense, can only be a pretence.

Unlike its predecessor, then, the post-Enlightenment view does not claim
that research serves, or can serve, universal interests, since there are none. It
also rejects the notion that there are political or practical goals that are in
intrinsic harmony with truth. Indeed, the concept of truth itself is frequently
jettisoned, at least as understood in terms of some kind of correspondence
between idea and reality. From this point of view, there is no such thing as
objective knowledge, there are simply 'knowledges' from different perspectives
that are likely to be in conflict, so that in a fundamental epistemological sense
all research is necessarily partisan. There is no rational basis for choosing
amongst these perspectives: we must commit ourselves to one or other of them
in an irrational, or at least non-rational, manner. Nor is there any guarantee
that pursuing research will have good and not bad effects. Given this, it is the
implications or consequences of a piece of research that are crucial, not its
'validity'; though, of course, its *perceived* validity may well affect those conse-

quences. The injunction that seems to follow is that researchers must seek to ensure, above all, that their work serves the cause to which they are committed. Thus, we find Foucault and Deleuze representing theory as no more than a means of challenging power, as a weapon (Foucault and Deleuze 1972).

The post-Enlightenment view has its sources in the work of nineteenth-century critics of Hegel, such as Kierkegaard and Nietzsche; and among the most influential twentieth-century versions of post-Enlightenment philosophy are existentialism and, more recently, post-structuralism and postmodernism. Thus, many existentialists argued against Cartesian, Hegelian and any other kind of rationalism.[19] They portrayed the human condition as involving, in Sartre's terms, the opposition between Being and Nothingness. He argued that human beings cannot be defined by a set of fixed qualities. We are self-creating in the sense that we determine what we shall be by the life choices we make. In this way, people project meaning on to a world that has no intrinsic rationality or meaning. Thus, while recognition of the meaninglessness of the world and the imposition of meaning on it are positively valued as the only authentic mode of human life, there can be no rational foundation, no universal justification, for the projection of any *particular* meaning on the world (Whiteside 1988: 110). The result of this is a sociology that sees conflict as inevitable, and a politics that offers no justification for compromise or negotiated settlement; quite the reverse, in fact, it validates wars to the death.[20] As Raymond Aron remarks in his book, *Marxism and the Existentialists*:

> The Sartrian consciousness is solitary, self-translucid, and alienated in matter; and, as a result of uniqueness, each man becomes the enemy of every other. It is only by revolt, in violent action, that men together escape solitude and inhumanity, pending their mutual recognition.
>
> (Aron 1969: 9)

And he concludes:

> If humanity begins with revolt, it must endlessly repeat an enterprise which cannot succeed and which cannot be abandoned.
>
> (Aron 1969: 10)

---

19 Existentialism's heritage is more complicated than this suggests. Matthews 1996 points out that Descartes bequeathed two lines of argument: rationalism and subjectivism. Existentialism rejects the former but falls squarely into the latter stream, particularly the work of Sartre.

20 This is a problem inherited from Nietzsche; see Pippin 1991: 199. Like other existentialists, Sartre attempts to overcome these implications of his position and to lay the basis not just for collective action for social change but also for the egalitarian community he desires. He does this through an elaboration of the centrality of the human desire for recognition by others. However, this attempt is not successful. On this aspect of his work, in comparison with that of his colleague Merleau-Ponty, see Whiteside 1988.

These implications of Sartre's perspective are worked out in the later writings of Frantz Fanon. He portrayed violence on the part of the Algerian resistance to French rule as not just a political necessity but as emancipatory in itself. At one point he comments:

> Violence alone, violence committed by the people, violence organized and educated by its leaders, makes it possible for the masses to understand social truths and gives the key to them.
>
> (Fanon 1965: 118, quoted in Caute 1970: 84)

The post-structuralism and postmodernism that came to dominate the Parisian scene in the late 1960s and early 1970s made no secret of its rejection of universal values. As a result, like existentialism, it adopted a relativism whereby partisanship can be no more than the serving of some particular ideal or interest; in a world where there is a plurality of such commitments, among which there can be no rational adjudication. For all these positions, all that can be involved in value commitment is a leap of faith.[21]

It should be said that this is not a conclusion that many existentialists and post-structuralists have consistently and explicitly embraced. But they have failed to provide any basis on which to build a positive justification for partisanship on one side rather than another. Indeed, it is fairly clear, I think, that no such justification is available within the relativistic framework to which they are committed. What has happened, commonly, is that, faced with an inability to justify their political convictions, they have reverted to Enlightenment philosophy, appealing to forms of historicism or to some notion of natural humanity, or have simply treated those convictions as givens.

We see the reversion to historicism in Merleau-Ponty's and Sartre's attempts to produce an existentialist Marxism. Even more revealing, perhaps, is the fact that Martin Heidegger, whose early work stimulated French existentialism, sought to justify his commitment to National Socialism in historicist terms, on the grounds that the 1930s represented a moment in the development of the world when a spiritual renewal was possible. While the revolution Heidegger wanted would have made Germany all-powerful, he believed that this was in the interests of Europe as a whole; that it was necessary if Europe were to be defended against the threat of Russia from the East, and of Americanisation from the West, these both representing the forces of planetary technology unleashed by metaphysical thinking. Indeed, in his view this spiritual revolution would save the world as a whole, since it would renew contact with Being (see Kisiel 1971; Sluga 1993; Rabinbach 1994).[22]

---

21 It is symptomatic that in the course of her postmodernist argument for partisan research, Griffiths (1998: 64 and 65) appeals to Kierkegaard.
22 Heidegger was not a historicist in the strict sense of believing the world to be on the way towards realisation of an immanent goal, but he does rely on a historical meta-narrative, in much the same way that Sartre and Merleau-Ponty relied on Marxism.

Existentialists were tempted by historicism, then, and many succumbed; albeit not always going in the same political direction. However, I think it is fairly clear that historicism and existentialism are incompatible at a fundamental level. This was obscured by the interpretations of Hegel that were prevalent in France in the 1940s (on which see Roth 1988). Nevertheless, existentialism is essentially individualistic and anti-rationalistic, whereas Hegel and Marx are collectivist and rationalist.[23]

Post-structuralists and postmodernists, unlike existentialists, have not usually reverted to historicism, having been effectively inoculated against it by structuralism. However, they do still sometimes seek to validate particular political projects, despite the fact that the framework within which they work cannot justify this. The most obvious example is Foucault's commitment to resisting knowledge/power, for example by supporting prisoners' groups. It is quite unclear what basis can be found within his philosophical position for the resistant and transgressive politics that he advocated (Walzer 1983; Dews 1986 and 1987; Habermas 1987). Instead, he seems to appeal implicitly to the authenticity of the marginalised, and thereby to some notion of natural humanity; despite his rejection elsewhere of all such ideas. And built into his conception of 'the people' as challenging 'power' are *necessarily* untheorised notions of freedom and equality. Much is inherited from Marxism here, despite the fact that the foundations of that position have been rejected.

In short, then, the post-Enlightenment view denies any harmony of values, and therefore any guarantee that the consequences of research will be beneficial. And it is taken to follow from this that it is the responsibility of researchers to carry out their work in such a way as to further the particular political or practical goals to which they are committed. What is often ignored, though, is that the post-Enlightenment perspective also undercuts any possibility of justifying particular value commitments. The result is that different researchers are free to promote quite different values through their research, nor is there any basis for arguing that those who pursue values to which we are opposed are wrong. We can, of course, declare that they are wrong; but that declaration can carry no more weight than their criticisms of *our* commitments.

Thus, the post-Enlightenment view provides no basis for choosing between, for example, Heidegger's commitment to National Socialism, Merleau-Ponty's early attachment to Leninism, Sartre's later association with Maoism, Foucault's particularistic activism, or Rorty's adherence to bourgeois liberalism. The result is a world in which there are groups with conflicting ideals battling against one another in the public arena, each accompanied by its own set of organic intellectuals. There is no scope for dialogue here, only for struggle. And it is a struggle in which there are not just two sides but rather a multiplicity of local parties fighting on different terrains and with diverse issues at stake.

Furthermore, in the context of a rejection of rationalism and of the very

---

23 The changes in Merleau-Ponty's position are symptomatic of the problem; see Whiteside 1988.

possibility of universally valid knowledge, the post-Enlightenment position implies a form of partisan research that amounts to the production of propaganda in support of some particular cause. Researchers become political strategy and public-relations experts. Appeal to knowledge or research findings on their part can only be a rhetorical ploy, and one whose force is likely to dissipate in so far as this post-Enlightenment view of research and its relationship to practice gains ground outside the academy. Thus, partisan research based on the post-Enlightenment view is a contradiction in terms. The very existence of research seems to be bound up with some notion that it is possible to produce, or at least to approximate, universally valid knowledge (see Hammersley 1999a).

Conclusion

In this chapter I began by seeking to clarify the meaning of the terms 'value neutrality' and 'partisanship'. Sometimes 'value neutrality' is taken to imply that research is or should be wholly independent of practical values, being concerned with the pursuit of theoretical knowledge for its own sake. Other proponents of this principle, notably Weber, while insisting that practical values must not be allowed to bias conclusions or be presented as validated by research, nevertheless recognise a considerable role for practical values; indeed, they require that social research be value-relevant. This still contrasts with currently influential advocacy of partisanship, though, which presents research as properly directed towards the achievement of practical or political goals.

I then went on to examine what seem to be the two main rationales for partisanship in research: the Enlightenment and post-Enlightenment views. I suggested that Enlightenment belief in the harmony of values is unsustainable. And one implication of this is that research governed by this orientation may be subject to bias. Given that the pursuit of the good will not necessarily aid discovery of the truth, any attempt to tailor inquiry to political or practical goals is likely to distort it. At the same time, the post-Enlightenment view leads to an impossible relativism; and thereby undercuts the distinction between research, on the one hand, and advocacy or propagandising, on the other.

My conclusion, then, is that neither of the philosophical rationales available for partisan academic research is convincing. Indeed, I believe that social research must necessarily be committed to value neutrality simply because it cannot validate value conclusions. While value judgements have a role to play in research, they should only be used as resources by means of which to select or construct value-relevant phenomena for factual investigation. And the potentially biasing effects of value commitment must be guarded against if we are to maximise our chances of producing sound knowledge.[24]

Of course, it might be argued that since we can never eliminate the potential

---

24 For discussions of the bias that can result from partisanship, see, for example, Brunton 1996, Foster *et al.* 1996 and Hammersley 1998a.

for bias, or even be absolutely sure that it is absent, the ideal of value neutrality serves no purpose – or, indeed, that it simply disguises the bias that is actually operating. But this is to assume that an ideal that is not, or even can never be, fully realised is of no value. This is true of some types of ideal, but not of all. Sometimes there is benefit even from the effort to achieve a particular goal, and in my view this is the case with value neutrality. The closer we can approximate to it, the less the danger of our political or practical values biasing our results. Furthermore, the principle of value neutrality also provides the basis for collective assessment by researchers of possible bias in their work. In both of these ways, that principle maximises validity, other things being equal.[25]

As I emphasised earlier, the principle of value neutrality does not rule out the selection of research topics on the basis of practical values or in accordance with the interests of a particular interest group. For Weber, practical values could play a legitimate role in defining the phenomena for investigation, and perhaps even in selecting relevant explanatory factors. Furthermore, practical values could be used as a basis for evaluations and prescriptions, so long as the status of these as theoretical rather than practical – as conditional upon the adoption of particular values – was made clear. In other words, research must not be used to try to justify commitment to one value rather than another, but it can demonstrate the practical implications of particular value positions.

Weber was one of the few social scientists in the early twentieth century to move away from what I have called the Enlightenment view. He was strongly influenced by Nietzsche, and therefore by post-Enlightenment ideas. But he saw scientific inquiry as an activity, indeed as a form of life, which has its own intrinsic rationale. According to him, while commitment to science cannot be justified in universalistic terms, once one has chosen this activity one must live out its principles to the full. In other words, one must pursue the truth wherever it leads, even when this carries implications that run counter to one's own interests or political values. To paraphrase the title of one of his most influential essays: science is a vocation (Weber 1948).

There is another side to Weber's position that is equally important. This is an insistence on the need to recognise the limits to what scientific research can achieve. This issue was not a matter of idle speculation for him. He had a practical concern both with protecting the legitimate autonomy of academics to teach and do research as they see fit against intrusions by the state, and at the same time with restricting to their proper bounds the power of academics over students, and their influence over the public generally.[26] The principle of value neutrality was intended to serve both these functions. Weber's view was that if academics overstepped the boundaries of their authority they undermined any

25 All this assumes, of course, that realism rather than relativism is the most defensible stance in epistemological terms. For arguments in support of this, see Hammersley 1992a: ch. 3; 1995a: ch. 1; and 1998b.

26 These concerns had particular significance in the German context of the time; see Ringer 1969.

defence of academic freedom against attacks on it by the state and other powerful interests (Scott 1995). In other words, he emphasised the fragility of the tacit agreement on the basis of which academic autonomy is tolerated. However, the principle of value neutrality was even more important for Weber as a defence of politics against science than it was as a means of protecting science from politics. He saw one of the prime dangers of the modern world as the misuse of science, and of formal rationality generally, in order to promote particular political ideals (Bruun 1972).

Partisan research carried out under what I have called the Enlightenment view is precisely an example of this misuse. It is pre-Weberian in its understanding of the relationships among values. But there are equally fundamental problems with post-Enlightenment partisan research. This is illustrated by the fact that those who explicitly adopt that position rarely keep within its bounds: they often rely on Enlightenment rhetoric, implicitly or explicitly, to try to justify their political commitments. And this is inevitable, since the post-Enlightenment view provides no basis for either research or politics as principled activities.

I would not want to suggest that Weber's methodological position is sound *in toto*; indeed, it suffers itself from the effects of value relativism, as critics from both ends of the political spectrum have pointed out (see Factor and Turner 1977). But, for the reasons I have outlined, it is difficult to see what other adequate basis there could be for social research than the principle of value neutrality. Taking sides *within* research is effectively to take sides *against* it. It involves either an appeal to a false harmony of values, or a systematic deception whereby political activists work under the cover of research and thereby undermine it.

2   Between Marx and Weber

C. Wright Mills on the role of the social scientist

A common view about the proper role of social research is that it should be concerned with identifying and understanding social problems, and perhaps also with developing and promoting solutions to them. This view is characteristic not only of those who see research as a 'professional' or 'technical' activity that properly serves the state and other institutions, but also of many who regard it as having a 'critical' political role that ought to challenge the status quo. Of course, these two views differ in how they formulate the character of social problems. In crude terms, the first either takes as given conventional definitions of what is and is not a problem – and of why it is or is not a problem – or seeks to identify social problems on technical grounds.[1] 'Critical' approaches, by contrast, typically question the official priority given to various problems, challenge the way they are currently formulated, highlight social problems that have been overlooked or neglected, and/or declare some officially defined problems to be spurious. And they do this on the basis of declared value commitments. Furthermore, among critical researchers there is resistance to treating problems as the product of individual pathology or even of localised social causes. The role of societal factors in generating social problems, and the responsibility of dominant groups for them, are emphasised.

One important source of this critical approach to social problems is the work of C. Wright Mills. In a well-known article published in the 1940s, he challenged the way in which 'social pathologists' studied social problems, criticising the fact that they took the framework of conventional society for granted, rather than examining its role in generating these problems. And the core theme of his later and even more famous book, *The Sociological Imagination*, is that it is the task of the social scientist to turn 'personal troubles' into 'public issues'. There, Mills presents social science 'as a sort of public intelligence

---

1 However, as Tumin (1965) points out, in practice even within this tradition there is a strong tendency for sociologists to emphasise problems that they themselves see as important, and to ignore others. A similar variation in response to candidate problems can be found in constructionist approaches; see Woolgar and Pawluch 1985.

apparatus' concerned with documenting the structural trends that produce social problems (Mills 1959b: 181).

During his lifetime Mills had considerable influence; certainly, his books sold in greater numbers than those of most sociologists.[2] In the years immediately after his death in 1962, both his example and his ideas shaped the thinking of the American New Left. And he remains a significant reference point in Anglo-American sociology today.[3] In this chapter I want to outline the model of the sociologist's role that Mills provides, against the background of some of the major influences upon him, and to assess the cogency of the case for that model.

Mills on the role of the sociological imagination

In *The Sociological Imagination* Mills argues that there is an acute need for social scientific ways of thinking in contemporary society. He puts forward several reasons for this: the increasing rapidity of social change; the move towards larger and larger forms of economic and political organisation; and the associated growth in the extent to which changes in one part of the world affect people living elsewhere. He argues that sociology is necessary for an understanding of the prevailing social forces, and that such understanding is essential if people are to be able to regain control over their own lives. This builds on the central theme in his substantive writings, particularly *White Collar* and *The Power Elite*, that a change has taken place within American society from a situation where decisions tended to be made on a local basis, and democratically, to a mass society whose members are isolated and dominated by powerful bureaucratic organisations (both commercial and governmental) and by a 'power élite' that controls them. In the new mass society, ordinary men and women do not understand what is happening, and they tend to see their problems in personal terms, overlooking the extent to which these are shared in common, and not realising the ways in which social factors lie behind them.

As is well known, Mills was very critical of the forms of sociology that predominated in America in the 1950s. In particular, he criticised what he dubbed 'grand theory' and 'abstracted empiricism'. He claimed that neither of these is well-designed to play the role that is required of social science. He judged grand theory, exemplified by the work of Talcott Parsons, as too abstract in its formulations, and as using language that makes it virtually incapable of

---

2 Aptheker (1960: 8) reports that *White Collar* sold 30,000 copies in its original edition and that the distribution of *The Power Elite* and *The Causes of World War Three* 'reached best-seller proportions'.

3 For the influence of Mills on the New Left, see Cleere 1971 and Miller 1986: 96. As evidence of his continuing influence, *The Sociological Imagination* is still in print, and there were around 800 citations of it between 1981 and 1997 according to the *Social Sciences Citation Index*. While generally enjoying a high reputation, this book has also recently been subjected to severe criticism: see Denzin 1990.

speaking to ordinary people. More than this, he saw this esoteric language as an obfuscation, as covering up defective sociological assumptions about the nature of modern societies. In particular, it neglected the extent of the concentration of power, played down conflict, and reified social forms rather than recognising their historical character. As a result, it obscured the extent to which social structures are the outcomes of political struggle, and are therefore open to change.

For Mills, abstracted empiricism was in some respects the mirror image of grand theory. Much as the latter fetishised concepts, this fetishised method, on the basis of a conception of science that was derived from positivist philosophy. Mills' main target here was the Bureau of Applied Social Research at Columbia University, run by Lazarsfeld, in which he had himself worked as director of the labour research division. He saw it as preoccupied with the collection of low-level facts needed by sponsors. As a result, its work lacked a well-defined theoretical framework, addressed trivial questions, and was therefore incapable of dealing with the important public issues that ought to be the focus of sociological analysis. Mills also argued that abstracted empiricism played an anti-democratic role, serving the bureaucrats who are involved in a system that oppresses ordinary people. Furthermore, the kind of research it stimulated was itself bureaucratic, reducing researchers to mere technicians. It involved a division of labour in which teams of interviewers were employed to collect data that were then analysed by project directors. Mills summarises the trend he is resisting in terms of the contrast between the sociologist as an independent scholar and the intellectual technician implementing methodological procedures:

> The idea of a university as a circle of professorial peers, each with apprentices and each practising a craft, tends to be replaced by the idea of a university as a set of research bureaucracies, each containing an elaborate division of labour, and hence of intellectual technicians. For the efficient use of these technicians, if for no other reason, the need increases to codify procedures in order that they may be readily learned.
>
> (Mills 1959b: 103)

In opposing both grand theory and abstracted empiricism, Mills appealed to what he referred to as the 'classic' sociological tradition, treating Marx, Spencer, Weber, Veblen and Mannheim as key exemplars (Mills 1960a). This tradition involves pursuit through empirical research of a form of theory that is less abstract than the grand theory generated by Parsons and his followers, and that is especially concerned with understanding the reasons for and consequences of historical change. Furthermore, while work in this tradition involves empirical analysis, its approach is flexible and imaginative, not tied down by methodological codifications in the manner of abstracted empiricism. Most significant of all, this type of research is focused on social problems that are identified as of crucial importance by the sociologist, who acts as an independent but politically committed intellectual. Data collection and analysis are directly driven by a concern with understanding each problem and its sources; and thereby with how it might be tackled. However, unlike some contemporary views of applied sociology, where the task is to formulate problems in such a way that they can be dealt with by government policies, in the case of Mills the solutions are expected to be more radical. Indeed, he sees it as the duty of sociologists to outline alternative possibilities no matter how Utopian these might appear from the point of view of conventional wisdom.

Another important feature of work in the classic tradition for Mills is that it is not hidebound by disciplinary distinctions. He points out that the sociological imagination is not the exclusive preserve of sociologists. Nor is research in the classic tradition addressed solely to other social scientists or to powerholders. It is designed to make publicly available the best knowledge there is, so as to provide a basis for enlightened democratic decisions. Thus, far from restricting the sociological imagination to an academic context, Mills emphasises that it can and should be found amongst journalists and non-academic writers, and that the audience which must be addressed is the general public. In this way, he resisted academic professionalisation as well as bureaucratisation (see Becker 1994).

As the basis for an assessment of Mills' position, in the next two sections I want to compare his view of the role of the social scientist with those that can be found in two of the most important influences on him: Marx and Marxism, on the one hand; and the work of Max Weber, on the other.[4]

Mills and Marxism

Mills' position has often been seen as lying between those of Marx and Weber, so that what he offers is regarded as a kind of Weberian Marxism or a form of radicalised Weberianism. While this is true in a superficial way, it hides much of importance. The impact of Marx on Mills must be understood in the context of other major influences on him – notably pragmatism and American liberal and radical thought – which were often themselves shaped by their own engagements with Marx and Marxism.[5] Mills blends elements from each of these influences to produce his own distinctive position. Nevertheless, the comparison with Marx is instructive.

Mills can be seen as taking over Marx's emphasis on the centrality of conflict in social life, on the importance of a historical perspective, and on the potential for progressive social change built into history. He also inherited something of

---

4 Mills describes Marx and Weber as 'the two sociologists who stand above all the rest' (cited in Press 1978: 135). Horowitz 1983 provides a detailed discussion of the wider range of influences that shaped Mills' work.

5 For a useful discussion of Dewey's role as a public intellectual and of his pragmatism, see Ryan 1995. For accounts of American radicalism in the twentieth century see Bottomore 1967 and Cooney 1986.

the polemical mode in which Marx and Marxists often wrote, and perhaps thereby the model of the critical intellectual that this tradition projects. However, he rejected what he saw as the one-factor determinism of Marxism, and the idea that the working class represents a revolutionary force in modern capitalist societies. He dismisses these as characteristic of vulgar Marxism, and draws a parallel between the role of this in the Soviet Union and that of liberalism in the West. As Eldridge comments, in Mills' view 'both [these] inheritors of the Enlightenment have ironically been transformed into instruments of unreason and unfreedom', so that 'we need to go beyond liberalism and beyond communism' (Eldridge 1983: 35). Mills sometimes put forward what he called 'plain Marxism' as an alternative to vulgar (and indeed to sophisticated) Marxism (Mills 1963). This involves accepting key ideas from Marx, but recognising that important social changes have occurred since he wrote, that not all of these have been in line with what he predicted, and that we can learn much about them from other writers in the classic tradition, as well as from empirical research into present realities.

Mills also differs somewhat from Marx in the conception of the ideal society that he uses as a yardstick for evaluating the current situation. Marx effectively denies that there is any model for this in the past or that the nature of postrevolutionary society can be predicted; though his ideals were necessarily influenced by his knowledge of earlier social forms. By contrast, to a large extent, Mills seems to operate on the basis of a Jeffersonian idealisation of late eighteenth- and early nineteenth-century North American society, a society of small farmers and craftworkers (Mills 1951: ch. 1).[6] In this respect, Mills' Utopia is close to that of many American liberals (and even to that of some on the political Right) in the way that it treats the virtues of an idealised small-scale society as the standard against which life in big cities or large nations is to be judged. However, he also makes politics, and in particular a notion of direct democracy modelled on the town meeting, central to his Utopia.[7]

It is more difficult to draw conclusions about the relationship between the role that Mills advocates for the social scientist and that proposed by Marx, because the latter wrote little about this issue. However, there is no doubt that what was central to Marx's intellectual orientation was the idea of the unity of

---

6 It should be noted, though, that this is not as sharp a contrast as some Marxist critics of Mills have suggested. The independent craftworker seems to have been at the heart of Marx's conception of labour, at least in his early writings.

7 This emphasis on democracy is close to Marx, on some readings; see, for example, O'Malley 1994. However, it is even closer to Dewey. Ryan summarises the political aspects of Dewey's project as 'building a revived Jeffersonian democracy in new conditions' (Ryan 1995: 327). Press (1978: 56) identifies a key difference from Marx here, that in Mills, as in Dewey, industrial capitalism is viewed negatively, whereas for Marx it was an essential prerequisite for the emergence of communism. On this basis, Press argues that Mills' 'image of man' is a bourgeois not a socialist one (Press 1978: 58).

theory and practice, and this will be my focus here.[8] This idea has several aspects. First of all, it involves an insistence that all thinking and writing are social in character. In more specific terms, they are generated – or at least shaped – by the material conditions of society. Unfortunately, this immediately plunges us into a major controversy within Marxism: about what constitutes the material component of society, and about what the relationship is between it and the ideas prevailing in that society. As we have seen, Mills rejects what has often been referred to as technological determinism or economism, whereby the forces of production or these together with the relations of production (defined in a narrow way) entirely determine the content of the superstructure (legal, educational, political and other institutions, as well as the ruling ideas). Many Marxists have also rejected this determinism; adopting concepts like 'dialectical relationship', 'relative autonomy', and 'determination in the last instance' to formulate the complex, and to a considerable extent bi-directional, process by which infrastructure and superstructure are related. And, indeed, these concepts seem essential to provide any scope for the political role of intellectual work.

A second dimension of the theory–practice relationship concerns what ought to be the nature of the connection between social scientists, or intellectuals generally, and the working-class struggle. And there are two aspects to this. One concerns the relationship between the knowledge produced by social science and what we might call the spontaneous consciousness of the working class. The positions taken by Marxists on this issue are usually closely related to their attitudes towards the role of the Party. Crudely speaking, on the one hand there are those who believe that the pressure for revolutionary change will, and must, come spontaneously from the working class; with that class developing for itself a true understanding of capitalist society and of the need for change. By contrast, what has come to be referred to as Leninism emphasises the role of the Party, not just in organising the political and military struggle but also in forming the consciousness of the working class: combating the dominant ideology and raising the orientation of the workers above what Lenin referred to as the level of 'trade union consciousness'. The first of these positions allows little role for specialised intellectual work, and I will not consider it further. The second raises the other aspect of the unity of theory and practice: the relationship between intellectuals and political parties. For some Marxists, intellectual work must be done as an integral part of political activism and therefore within the context of Party control. By contrast, others see intellectual work as needing to be more autonomous, though usually still closely connected with political commitment and practice.

One way to explore this contrast is to look at two influential twentieth-century Marxists who, while sharing a Leninist position, represent very different approaches in this respect: Gramsci and Althusser.

---

8 For information on Marx's political activities and how these paralleled his theoretical work, see McLellan 1973 and Gilbert 1981.

Gramsci

Gramsci draws a distinction between the sense in which everyone is an intellectual – just as everyone performs some elements of more specialised activities (we are all tailors and cooks to some degree, to use Gramsci's own examples) – and the specialised function of the intellectual in modern society. It is not very clear how he defines that latter function in specific terms. And, indeed, given the universality of intellectual activity, perhaps it would not be reasonable to expect any sharp distinction; but rather only a rough scale running from those groups who no one would deny are intellectuals through to those who are more borderline – in that their specialised task has only a marginal relationship to the production and dissemination of ideas or information. This uncertainty about the boundary around what 'specialised intellectual' refers to also arises from Gramsci's conception of the dialectical relationship between theory and practice: his insistence that intellectuals are inevitably engaged in political praxis; that their thinking arises out of that praxis; and that it should function to clarify and redirect their own and others' actions.

As is well known, Gramsci also drew a distinction between organic and traditional intellectuals. The root of this distinction is the closeness and explicitness with which the work of intellectuals is related to the activities of the class they represent. An organic relationship is one in which the dialectic between thought and action flourishes, even if the thought and the action are to some extent carried out by different people. 'Organic' here is presumably a bodily metaphor, and the suggestion is that intellectuals serve as one specialised organ in the body politic of the class that they represent. By contrast, traditional intellectuals represent a deformation of this relationship: their thinking continues to have its origins in the class they serve, but their thought no longer guides the action of that class. It comes to function only as propaganda, for which the traditional intellectuals' apparent independence from politics serves as a disguise. Thus, Gramsci sees the clergy as having once been in an organic relationship with the landed aristocracy but as having turned into traditional intellectuals. This dislocation in the functioning of the body politic is something that occurs once a social class has come to power, and especially when its reign as the ruling class is nearing its end – when it has exhausted its progressive political role; though, of course, propaganda may prolong that life beyond the point at which material factors demand change.[9]

There is no doubt that Gramsci believed that the proper relationship of intellectuals to the working class in its struggle for power is an organic one. He sees that relationship very much in terms of what has come to be called 'consciousness-raising', though this is not simply the imposition of 'true working-class consciousness' on the masses. What is involved is mutual discovery of the nature of capitalist society and of how it can and must be overthrown, thereby

---

9 Gramsci's ideas about the role of intellectuals are to be found in Hoare and Nowell Smith 1971.

creating the 'intellectual–moral bloc' that is necessary for successful action. Gramsci's plan to write a modern counterpart to Machiavelli's *The Prince* captures a great deal of what he saw as the role of the intellectual who is organically tied to the working class. The task was the self-education of the proletariat, to train it to become the ruling class of the future (Joll 1977: ch. 9). Central here is the work of divesting politics of the false ethical content created by the traditional intellectuals who serve the currently dominant classes. Gramsci did not take this to mean that what had been produced by traditional intellectuals could simply be ignored by revolutionary intellectuals. Locked into it was much that could be of value, but what was of value would only be revealed in the dialectical relationship between intellectual work and political action based on the experience of the working class.

Moreover, for Gramsci the task of discovering true working-class philosophy is not a purely cognitive matter, it depends on 'feeling the elemental passions of the people' and 'connecting them dialectically to the laws of history, to a superior conception of the world' (quoted in Joll 1977: 101). So, what is required is 'organic participation in which feeling and passion become understanding and thence knowledge', since 'then and only then is the relationship one of representation' (quoted in Joll 1977: 102). Here we have a model of the body politic in which, to a large extent, the masses provide the instinct and passion that are the driving force for the struggle, while the Party, conceived as the intellectual advance-guard, transforms this into knowledge that can direct the struggle and bring about victory. Of course, this is too simple. As already noted, for Gramsci everyone is an intellectual to some degree, and the specialised intellectual must be in contact with the masses and be directly involved in political activity. The dialectical relationship between feelings and thought within each individual, which takes a somewhat different form according to whether or not that individual is part of the intellectual organising élite, must be reinforced and transformed by the dialectical relationship between that leadership and the rest of the Party. And this requires not just contact between them but also some social mobility: any closing off of the Party leadership from its membership would turn the latter into a permanent élite and undermine its role in bringing about progressive social change.

Gramsci's view of intellectual work may seem to reduce it to an instrumental matter of whatever functions to serve the interests of the Party, these being regarded as identical to those of the working class. It is an impression that is reinforced by his appeal to Machiavelli, and by vulgar interpretations of the latter's ideas.[10] However, while instrumentalism is certainly present, it arises in the context of a distinctive interpretation of the work of Marx. As Merrington (1977: 141) points out, a key feature of Gramsci's work was his active rethinking of Marxism in the new post-First World War context. Equally impor-

---

10 For a historically sensitive interpretation of Machiavelli, see Skinner 1981.

tant is that Gramsci's ideas were strongly influenced by Croce, whose philo-sophical outlook was Hegelian. Gramsci read Marx from this perspective, and thereby understood him in a way that conflicted sharply with the orthodox Marxism of the time. The latter emphasised the scientific character of the laws of historical development on the basis of which the political success of the working class was guaranteed. Gramsci also saw history in terms of teleological development towards the realisation of true humanity, but in his view this development could only occur through class conflict, through the activity of the working class. It was not inevitable, but had to be worked for. And the success of the struggle would depend in large part on what we might call the cultural stage of development of the working class.

This was not simply a matter of that class having the ideas, moral qualities, etc. that would serve the struggle. What worked in political practice was not a matter of happenstance or local contingency. Rather it was built into the logic of history. A true philosophy was waiting to be discovered by the working class, not least through their experience of the class struggle, and this was a philos-ophy that provided for the eventual victory of that class, a victory that would confirm but not determine that philosophy's validity. From this point of view, both theory and reality are socio-historical products, but there is a mismatch between them; and overcoming this requires changing the world as well as developing the theory. Without this overarching process, all that would be involved is another episode in the 'circulation of élites'. In this way, Gramsci steered a course between orthodox Marxism, on the one hand, and the pessimistic 'machiavellianism' to be found in the work of Mosca, Sorel and Pareto, on the other.

A significant aspect of Gramsci's perspective for my purposes here is his emphasis on the contribution of intellectual hegemony to the continuing ability of the ruling class to keep control. What followed from this was the urgent need for working-class parties to develop *intellectual* influence, not only within that class but also beyond it, if any future revolution was to be successful. And that made the role of the intellectual who was organically related to the working class of central importance from Gramsci's point of view. Here, then, we have one influential Marxist model of, and rationale for, the work of the intellectual.

Althusser

Like Gramsci, Althusser also resisted the claims of traditional intellectuals to represent Humanity. That was, indeed, one of the keystones of his opposition to 'humanistic' Marxism. For him Marxism was the science of history, and it was necessarily tied to the interests of the working class; though, of course, the reali-sation of those interests was held to serve the long-term interests of all. There are some other respects in which Althusser's position was similar to that of Gramsci as well. One was that both were Leninists, in the sense of emphasising the directive role of the Party, both in the education of the working class and in providing political leadership. And, like Gramsci, Althusser regarded the task of the intellectual as requiring direct involvement in the Communist Party. He was a member of the French party for most of his life, through a period in which many other intellectuals left over its response to the Hungarian uprising, its effective support of French Government policy in Algeria, its response to the 'Prague Spring' and the Soviet invasion of Czechoslovakia, and its attitude to the 'events' of 1968.

However, by contrast with Gramsci, Althusser was a university teacher and was not active in the party leadership. While he believed in an organic relationship between the science of history and working-class struggle, for him that involved a sharp separation of functions, and this was closely related to his emphasis on the scientific character of Marxism. For Althusser, theoretical work was in itself a form of political practice ('the class struggle in theory'), but it was distinct from other kinds of political practice in its capacity to produce sound knowledge. Thus, Althusser drew a distinction between technical practices, which involve using means to achieve practical ends, and theoretical practices, which produce knowledge; though he saw scientific knowledge as one of the means employed by technical practices. Indeed, he regarded the validity of the ideas on which political practice is based as crucial to its success. He recognised that technical practices not only draw on scientific ideas but also spontaneously generate their own. However, he argued that these need to be corrected and developed through theoretical practice, and he saw this as the distinctive task of the intellectual. For these reasons, he did not believe that the actual beliefs of the working class are epistemologically privileged. And he saw the university as part of the technical not the social division of labour, and therefore as able in principle to promote forms of science that are free from the effects of ideology. He saw the revolutionary intellectual-as-theoretician as 'subject neither to the ideology of the bourgeois University nor to the stale orthodoxies of the Party, [as possessing] direct and unmediated access to the science of revolution' (Khilnani 1993: 94).[11]

One result of this emphasis on the role of science is that the focus of Althusser's work is more remote from particular political issues than Gramsci's, at least before the latter's period of incarceration. Most of Althusser's work was concerned with correcting what he saw as the intellectual errors that were prevalent within the French Communist Party. These informed not just Stalinism but also the reaction against it that had followed Khrushchev's 'secret' speech on 'the cult of personality' in 1956. What he offered was a *'left wing critique of Stalinism'* (quoted in Elliott 1987: 15). Althusser believed that what was necessary to provide the basis for this was a correct reading of Marx's work, and this is what he set out to provide. Central to his position was the argument

---

11   There is a dispute about how much Althusser's views changed over time. For a different view from Khilnani, see Elliott 1987.

that there is a radical discontinuity between Marx's early and later writings, and he insisted on the superiority of the latter. What these provided was a science of capitalist society of a structuralist kind. In providing this new reading, Althusser drew not just on the structuralist ideas that were emerging in France at the time, but also on Lacan's revisionist account of psychoanalysis – which he saw as paralleling his own approach to Marx – and on the work of Bachelard, Canguilhem and others in the philosophy of science (see Elliott 1987). What was central to all of these was rejection of the idea that history or knowledge are the product of a constitutive subject, whether individual or collective. Instead, Althusser viewed history as 'a process without a subject' that constitutes and distributes human subjectivities according to their functions in an ensemble of economic, political and ideological structures, each of which is subject to its own particular laws of development.

An important aspect of Althusser's approach, for my purposes here, was his insistence on the independent role of intellectuals within the Party, following a period in which they had been treated as at the disposal of the Party's leaders (see Khilnani 1993). Althusser criticised the dogmatism and pragmatism to which this had led, claiming that the French Communist Party was heir only to a political and not to an intellectual tradition. He insisted that the task of Party intellectuals was to provide the scientific knowledge that should be the basis for Party policy, which it was then the task of the Party to implement. And he was responsible for developing a group of young intellectuals at the École Normale Supérieure who were members of communist organisations and who, initially, promoted his point of view.

So, Althusser provides a rather different model for the role of the Marxist intellectual from Gramsci. Like the latter, he sees the intellectual as properly operating within the Communist Party, and both of them assign considerable importance to the role of the intellectual for the success of working-class struggle. Thus, they both saw theory as necessarily playing a directive role in shaping political practice. However, Althusser differs from Gramsci in several important respects. One is his insistence on the authority of the specialised intellectual within the Party, and on the autonomy of theoretical work from more direct forms of political struggle. Moreover, theoretical practice is seen as producing knowledge by applying a scientific approach, rather than achieving this through a direct relationship with working-class experience of political struggle. By contrast, Gramsci sees intellectuals as organically related to the working class, and assumes much closer – albeit dialectical – relationships among working class consciousness, political activism and intellectual work. Indeed, he saw the emphasis on scientific knowledge, both within Marxism and outside, as positivist, and as stemming from capitalist ideology. This is closely associated with the fact that his view of Marxist theory was thoroughly Hegelian, whereas Althusser rejected Hegel and those interpretations of Marx which emphasised what he had inherited from that source. Finally, Althusser differs sharply from Gramsci in abandoning the teleological view of history in terms of which truth and justice are the realisation of human species-being.[12]

Mills and the Marxist model of the intellectual

In the previous section I tried to show something of the range of models of the role of the intellectual to be found within Marxism. However, Mills' approach differs in important ways from both of the models I have outlined. In his early work, concerned with trade unions, Mills identifies several different roles that intellectuals can play in relation to those organisations: dependent staff specialists, party intellectuals, freelance intellectuals, and union-made intellectuals (Mills 1948a; see Cleere 1971: 102–4). It is quite clear from his discussion of these roles which one he believed to be the most valuable: the union-made intellectual is presented as combining the advantages of all the other types. To some extent, this implies a Gramscian view of the organic relationship between theory and practice; though it also involves considerable emphasis on the autonomy of the intellectual from the union leadership (a leadership that was far from engaging in revolutionary activity at the time). Furthermore, the way that Mills operated himself implied a much more distant relationship to active political organisations even than Althusser's; in his own terms, he was closest to the freelance intellectual, the independent critic of society.[13]

Like Althusser, Mills worked in a university and emphasised the role of scientific work as an activity in its own right, autonomous from practical politics.[14] However, in many ways, the character of his work was closer to that of Gramsci in its emphasis on historical and cultural understanding. And, by contrast with both, he was not closely affiliated with a political party or with any particular Leftist group, nor did he see political parties as the main vehicle by which intellectual work could have political impact. Instead, he emphasised its contribution to public debate. He seems to have believed that through such debate people's minds could be changed and that this would lead to transforma-

---

12 In doing so he leaves the status of truth and justice very uncertain, because they have none of the philosophical props that previously sustained them. These values seem to lie neither in the thought and practice of individuals nor in the dialectical progress of History. Indeed, Althusser inherits all the problems that attend the notion of structuralist science, both as regards what interpretation is to be given to the concept of truth and the relationship between knowledge and action. As Matthews (1996: 133) comments: 'Marxism as a theory of revolutionary action seems to require the very universal "humanism" which Althusser's Marxism, as a science of existing society, rejects.'

13 Of course, this may have reflected the options available to a Leftist American intellectual in the late 1940s and 1950s.

14 Press (1978: 31) points out that there may be a conflict between being a 'free scholar' and belonging to a university, and Mills certainly experienced conflict between his own mode of operation and what was expected of sociologists at Columbia University in the 1950s; see Horowitz 1983.

tive political action. This indicates not only that Mills was not a Leninist but also that in this area he owed more to Dewey than to Marx. While he broke with Dewey and the other pragmatists in the emphasis he gave to the importance of sociological knowledge of contemporary society and of its historical development, to a large extent he inherited their view of how scientific thinking could shape collective political action, and the form the latter should take. Despite Dewey's many frustrations over the reception of his ideas, and about the development of American society, he retained a belief in the common-sense of ordinary people. Indeed, Dewey believed that the central requirement for the revitalisation of American democracy was the transformation of a mass into a public. Mills took over this view, arguing that mass action had to be brought under the control of reason to create a public that could subject élites to democratic control. He saw the role of intellectuals as crucial to this, and he hoped that they could kick-start the formation of an organised and critical public. As Gillam comments, 'Mills never entirely lost confidence that revelation of the facts or truth could bring once-apathetic citizens dashing forthwith to the barricades. He continued to believe that reason, widely apprehended, must necessarily transform "masses" into "publics"' (Gillam 1977/8: 80).

What was required, then, was for the mass of ordinary people to form themselves into a public, to draw on the sociological imagination, and to exploit the scope for democratic forms of organisation that still existed in American society. In this way, they could take control of social developments that had got out of hand, which were the source of the social problems they suffered.

Mills and Weber

Mills' debt to Weber is more complex than his debt to Marx. Of course, Weber's own relationship to Marx has long been a matter of contention (see Antonio and Glassman 1985); and, on some interpretations, the sort of integrated position represented by Mills involves no basic contradiction. However, there are good reasons to argue that despite some similarities, and despite Weber's great respect for Marx as a social analyst, the basic orientations of these two representatives of the classic tradition of sociology are fundamentally different (Löwith 1960; Runciman 1963). Given this, those like Mills who seek to draw on the work of both these writers will be faced with some fundamental choices, or will make such choices whether they are aware of it or not.

In fact, Mills does not seem to have recognised how sharp the conflict in approach is between Marx and Weber.[15] This perhaps arose in part from the

---

15 At one point he comments, 'I think it is not unreasonable to say that ... [in adding status or prestige to the economic category of class] Weber completed the uncompleted work of Marx' (Mills 1960a: 13).

difficulties involved in interpreting Weber. His work is, if anything, even more obscure in motive and message than that of Marx, and there is also a significant difference in the clarity of their writing (see Tribe 1988: 10–14). Moreover, the distinctiveness of Weber's orientation only stands out more clearly today as a result of revisionist accounts that stress the distortions involved in the reception of his work by Anglo-American scholarship (see, especially, Mommsen 1984; Turner and Factor 1984; and Hennis 1988).

With Hans Gerth, Mills was editor and translator of the material included in *From Max Weber*, probably the most influential collection of extracts from Weber's work to be published in English. And the similarities between Mills and Weber – in terms of substantive sociology, political ideas and their conceptions of the role of the social scientist – are clear enough. For example, both share with Marx an emphasis on the inevitability of conflict in modern society and on the role of group interests in producing this. Furthermore, most of the respects in which Mills' sociological views deviate from those of Marx are in the direction of Weber: notably, his rejection of the philosophy of history that underpins Marx's work; and his stress on the independent role of ideas, and of political and status groupings over and above social class divisions. Indeed, both Weber and Mills have been accused of viewing Marx as a crude, economic determinist; with the result that their actual distance from him is exaggerated (see Aptheker 1960).

In political terms, as well, there are important similarities between Weber and Mills. In particular, both had an antipathy towards bureaucracy. Weber regarded the power of the civil service in Germany as a threat to the proper role of politics in that country. More generally, he saw its growth as part of a trend that threatened to result in Western societies becoming locked in an 'iron cage' of rational administration which threatened human freedom (see Beetham 1985). Similarly, Mills criticised bureaucracy as the dominant form of oppression in modern societies. And, in both cases, their objection to it arose to some extent from a nostalgia for the past: regret at what had been lost as a result of the growth of capitalism and bureaucracy. At the same time, this was accompanied by a recognition that the course of history could not be reversed. Thus, the work of Weber and Mills displays a poignant mixture of pessimism and hope about the possibility of regaining what they believed was essential to a truly human life; though Weber is much closer than Mills to seeing history in terms of tragedy.

Finally, there is at least a superficial similarity in the roles that Weber and Mills prescribed for the social scientist, and that they themselves played. Both stressed the importance of empirical analysis, as against moralising or philosophical speculation, and yet also emphasised the contribution of theory designed to conceptualise patterns of historical change and future possibilities. Moreover, for both, the value of social science lay in its capacity to illuminate what is and is not possible in particular historical circumstances, and thereby to serve political action. And, in personal terms, they were both intensely political men, engaged in recurrent debate about contemporary issues. Their writings often adopted what might be called the heroic mode, challenging currently influential ideas and powerful opponents, rather than painstakingly adding small items of knowledge to a cumulative body of knowledge.[16]

Despite these similarities, however, there are some fundamental differences between Weber and Mills. While both opposed bureaucratisation, they did so within the context of very different theoretical and political perspectives. This is reflected in the fact that the term 'bureaucracy' carried divergent meanings and significance for them. Weber did not deny the efficiency of the German civil service, nor its proper role in German society. He saw modern rational bureaucracy as the most efficient form of administration, and as desirable for that reason. Nor, perhaps even more significantly, did he deny the value of bureaucracy within political parties. This was the focal point of his disagreement with Michels. He agreed with the latter's analysis of the way in which the German Social Democratic Party had become bureaucratised and the effects of this on its political orientation, agreeing also that this was a tendency characteristic of modern political parties (an 'iron law of oligarchy'). However, before Michels was converted to fascism, he had contrasted this bureaucratisation with a model of direct democracy that he believed ought to operate within Left-wing parties. Weber, by contrast, saw the emergence of 'machine politics' as an essential feature of modern democracy, and as facilitating the role of charismatic political leaders that he regarded as essential if the iron cage was to be avoided. He opposed bureaucratisation only to the extent that it over-extended its authority into the realm of political decision-making.[17] By contrast, for Mills the term 'bureaucracy' referred to large-scale organisations in which there is a hierarchical structure of command, so that those at the bottom are required simply to carry out orders, rather than participating in executive decision-making. He objected to the very character of these organisations, and to the fact that they had gained the power to dominate whole communities. He regarded the trend towards large-scale organisation, which was still expanding across American society, as a threat to democracy; indeed, he believed that it undermined America's claims to be a democratic nation.

More fundamentally, even the common commitment of Weber and Mills to the values of freedom and democracy hides important differences. They interpret these concepts in discrepant ways. Of course, both concepts have complex histories in which quite diverse meanings have developed and become intertwined. In the case of 'freedom', neither Weber nor Mills is very explicit about the interpretation being employed. And while both writers seem to

---

16 And this despite Weber's praise for the vocation of the scientist in precisely these terms (Weber 1948). On the parallels that Mills probably saw between himself and Weber, see Horowitz 1983: 46–7.

17 For a useful discussion of the significance of bureaucratisation for Weber, see Mommsen 1989: ch. 7.

combine concern with positive and negative forms, they do so in different ways.[18]

One important ingredient in Weber's understanding of freedom was the Kantian idea that it involved conformity to a rational principle that the individual had legislated for him or herself. And built into this is the notion of freedom through self-constraint that was central to 'the German idea of freedom' (see Krieger 1957). Another element of Weber's approach is the influential ideal of 'cultivation', which demands the development of individual character out of the objective cultural materials available, these being fashioned into a unique and striking unity (see Ringer 1969: 108). This cultivated personality was seen as characterised by inner freedom; and this was treated as superior to, indeed as necessary for exercising, other kinds of freedom, both positive and negative. Moreover, despite its apparent individualism, this notion of cultivation was very closely associated with a conception of the nation as a community standing above purely individual or sectional interests, a community having its own distinctive cultural character. In these terms, true freedom was often interpreted as devotion to the nation.

At the same time, there are also signs in Weber of the influence of Nietzsche, for whom free action involved the transgression of conventional or customary modes of thought or action.[19] This is closely related to Weber's view that actions are based on fundamental values whose validity cannot be rationally demonstrated, so that commitment to them involves a leap of faith. In these terms, freedom is something that is displayed by great individuals; though there may have been a sense for Weber in which followers exercise positive freedom by participating in the selection and support of their leaders.

By contrast, Mills adopts a more egalitarian conception of freedom, in terms of the power to control one's own life, a power that he believes everyone should have. In large part, this is negative freedom, as in the case of the craftworker or university academic properly engaged in work that is to a considerable extent under his or her own control; the contrast being with the subordination built into bureaucracy. This is the basis for Mills' opposition to the development of complex technical divisions of labour, whether in

18 Positive freedom is achieved through participation in politics, in other words through collective self-government; though the nature of the participation envisaged can vary. By contrast, negative freedom concerns the degree of autonomy that can be exercised by any individual in relation to others, and particularly in relation to state institutions (see Berlin 1969). These two kinds of freedom are central to what have come to be referred to as the republican and liberal traditions, respectively; though each of those traditions is internally diverse.

19 Here it is of significance that opposition to being ruled by convention was central to the Anglophobia that was characteristic of many influential Germans at the time, though Weber was far from Anglophobic; see Roth 1993.

the factory, the office or the university; on the grounds that this leads to alienation in very much the way that Marx had argued. Along these lines, in the political realm, Mills points to the way in which military, political and corporate interest groups control the state, and stifle the voices of individuals. And, in universities, there is the development of technical bureaucracies and of the abstracted empiricism associated with them. At the same time, Mills also stresses the positive aspect of freedom, in terms of democratic participation in decision-making in both political and industrial realms. His ideal seems to be direct democracy, in which everyone's voice is heard and counts; though he also stressed the need for citizens to be educated for political participation (Press 1978: 60).

Weber's commitment to democracy is famously ambivalent, partly because it seems to be in conflict with his concept of freedom. And while he argued that democracy was a necessary feature of modern politics, especially in Germany after the First World War, the democracy he favoured was certainly not of the direct kind. He regarded that as neither possible in the modern world nor as a desirable ideal. Indeed, what he advocated was not even representative democracy in the strict sense of that term. What was central was the capacity of a population to select its leaders freely through elections. However, he did not see politicians as mandated to promote a particular set of policies, or even as charged with the primary responsibility of furthering the interests of those whose support they received. Rather, the task of the politician was to put forward a personal vision based on value principles, albeit one that would attract a following, and then to seek to impose that vision on the world by gaining power through competition with other political leaders. For Weber, the essence of politics was the struggle among individual political leaders who represented fundamentally different points of view.

Thus, Weber and Mills also differ in their concepts of democracy and in the reasons for their commitment to it. For Weber, democracy was a means and not an end, whereas for Mills it was an ultimate value. Furthermore, underlying this difference is a fundamental divide in modern political thought: between those for whom the goal of politics is the mundane one of making human life less nasty and short; and those who see its goal as the noble one of realising true human values. Of course, there are many who have tried to transcend this divide. These include some liberals, Marxists and others who treat democracy as offering an improvement in the quality of life in terms of the meeting of basic human needs and at the same time the freedom of all to engage in higher cultural pursuits. Mills falls clearly into this camp; Weber does not.

In Weber's case, what is reflected here, in part, is the influence of Nietzsche. For the latter, human nobility and excellence are paramount and are seen as arising out of struggle. And this quite explicitly involves the creation of an élite that depends for its existence on the slavery of the many, who are necessarily inferior. While Weber certainly does not endorse this extreme view, he is much closer to it than is Mills.[20] Weber's view of the heroic political leader proclaiming his own values and seeking to lead the populace, and his recognition that both this and the operation of the state depend on hierarchical forms of administration, make it clear that the bulk of the population are not free to follow their own gods. Nor was his fear of the iron cage an egalitarian one. Like Nietzsche, what he was afraid of was the disappearance from history of great men (and, perhaps, women), not the enslavement of the many.[21]

To some extent, Weber seems to have transposed Nietzsche's cultural élitism into German nationalism, where Nietzsche rejected nationalism and even advocated a united Europe (Ansell-Pearson 1994: ch. 4). Thus, Weber viewed national politics in the context of the political and military struggle among nations to achieve world power. He wanted Germany to be the equal of other Western nations; both in its direct relations with them, and in its control of an empire in the 'less civilised' areas of the world. He believed that it was only as a great power that the distinctive potential of German culture could be realised (see Mommsen 1984). This kind of nationalism was not unusual in Germany in the second half of the nineteenth century, up to and beyond the First World War, and marked Germans off from 'the West' (see Ringer 1969: 100–1); though Weber's views about what was necessary for the achievement of Germany's proper place in the world *were* distinctive.

The contrast with Mills here could not be sharper, given the latter's commitment to a negotiated world peace in which the United States would give up its dominant military position. Indeed, there is some evidence to suggest that the 'crackpot realism' (Mills 1958) that Mills criticises was itself derived from Weber, in the form of Morgenthau's work on international relations (see Turner and Factor 1984: 168–78). That Weber was a German nationalist is well known. What was less strongly emphasised in the early Anglo-American literature, including Gerth and Mills' introduction to *From Max Weber*, was that this nationalism followed from his views about the nature of politics and freedom in the modern world.

There are fundamental differences between Mills and Weber, then, and in part these reflect a conflict between what I referred to in the previous chapter as Enlightenment and post-Enlightenment thought. Mills recognised the role of

20 As Ansell-Pearson and Conway point out, Nietzsche's political views were complex and changed over time, like other aspects of his philosophy (Ansell-Pearson 1994; Conway 1997). For discussions of the influence of Nietzsche on Weber, see Fleischmann 1964; Shapiro 1978; and Eden 1987. It is worth noting, though, that Mills was often accused of élitism (see, for example, Gillam 1977/8: 78), and to a large extent what he bemoaned in what he saw as the disappearance of genuine democracy was a decline in the power of intellectuals. See Mills 1955.

21 On this aspect of Nietzsche's philosophy, see Conway 1997: ch. 1. While Weber departs from Nietzsche's treatment of art as the highest value to which all else must be sacrificed, he does nevertheless seem to be committed to an aesthetic view of politics, in the sense that the key value is the cultivation of character (see Hennis 1988). On this aspect of Nietzsche, see also Nehamas 1985.

irrational forces in social life, and as a result was less than fully optimistic about the prospects for the kind of social change he wanted. Nevertheless, he retained commitment to Enlightenment values, and in particular to belief in the close relationship between the pursuit of knowledge and the achievement of a better society. Horowitz comments that, 'Mills was above all a man of the enlightenment, a believer in the practical worth and consequence of ideas' (Horowitz 1963: 15). Thus, he assumed that social problems had intellectual causes and could be resolved by intellectual means. Similarly, Gillam has pointed out that Mills shared a commitment to the 'critical ideal' with the historian Richard Hofstadter, who was an early friend: the belief that scholars should be intellectuals – confronting, and expressing clear views about, the big issues. And closely associated with this was the assumption that ideas could have powerful political effects. Talking about Hofstadter, Gillam remarks that he:

> constantly assumes, not only that defects of intellect lie at the root of our problems, but also that it is still possible to reason our way out of trouble by coming to grips intellectually with 'what is happening in the world'.
>
> (Gillam 1977/8: 77)

Much the same could be said of Mills. For him, 'The unmasking of lies which sustain irresponsible power is the political calling of the intellectual' (quoted in Miller 1986: 86). And he believed that many contemporary intellectuals were not living up to this duty:

> There are many illusions which uphold authority and which are known to be illusions by many social scientists. Tacitly by their affiliations and silence, or explicitly in their work, the social scientist often sanctions these, rather than speak out the truth against them. They censor themselves either by carefully selecting safe problems in the name of pure science, or by selling such prestige as their scholarship may have for ends other than their own.
>
> (Mills 1944: 302)

Thus, while Mills believed that 'in his natural state man is essentially irrational, a creature who responds to impulses, political slogans, status symbols, etc.', nevertheless sociology 'could provide [the] means by which man casts off an egoistic, sectarian and mythic pride and grows to maturity' (Horowitz 1963: 16). It could do this by helping people to 'know where they stand, where they may be going, and what – if anything – they can do about the present as history and the future as responsibility' (Mills, quoted in Horowitz 1963: 16).

Not surprisingly, perhaps, Weber and Mills are also at odds over the question of the role of the social scientist, despite some superficial similarities. Both stressed the differences but also the close relationship between scholarship and political activity. Thus, Mills draws a clear distinction between intellectual and political activity and insists that intellectuals must continue with their task, not give it up for politics (Mills 1959b: 192). He comments, 'the role of the social scientist requires only that he or she get on with the work of social science [and] avoid furthering the bureaucratisation of reason and of discourse rather than getting involved in political activity directly'. However, this was because he saw sociological work as itself playing a progressive political role. He believed it to be intimately connected with universal values, and thus as properly value-laden. Horowitz comments: ' for Mills ... sociology could *cure* human ills as well as explain them. And any science concerned with human beings had to have this prescriptive value – just as medicine and psychology' (Horowitz 1963: 16–17). In this, Mills relied on those strands in the classic tradition that claim to be able to derive evaluations directly from the analysis of society, notably Marxism.

However, equally important here was the influence of pragmatism, and especially of Dewey. Like Marx, Dewey followed Hegel in rejecting the fact-value distinction. It was one of several dichotomies that had to be, and could or would be, transcended. For Hegel and Marx this was to occur through historical development, which would reach a point where the real became rational and the rational real. Dewey put forward a less historicist argument, insisting that the distinction between goals and means is a functional and not an absolute one. Correspondingly, there is no fixed realm of facts separated from a realm of values; there is a single realm of value-laden facts (Dewey 1939). Ryan says of Dewey that although he 'seemed to have turned ethics into sociology; it was a sociology of a peculiarly moral kind' (Ryan 1995: 178). And that description would apply to the work of Mills as well. It rests on the assumption that evaluative and prescriptive conclusions can be derived from scientific or rational analysis of social conditions. This is the reason why Mills' writing is full of evaluative judgements.[22] Reviewing *White Collar*, Macdonald praises Mills for reviving 'the old-fashioned custom' of 'mixing moral judgements and aesthetic impressions into his sociology' (Macdonald 1974: 295), and this praise is offered in a review that is otherwise rather hostile. In fact, at one point Macdonald comments: 'in this book, Mills is a propagandist rather than a thinker' (Macdonald 1974: 297).

Weber too sees social scientific work as playing an important political role; but this is in the context of the pursuit of goals chosen from incompatible and competing ideals, rather than a coherent set of universal values. Weber argues that conclusions about the desirability or otherwise of particular situations, policies, etc. cannot be founded solely on empirical analysis but must also involve ultimate values. Moreover, since those values are multiple and necessarily in conflict, there are no grounds for assuming that they can be reconciled in a

22 There are differences between Mills' first three books and *The Causes of World War Three* and *Listen Yankee*, in this respect. Mills referred to the latter as pamphlets, and they are overtly political statements. However, this difference is one of degree. Eldridge (1983: 44) comments, 'Writing in the end comes to be defined by Mills as a form of cultural struggle'. In my view, to a considerable extent, that is how he saw it from early on. Indeed, there are commentators who have denied any significant break between Mills's early academic and later political works in this respect; see Martindale 1975.

rational consensus. It is for this reason that he sees struggle or conflict as essential to human life, and the qualities relevant to it as the only ones that are of transcendent value. This was the basis for his disagreement with influential members of the *Verein für Sozialpolitik*. They represented the tradition of German historical economics, in which he had himself been trained, and in which he continued to work throughout his life, in many ways. But, as a result of the influence of Nietzsche and neo-Kantianism, he came to reject the way in which many German social scientists built value judgements into their work. He regarded this as an aspect of the rationalisation of politics, as facilitating its reduction to the administration of things.

So, Weber saw it as essential to make clear the limits to what science can tell us, to emphasise that it cannot validate value judgements and should not be treated as if it can. On this basis, he argues that scholars must not build evaluations and prescriptions into their concepts or conclusions in such a way as to obscure the ultimate values involved. Any evaluations or prescriptions included in scientific work must be conditional on explicitly expressed ultimate values. Moreover, the immediate purpose of research is to produce value-relevant factual knowledge, not to say what is wrong or what is to be done. Only in this way, he believed, could it avoid contributing to the rationalisation of politics that he feared was the future for the West.[23]

Conclusion

In this chapter I have examined the view of the social scientist's role to be found in the work of C. Wright Mills, comparing this with what is implied by two of the major influences on him: Marx and Marxism, on the one hand, and Weber, on the other. Mills shared what we might call the progressivism of Marx (along with that of Dewey), belief in the possibility of bringing about a form of social life that would realise human ideals; though he did not take over Marx's views about the role of the proletariat or about the determining role of economic factors in social change. Nor did he accept or adopt any of the models of the party intellectual to be found within Marxism. Furthermore, to a considerable extent, where he differed from Marx he drew on Weber, for example in emphasising the role of ideas and politics in history. However, despite superficial similarities in their concern with bureaucracy, freedom and democracy, Mills and Weber differed profoundly in their interpretations of those concepts. As a result, they also differed in their views about the relationship between social science and politics. Both draw a distinction between these two activities, while

23 It has been argued that Weber did not live up to his own methodological ideals, and that his scholarly and political writing cannot be clearly separated. For example, Mommsen describes him as standing 'on the threshold between politics and science' (Mommsen 1989: 7). However, this arises in large part from changes in Weber's views about the relationship between research and political policy, on which see Sharlin 1974. Moreover, there is a clear difference in tone between the later academic writings of Weber and even the earlier ones of Mills.

insisting on their close relationship. However, where Weber argues that social research should strive to be value-neutral, in the sense of limiting conclusions to factual descriptive and explanatory ones, Mills' own work is explicitly evaluative; he sees the role of the intellectual as to create an informed and radical public that will challenge those who currently exercise power, and thereby facilitate progress towards the realisation of human ideals.

These comparisons with Marx and Weber highlight a number of problems with Mills' conception of the role of the social scientist. Important from the Marxist side are questions about effective strategies for change. Mills believed that work informed by 'the sociological imagination' could shape public opinion, and thereby generate political action to transform American society. Yet this is at odds with Marxist analyses of modern societies, and even with his own account of the control exercised by the power élite. In other words, the criticism is that there is no effective mechanism by which Mills' analysis of social problems could be transformed into action; since it neither services the state nor shapes the practice of an oppositional political movement. Instead, Mills placed reliance on the possibility of creating an active and rational public opinion informed by research, and on the effectivity of this in changing social conditions. Despite his considerable doubts about American democracy, he nevertheless assumes that the voice of the people can overcome the control exercised by the power élite and the large-scale bureaucracies, whose dominating role he had himself documented. He also assumes that, ultimately, the reception of research findings by the public will be rational, rather than being hemmed in by interests or ideology, so that social research could lead directly to the widespread acceptance of progressive political conclusions. On this basis, Mills hoped that the freelance intellectual could play a far more powerful role in modern societies than seems likely to be the case (see Rule 1978: 53–5).

The criticisms of Mills that arise from the Weberian side are, if anything, even more fundamental. They relate to the production of knowledge as well as to its effectivity. First of all, Weber places more emphasis on the dangers of bias coming from the value commitments of the researcher than Mills seems to do. While the latter treats sociology as a craft, and recognises that it can be distorted by ideology, there is little sign of caution within his own work about the ways in which his political values might affect his empirical conclusions. Indeed, the conception of scientific work presented in the methodological appendix to *The Sociological Imagination* is one that plays down the significance of both rigorous hypothesis-testing and of the kind of open-ended collection and analysis of data characteristic of, say, grounded theorising. In that appendix Mills says at one point:

> Now I do not like to do empirical work if I can possibly avoid it. If one has no staff it is a great deal of trouble; if one does employ a staff, then the staff is often even more trouble. ... There is no more virtue in empirical inquiry as such than in reading as such. The purpose of empirical inquiry is to settle disagreements and doubts about facts, and thus to make arguments more

fruitful by basing all sides more substantively. Facts discipline reason; but reason is the advance guard in any field of learning.

(Mills 1959b: 205)[24]

The concern that such comments raise about the quality of his empirical research is reinforced by the account of Goldsen, one of his team when he worked for the Bureau of Applied Social Research:

> In the days when we worked together on *Puerto Rican Journey*, I found much pleasure and excitement in wandering around Harlem and East Bronx, chatting, drinking coffee with Puerto Ricans, questioning, arguing, wondering, commiserating, checking. Mills rode around Harlem and East Bronx in his impossible open jeep. He did not interview migrants or try to share their views. He interviewed English-speaking officials and intellectuals. He took everything else in through his eyes and his pores. He also read everything he could get hold of on migrations. His brilliance when we discussed these works always gave me new insights and ideas and understanding, and it raised even the most pedestrian writings above their own level. Mills never felt he had to study our interviews or analyze them. He culled them and quickly pounced on the nuggets that would make the main points he had blocked out for his looking and reading. The staff did the detailed analysis.

(Goldsen 1964: 90–2)

This tendency to use evidence to develop and support a position is reflected in his mode of writing. As Miller remarks: 'To win an audience, he was prepared to sacrifice subtlety, nuance, the patient evaluation of contradictory evidence – in short, the virtues of dispassionate scholarship' (Miller 1986: 99–100). This judgement echoes earlier much more severe critiques. In a review of *The Sociological Imagination*, Edward Shils described Mills as 'in part prophet, in part a scholar, and in part a rough-tongued brawler – a sort of Joe McCarthy of sociology, full of wild accusations and gross inaccuracies, bullying manners, harsh words and shifting grounds' (Shils 1960: 77–8). Similarly, in response to 'Letter to the New Left', in which Mills criticised him, Daniel Bell describes Mills' style as 'explosive, detonative rather than denotative' (Bell 1980: 138). He comments that 'no point is ever argued or developed, it is only asserted and reasserted. This may be fine as rhetorical strategy, but it is maddening for anyone who does not, to begin with, accept Mills' self-election as an ideological leader' (Bell 1980: 140–1).

Another criticism that can be made of Mills' position from a Weberian point

---

24 What Mills is reacting against here is empiricism, and probably not just the abstracted empiricism of Lazarsfeld but also ethnographic empiricism; see his review of Westermarck (Mills 1948b).

of view concerns the relationship between research findings and political conclusions. As already noted, like Marx and most Marxists, Mills is wedded to an Enlightenment, rather than a post-Enlightenment, point of view. As a result, he retains a belief in the possibility of consensus about the nature of the good life, and therefore about political action directed towards realising it. And he sees sociology, in the broad sense, as playing a crucial role in shaping and bringing about that consensus. Yet there is no reason to believe that such a consensus is possible, given value pluralism. Furthermore, social science cannot on its own indicate what form the good society should take.

In insisting on the separation between facts and values, and on the conflicting value commitments to be found in Western society, Weber effectively undercuts the determinative role of social science in relation to political practice that both Mills and the Marxists assumed to be possible and desirable. He saw research as contributing to political deliberation and action, but it could only provide a necessary political realism. It could not, and should not attempt to, determine which of various feasible political goals are to be pursued. By contrast, Mills' Enlightenment orientation leads him to treat the validity of his assessment of the oppressive character of modern bureaucracy, of the power élite, of the role of the great powers (and especially the United States) in international relations, as obvious; as something that everyone who is rational and of good will must recognise. And the other side of this is the assumption that those who do not find his argument compelling must either be defective in intelligence or have ulterior motives. This is reflected in the rhetorical strategies that he employs, such as his use of the term 'crackpot realism' to refer to those who believe that nuclear deterrence is a sound policy in international relations.

One does not have to accept Weber's value irrationalism, or his nationalism, in order to find his view of the role of the social scientist convincing. Indeed, one does not even have to accept value pluralism. All that is necessary is recognition that in many value disputes there is scope for reasonable disagreement (Larmore 1996), and that value conclusions cannot be derived from factual premises alone. Nor is this to imply that social scientists can play no role in politics of the kind that Mills sought to play: criticising current social arrangements, policies, etc. What it does mean, though, is that they must not claim or imply that the stand they take derives entirely from social science; in other words that the criticism is validated by research. Indeed, it should be made clear that quite different value conclusions could be reached on the basis of the same social scientific findings. A second point is that these criticisms will need explicit value argument as well as appeal to factual information, if public discussion is to take a rational form. In my view, Mills' work fails on both these counts. First of all, his social scientific work is not clearly separated from his political arguments, and one result of this is that his conclusions are rarely supported effectively by evidence: he takes them to be valid too readily. Secondly, his conclusions are presented as if the value assumptions on which they rely are patently the only rational ones. And this ill serves the kind of democratic discussion to which he was himself committed.

As I noted earlier, Mills' influence has been substantial. Moreover, it seems likely that, to a large extent, this has stemmed from the ambiguities within his position. What he appears to offer is a model that combines the traditional virtues of science as a specialised craft with the role of the intellectual as supplier of a comprehensive worldview, one that tells us what is right and wrong with the world and what needs to be done to remedy it. This is very similar to the appeal of Marx; but Mills' model of the intellectual is not tarnished by the autocratic, indeed anti-intellectual, record of Marxism in power.

There are respects in which Weber's combination of the role of scholar with that of political adviser and would-be politician may seem to conform to the same model. But Weber's methodological arguments subvert this conception of the intellectual as harbinger of a rational society. These arguments imply that it is important to make a distinction between the role of the social scientist and that of the intellectual. They require social scientists to restrict themselves to factual conclusions *when writing as social scientists*. This does not rule out their documenting value-relevant features of particular situations, offering explanations for those features, or indicating what would be likely to happen if a particular policy were to be implemented. But it *does* rule out their arguing for or against the importance of particular problems and the adoption of particular policies. As individuals they may, of course, participate in public debates to present their own views, but they should not appeal to scientific authority to validate those views; even though, like others, they can call on research findings in supporting their case. To claim scientific authority for their political conclusions would be to abuse science, and to distort the political process in precisely the way that Weber feared. In my view, this is an offence that Mills commits.

3   Which side was Becker on?

Questioning political and epistemological radicalism

Howard Becker's article, 'Whose side are we on?', published in 1967, has been very widely cited in the literature of the social sciences.[1] Furthermore, there is considerable consensus about its message. It is generally taken to argue that sociologists are inevitably partisan, and that they should be explicitly so. Gouldner provided one of the earliest and most influential interpretations along these lines, even though he was critical of the *kind* of partisanship he took Becker's article to imply (Gouldner 1968). And we find much the same interpretation prevailing today. Thus, writing in 1995 about the work of the 'second Chicago School', Galliher describes the message of Becker's article as follows:

> he argued that since some type of bias is inevitable in all research on human subjects, to gain a full understanding of the world it is essential that we consciously take the perspective of the oppressed rather than the oppressor.

And he adds that: 'Becker's labelling theory of deviant behavior is consistent with his admitted political bias' (Galliher 1995: 169–70). This is what I will call the radical reading of Becker's article, and I will begin by explicating it. Later, I will argue that, while there are important ambiguities, this interpretation of the article is misconceived.[2]

---

1 In the Social Sciences Citation Index there were over a hundred citations of this article between 1980 and 1996.
2 Much the same misinterpretation is to be found in some discussions of Goffman's *Asylums*. For example, Fine and Martin interpret his comment that 'to describe the patient's situation faithfully is necessarily to present a partisan view' (Goffman 1961: x) as evidence that the book was intended as a 'political tract' (Fine and Martin 1990: 110) that uses 'literary terrorism' (1990: 99) to present psychiatric institutions as 'dehumanizing' (1990: 109), and patients as 'morally preferable to their keepers' (1990: 91). According to these authors Goffman uses satire, and other rhetorical devices, as a weapon to remedy the gap between how things are and how they ought to be (1990: 101). In my view, Goffman's position is very similar to that of Becker. In the Preface to *Asylums* he refers to his work as 'pure research', without any trace of irony. And elsewhere he describes himself as an urban ethnographer in the tradition of Hughes, and indicates his commitment to the regulative ideal of 'value-freedom' (Verhoeven 1993: 318–19).

The radical reading

There are several features of 'Whose side are we on?' that seem to imply advocacy of partisanship. The title itself assumes that we are forced to choose sides. And this is reinforced in the opening section of the article where Becker rejects value freedom as impossible, and explicitly states that 'the question is not whether we should take sides, since we inevitably will, but whose side we are on' (1967: 239). Moreover, against the background of Becker's work in the sociology of deviance, the implication seems to be that we should side with those in a subordinate position; hence Gouldner's labelling of Becker's position as 'underdog sociology' (Gouldner 1968). Thus, what is proposed could be described as radical in political terms, even though Gouldner argues that it is not radical enough and may still function to support the liberal establishment.[3]

Furthermore, on this reading Becker's article involves epistemological as well as political radicalism. For example, he remarks that: 'there is no position from which sociological research can be done that is not biased in one way or another' (1967: 245). The implication, it may seem, is that there is no objective viewpoint: people in different social locations necessarily have different perspectives, and the researcher must simply adopt one or other of these. This is the kind of relativism that has sometimes been associated with radical versions of the sociology of knowledge, in which 'truth' is no more than what passes for knowledge in a particular community, or what an individual decides is true for him or herself.[4]

This radical reading of Becker's article probably accounts for much of its continuing popularity: it is consonant with the growing influence in many areas of the social sciences of both political and epistemological radicalism, in the form of 'critical' approaches, of constructionism, and of postmodernism. And, as already noted, support for this reading of the article can be provided by seeing it in the context of the labelling theory of deviance, to which Becker made a major contribution in the 1950s and 1960s. In fact, we can treat the article as in some respects an application of labelling theory to the case of sociological work itself.

Labelling theory transformed the field of research on crime and deviance in several ways. Most obviously, it expanded the focus of enquiry to include the processes by which particular types of act, and particular people, come to be labelled as deviant. In this way, the labellers as well as the labelled became objects of study. More fundamentally, on some interpretations, deviance was no longer to be treated as an objective feature of the world whose character could be taken for granted in order to explain why it happened, why changes in its incidence took place, why some groups engaged in more crimes of particular kinds than others, and how crime rates could be reduced. Rather, what counts

---

3 Gouldner softened his attitude towards Becker's position later; see Gouldner 1973a: 463 and
   1973b: xiii. As we shall see, their positions have important similarities as well as differences.
4 For an interpretation of Becker's article along these lines, see Riley 1974a.

as deviance was now treated as a matter of social definition, so that the labelling process came to be regarded as *constitutive* of deviance rather than as merely identifying independently existing offences more or less accurately. In other words, 'deviance' was defined as 'behaviour labelled as deviant', with labelling as a process of social construction that is open to sociological study, and that must be studied if work in the field is not simply to take over the common-sense perspective promulgated by powerful groups in society.

There were two main elements of the argument for this new focus on the social construction of deviance. First, it was pointed out that there is substantial variation across societies in what activities are and are not counted as offences, in either legal or moral terms, with changes in this occurring over time. Furthermore, it was argued that what is and is not an offence in a society in a particular period is to some extent the result of the work of moral entrepreneurs. Moral panics engendered by such entrepreneurs can result in major shifts in attitude towards various sorts of activity, on the part of both the public and government authorities. And, in this way, they can succeed in getting legislation passed to outlaw activities that had previously been legal; though, of course, there may also be campaigns to legalise what was previously prohibited. Changes in attitudes towards and laws about alcohol use, abortion and homosexuality are key twentieth-century examples.

The other main element of labelling theory was an emphasis on the contingency of the relationship between offence and punishment. There are several aspects of this. Different groups in society are subject to different levels of surveillance, so that offences on the part of some people are more likely to come to the attention of law enforcement agencies than are those of others. This is most obviously the case with those who have a criminal record, but it is also generally true in Western societies that the activities of the working class and of particular minority ethnic groups are subjected to greater surveillance than those of middle-class members of the ethnic majority. And further elements of contingency occur in the actual identification of offences, and in responses to them. First of all, the meaning of any rule involves an element of indeterminacy, so that judgement or decision-making is involved about whether it applies in a particular case. Secondly, even when an offence has been identified, discretion is exercised by onlookers in reporting it, and by the police in pursuing investigation of it, so that some types of people may be much more likely to be prosecuted than others, even for the 'same' offence. Thirdly, the courts also involve contingencies that introduce further indeterminacy into the relationship between offence and outcome, for example as regards the securing of legal representation, and in the way that plea-bargaining and courtroom interaction operate.

These two arguments – about intercultural variation in moral and legal rules, and about contingencies in their application – throw doubt on the idea that there are intrinsic differences in causal terms between deviant and non-deviant activities: the same behaviour will be judged deviant in some circumstances but not in others. Above all, labelling theory represents a challenge to the idea that deviants differ psychologically from non-deviants, perhaps suggesting more generally that psychological explanations are of little use in this field. This is reinforced by the argument that even the most hardened criminal conforms to moral and legal rules most of the time: he or she is deviant only in some particular respect and on some occasions. On these grounds, it is insisted that deviant activities should be investigated by sociologists rather than by psychologists, and that this should be done in exactly the same way as with any other form of social activity, employing standard theoretical and methodological resources (see Polsky 1967). No difference in fundamental character should be assumed, even between the social organisation of crime and that of law enforcement. Both must be studied in much the same way. On top of this, some commentators also drew practical and political conclusions, for example in support of policies of 'radical non-intervention' (Schur 1973).[5] Indeed, on some views, deviance was to be regarded as representing political resistance to the dominant social order (see Taylor *et al.* 1973).

Against the background of labelling theory, it is significant that in 'Whose side are we on?' Becker focuses primarily on *accusations* of bias, rather than on bias itself. He is mainly concerned with the conditions under which such accusations arise. He identifies two types of situation: what he calls the non-political and the political. In the former, there is a largely uncontested credibility hierarchy in terms of which those at the top of an organisation or community are assumed to know best. While subordinates may privately hold views that contradict official ones, they are not politically mobilised and their views are not publicised. In this situation, Becker suggests, accusations of researcher bias are likely to come from superordinates, and will arise only when the social scientist does not conform to official views, for example by taking seriously the dissident perspectives of subordinates. In the *political* situation, by contrast, there is a much more open conflict of views, with subordinates being mobilised against superordinates, and their perspectives promoted. As a result, there is no agreed credibility hierarchy. Here, accusations of bias can come from either or both sides, depending on the interpretations of the situation the sociologist adopts.

What this analysis implies is that, as with other kinds of deviance, 'bias' does not refer to some intrinsic feature of the behaviour involved: it is a matter of social definition. Accusations of bias are a product of the situation in which the sociologist works, and it must not be assumed that a research study that is accused of bias is defective or culpable in some naturally given sense. While it may be biased from one point of view, it need not be from others. For instance, it may be seen that way by the powerful but not by the powerless. And the conclusion drawn from this by those who adopt what I am calling the radical

---

5 Discussing delinquency, Schur comments that 'the basic injunction of radical non-intervention is "leave kids alone wherever possible"' (1973: 154), and that 'if the choice is between changing youth and changing the society (including some of its laws) the radical non-interventionist opts for changing the society' (1973: 155). See also Becker and Horowitz (1970) on the 'culture of civility', discussed later in this chapter.

reading of Becker's article is that the sociologist is simply faced with a choice about whose perspective to adopt, with bias being a function of the relationship between that decision and the dominant views within the situation studied. If the researcher takes the point of view of the powerful, there are unlikely to be accusations of bias, at least in the non-political situation. However, if the point of view of subordinates is adopted, the sociologist will probably be accused of bias whatever the situation. On this radical reading of the article, 'bias' is a relative and contingent matter that depends on who is in power and the stance the researcher takes towards them.[6]

Some contrary indications

It is quite clear, then, that there are elements of 'Whose side are we on?' that can be read as insisting on the inevitability of bias: that the researcher cannot avoid taking sides, and that he or she will often be accused of bias, especially by those in power. Furthermore, in line with Becker's work on labelling theory, bias is presented as a contingent product of the situation in which sociologists work, rather than as an intrinsic characteristic of that work. And these elements of the article have often been taken to imply that Becker was recommending active partisanship: that we must choose whose side we are on.

At the same time, however, there are features of the article that do not fit this radical reading of it. We can get some purchase on a different interpretation by noting an important ambiguity in labelling theory that was highlighted by a number of commentators (Pollner 1974; Rains 1975; Fine 1977). Labelling theorists did not consistently deny that deviance exists independently of its labelling by law enforcement agencies and others. The idea was sometimes retained that deviance is a feature of particular forms of action, rather than simply a product of societal reaction. An example of this ambiguity is to be found in a typology presented by Becker in his book, *Outsiders* (see Figure 3.1).

Despite his constructionist slogan that 'deviant behavior is behavior people so label' (Becker 1973: 9), in this diagram Becker acknowledges the possibilities both of a person being 'falsely accused' and of 'secret deviance'. And these assume that deviance can be identified by the analyst independently of whether or not it has been officially labelled as such. Indeed, even the analytic distinction between obedient and rule-breaking behaviour seems to be unsustainable from a constructionist point of view.

In identifying this ambiguity, labelling theory's critics argue that it runs together two incompatible positions. The first is the constructionist approach that underpins what I have referred to as the radical reading of Becker's article. If this is applied consistently, the exclusive focus of analysis becomes the social

---

6 For another application of what I am calling epistemological radicalism to the concept of bias, see McHugh *et al.* 1974. Earlier, Blum (1970) and McHugh (1970) had applied the same approach to deviance.

	TYPES OF BEHAVIOUR	
PERCEPTIONS OF BEHAVIOUR	Obedient behaviour	Rule-breaking behaviour
Perceived as deviant	*Falsely accused*	*Pure deviant*
Not perceived as deviant	*Conforming person*	*Secret deviant*

Figure 3.1 The relationship between labelling and behaviour
Source: Derived from Becker 1973: 2

processes by which deviance is defined, and in particular the discursive strategies that are employed to do this. Deviance has no existence independently of these strategies and therefore cannot be studied in itself. Indeed, the specific concern with law and its enforcement may largely disappear in favour of an interest in the practice of deviance attribution wherever it occurs.[7]

The other version of labelling theory does not involve this kind of epistemological radicalism, but rather a realist view that treats activities as deviant or not deviant in terms of their relationship to some set of moral or legal rules, irrespective of whether they have actually been so labelled. Indeed, one of the central interests is the degree of mismatch between what *could be* labelled as deviant and what *is actually* labelled, drawing attention to the possibility of *discriminatory application* of the rules.[8] Another focus is on the *effects* of labelling, in particular on the possibility that it might amplify deviance.

First of all, then, this approach emphasises that variation in the application of rules may involve discrimination against particular groups, and even the creation of spurious offences. In his Foreword to Selby's *Zapotec Deviance*, Becker notes that, if people in the traditional Mesoamerican community that Selby studied 'can routinely discover witches who we know do not exist', this shows the necessity of keeping the possibility in mind 'that [in mainstream American society] physicians and policemen find lunatics and criminals where none exist' (Becker 1974: x–xi). Secondly, the concern with deviance amplification points to another way in which state agencies can generate deviance: through the consequences of labelling. Contrary to the official view that prosecuting deviants has a deterrent effect, labelling theorists argue that it may

---

7 This is the position adopted by Kitsuse; see Kitsuse 1962 and Rains 1975. It has subsequently been extended to the study of social problems generally; see Spector and Kitsuse 1977 and Ibarra and Kitsuse 1993. See Holstein and Miller 1993 for diverse assessments of Kitsuse's 'strict constructionism'.

8 Thus, Lemert was concerned with assessing the difference between warranted and unwarranted societal reaction; see Rains 1975. See also the attempts of Goode and Ben Yehuda (1994: ch. 3) to define 'moral panic' as an excessive or unwarranted societal reaction.

actually cause further deviance. This can occur both as a result of changes in deviants' situations (removing their normal means of maintaining a livelihood, undermining their relationships with kin and friends, etc.) and as a result of redefinition of their identities (whereby they come to see themselves wholly in terms of the deviant identity, and start to value that identity in order to preserve self-esteem).[9] Indeed, one writer suggests that deviance amplification may actually be functional for social systems, since deviance is essential for their 'boundary-maintenance' (Erikson 1964 and 1966).

The constructionist and realist versions of labelling theory are incompatible. It is not possible to identify discriminatory or spurious labelling if deviance cannot be identified independently of the labelling process. Similarly, the concept of deviance amplification requires that the actual level of deviant activity be measurable by the analyst in order to show that it has increased, a possibility that constructionism denies.

In 'Whose side are we on?' this ambiguity in labelling theory has a direct parallel. On the one hand, as already noted, Becker seems to define 'bias' in terms of accusations of bias, explaining how bias arises not by referring to the behaviour of the researcher but to the conditions in which he or she works, and the interests of powerful others. Thus, he seems to treat bias as nothing more than behaviour on the part of the social scientist that is so labelled. And this constructionist view corresponds with more recent arguments to the effect that notions of objectivity and bias are ideological, designed to ensure that research supports the interests of dominant groups; or at least that their legitimacy is relative to a particular epistemological paradigm (see, for instance, Harding 1992). On the other hand, Becker's discussion of bias in 'Whose side are we on?' extends beyond a concern with external accusations of bias, and in doing so he deviates from the constructionist position in two important respects.

First of all, he notes in passing that sociologists may suspect *themselves* of bias for much the same reasons as do others. In parallel terms, it was sometimes explicitly recognised by labelling theorists that deviants are often only too aware that they are engaging in activities that would be regarded as deviant by others. Attention was thus given to the ways in which justifications or excuses are used by deviants to account for their actions, explaining why their actions are legitimate or allowable despite the appearance of immorality or the fact of illegality (Cressey 1950 and 1953; Sykes and Matza 1957; Matza 1964).[10] Moreover, it is only a short step from this to acknowledging that actors may sometimes engage in activities that *they themselves* regard as illegitimate, or at

9 See, for example, Ray 1961.
10 The case of political deviance is particularly interesting since here the activities may be engaged in precisely *because* they challenge the rules. Of course, not all acts that are defined as deviant by actors will be officially labelled as deviant, and there will also be acts that are officially labelled where the actor was never aware of that possibility.

least see their behaviour as culpable.[11] What these points suggest is that notions of normality, morality and law are frequently built into the very performance of actions, long before any societal reaction. In parallel terms, Becker recognises that researchers are guided by methodological considerations about what conclusions should and should not be drawn on the basis of the evidence collected, what further evidence may be required, etc. In other words, potential bias is a focus of concern for researchers themselves, not just for other interested parties.

This first point is not necessarily incompatible with social constructionism, however. It may be argued that self-labelling is a product of the internalisation of the dominant social norms by the deviant. And this argument can be applied to the case of research, with concepts like objectivity being presented as the product of a methodology that is infused by the culture of positivism or by patri-archal ideology. While it does not follow that simply because social norms are internalised they must be socially oppressive, this often seems to be assumed. And one reading of the whole modernist project in epistemology suggests that its logical end-point is the conclusion that any notion of method, or any concept of truth as external to the researcher, is a constraint on freedom (Pippin 1991).

However this may be, the second respect in which Becker moves beyond a concern with external accusations of bias cannot be reconciled with the radical reading of his article. Early on, he draws a distinction between why accusations of bias are made and the truth of those accusations, a distinction that is not formulatable within constructionism:

> I will look first … not at the truth or falsity of the charge [of bias], but rather at the circumstances in which it is typically made and felt. The soci-ology of knowledge cautions us to distinguish between the truth of a statement and an assessment of the circumstances under which that state-ment is made; though we trace an argument to its source in the interests of the person who made it, we have still not proved it false.
>
> (Becker 1967: 240)

Here Becker commits himself to a moderate approach to the sociology of knowledge, rather than to what I referred to earlier as its more radical form.[12] Moreover, he promises to address the issue of the validity of accusations later. And, indeed, three-quarters of the way through his article, he returns to this issue. He comments: 'What I have said so far is all sociology of knowledge, suggesting by whom, in what situations and for what reasons sociologists will be

---

11 One area where this has been recognised is in studies of illness as deviance. See, for example, Lorber 1967.

12 For discussions of different versions of the sociology of knowledge, see Curtis and Petras 1970, Hamilton 1974, and Hekman 1986.

accused of bias and distortion' (1967: 245). And what he says in the closing pages of the article conflicts with what is implied by the 'radical' reading of it.

First of all, he recognises that the researcher can take account of more than one perspective, rather than simply having to line up with one side or the other. Thus, he writes, 'no matter what perspective he takes, [the sociologist's] work either will take account of the attitude of subordinates, or it will not'. Here the question being addressed no longer seems to be whose side the researcher is on but rather whether he or she simply adopts the views of the powerful or takes account of those of the less powerful as well. Moreover, Becker notes that the distinction between a superordinate and a subordinate is a relative one. He comments: 'Is it not true that the superordinates in a hierarchical relationship usually have their own superordinates with whom they must contend?' (1967: 246). And he continues:

> if a prison administrator is angered because we take the complaints of his inmates seriously, we may feel that we can get around that and get a more balanced picture by interviewing him and his associates. If we do, we may then write a report which *his* superiors will respond to with cries of 'bias'. They, in their turn, will say that we have not presented a balanced picture, because we have not looked at *their* side of it. And we may worry that what they say is true.
>
> (1967: 247)

Becker points to the problem of 'infinite regress' here: 'for everyone has someone standing above him who prevents him from doing things just as he likes'. Thus, he concludes, 'we can never have a "balanced picture" until we have studied all of society simultaneously', adding 'I do not propose to hold my breath to that happy day' (1967: 247).

From this it seems that the problem is not that an objective or balanced view is impossible in principle but rather that it is very difficult to achieve in practice, and that we have to carry on with our work before it is achieved (indeed, if we did not do so it could never be achieved). This is reinforced right at the end of the article when Becker writes:

> It is something of a solution to say that over the years each 'one-sided' study will provoke further studies that gradually enlarge our grasp of all the relevant facets of an institution's operation. But that is a long-term solution, and not much help to the individual researcher who has to contend with the anger of officials who feel he has done them wrong, the criticism of those of his colleagues who think he is presenting a one-sided view, and his own worries.
>
> (1967: 247)[13]

---

13 There are echoes here of the concept of the mosaic that Becker introduces in another article, with each study contributing a new piece that adds to the overall picture (Becker 1966).

The second kind of evidence against the radical interpretation of Becker's article to be found in its closing pages is the fact that he not only recognises that accusations of bias may be true, but also that it is the researcher's responsibility to try to avoid bias. He writes: 'our problem is to make sure that, whatever the point of view we take, our research meets the standards of good scientific work, that our unavoidable sympathies do not render our results invalid'. He then elaborates on this, noting the ways in which 'we might distort our findings, because of our sympathy with one of the parties in the relationship we are studying, by misusing the tools and techniques of our discipline'. And he insists that: 'by using our theories and techniques *impartially* [emphasis added], we ought to be able to study all the things that need to be studied in such a way as to get all the facts we require, even though some of the questions that will be raised and some of the facts that will be produced run counter to our prejudices'.

Indeed, Becker warns against what he refers to as 'sentimentality': the refusal to investigate some matter that should properly be regarded as problematic. And he clarifies this as follows: 'We are sentimental, especially, when … we would prefer not to know what is going on, if to know would be to violate some sympathy whose existence we may not even be aware of.' He concludes this part of his argument as follows: 'Whatever side we are on, we must use our techniques impartially enough that a belief to which we are especially sympathetic could be proved untrue. We must always inspect our work carefully enough to know whether our techniques and theories are open enough to allow that possibility' (1967: 246).

These comments conflict sharply with the reading of Becker's article as advocating political and epistemological radicalism in the form of partisanship. Emphasis on the need for researchers to be as impartial as possible is discrepant with the idea that they are unavoidably or justifiably partisan. Moreover, in these passages, Becker explicitly recognises that bias is not simply constituted by accusations of bias: that there is a real danger of researchers allowing their analyses to be swayed by their sympathies, *and* that this source of bias can be (and ought to be) minimised by taking precautions against it. What is implied here is a rather conventional conception of the requirements of social scientific work; indeed, one that can be labelled as adherence to the principle of value neutrality (see Becker 1973: 198). It is assumed that there are real phenomena to be described and explained, phenomena that exist independently of our interpretations of them. And Becker sees science as having privileged access to knowledge of these phenomena as a result of its methodological orientation, which should be geared to the production of objective knowledge through efforts to avoid bias.

Resolving the ambiguities

The obvious question that arises from this discussion is: which interpretation of Becker's article is correct? Which side was he on? Was he recommending

political partisanship or scholarly detachment? Was he proposing a constructionist account of bias or a more traditional realist one?

Of course, there are those who would argue that these questions are un-
answerable. In fact, this conclusion may be derivable from social
constructionism itself. Constructionists often deny that meanings are inherent
in texts, any more than they are inherent in actions, insisting that they are
constructed by readers. In these terms, Becker's article is open to being read in
different ways: as politically and epistemologically radical but also as advocating
a more conventional scholarly position. For constructionists there can be no
way of adjudicating between these two readings in terms of accuracy, though
they may seek to discriminate between them in value terms (judgement about
this necessarily being subjective) (see Fish 1989).

However, it is worth noting that, in responding to criticism of his article,
Becker does not conform to a constructionist approach. First of all, he appeals
to what he intended to say and the possibility of this being misinterpreted.
He begins his response to Riley's claim that he denies the principle of objectivity as follows: 'Riley may have a quarrel, but it isn't with me. Evidently
I failed to make the argument of my paper sufficiently unambiguous to prevent
the misinterpretation of my position that he has made' (Becker 1971: 13). In
this way, the form of Becker's response may be taken as evidence against the
radical reading of his article. Moreover, this is confirmed by the *content* of his
response. He distinguishes between two types of bias: as 'favoring or appearing
to favor one or another side in a controversy', and as 'statements of fact that are
demonstrably incorrect'. And he indicates that his main focus in the article was
on the first not the second, and that he was not denying the possibility of objective knowledge. He writes: 'Saying that our research, insofar as it deals with
matters of public concern, will inevitably confirm or impugn conventional
wisdom on those matters in no way suggests or implies that objective research is
not possible' (Becker 1971: 13).[14]

There is strong evidence, then, from both within 'Whose side are we on?',
and from Becker's response to criticism of it, which counts against the radical
reading. However, this conclusion does not entirely resolve the ambiguity we
have identified in the article. It does not explain how the evidence that

---

14 A constructionist might respond to this evidence by denying that writers have any privilege in
identifying the meaning of what they wrote (perhaps also pointing out that, in any case, we
have to *interpret* their meta-comments about it, these also not being open to a 'correct' interpretation). And it is true that there are good reasons not to assign a writer absolute
epistemological privilege: memory is subject to erosion and distortion over time, the writer
might have an interest in lying, and the writing process is never entirely under his or her
control. However, we can accept these points without denying that the writer usually has additional data available compared to the reader, and that his or her account of the intended
message ought to be taken seriously. But, in any case, the constructionists' arguments can be
turned back on themselves: how can we interpret what a constructionist says as representing
constructionism without seeking to construct some sense of what he or she intended to say?

supported the radical reading is to be reinterpreted. When faced with an ambiguity, initially at least, we should act on the assumption that there was a coherent message, and explore ways in which the ambiguity could be a product of misreading.[15] This does not mean that we cannot subsequently conclude that there is a fundamental inconsistency in Becker's position, but rather that we should only reach that conclusion after all the plausible ways of eliminating it have been explored. Nor are we prevented from criticising Becker's position in other ways; but it is important that we try to ensure that we do so on the basis of a sound understanding of what his position is.

It is worth noting that Becker does not seem to regard his arguments as carrying contradictory implications in either political or epistemological terms (Becker 1973), and I want to suggest that this is understandable given the background assumptions on which he relies.

Political radicalism

To point up the ambiguity in Becker's article, we might say that he argues both that we cannot avoid taking sides and that we should avoid taking sides. But, in large part, this ambiguity stems from his use of the terms 'bias' and 'taking sides' to cover several different matters. And there is a way of summarising his argument that removes this ambiguity, and which accounts for all of the data in the article:

> Becker employs three definitions of bias in terms of which researchers *cannot avoid* being biased. First of all, researchers are constantly in danger of being biased, in the sense of being accused of bias, because of the nature of the situations in which they work. In much of his discussion, and in line with some interpretations of labelling theory, Becker does not distinguish explicitly between such accusations and actual bias on the part of the researcher, even though there are other places where he recognises this distinction. The second sense in which bias may be unavoidable is that researchers often have more sympathy for some of the people in the situations they study than for others; and as a result they may find the views of those people especially plausible. This follows from the fact that researchers are human beings, that they themselves belong to society and will therefore have their own commonsense assumptions, political views and personal preferences. A third sense in which sociologists cannot avoid being biased is that they cannot take account of every possible point of view: there is a practical limit to the number of perspectives that can be incorporated into any study. As a result, there is always the danger that some key feature of a

---

15 This can be justified by what is often called the principle of charity; see Grice 1989. See also Gadamer's argument that interpretation involves projection of a coherent whole (Warnke 1987).

situation has been overlooked because the particular perspective from which it would have been highlighted was not used in the analysis.

Becker also uses a fourth sense of 'bias', in terms of which we *need not*, and *should not*, be biased. By using our disciplinary theories and methods we ought to be able to avoid external pressures or internal sympathies leading us into systematic error, and we must take all available precautions against this.

It is a key feature of Becker's position that the relationships among these four types of bias are not tight. Thus, not being biased in the final sense does not ensure that researchers will not be viewed as partisan. Indeed, in many circumstances it is precisely when they do their work well that such accusations are most likely to arise. Becker's discussion of the political and non-political situations is intended to demonstrate this (see also Becker 1964). Similarly, he does not see any necessary relationship between being more sympathetic to the views of one party in a situation and systematic error. By taking the proper precautions, 'sentimentality' should be avoidable. So, in large part, the ambiguity of Becker's article stems from his failure to indicate clearly which of these four senses of the term 'bias' or 'taking sides' he is using at any particular point; and/or from the failure of readers to recognise this from the relevant contexts of use.

The above argument suggests that the politically radical reading of 'Whose side are we on?' is mistaken: Becker was not proposing that researchers must choose which side they are on and do research in such a way as to serve it. Nevertheless, I suspect that there *is* still a sense in which Becker sees sociological research as politically partisan: *in its effects*. In his response to criticisms of labelling theory, he comments at one point: 'interactionist theories look (and are) rather Left. Intentionally or otherwise, they are corrosive of the conventional modes of thought and established institutions' (Becker 1973: 197). And, in an article co-authored with Irving Louis Horowitz, he argues that sociologists cannot help being politically radical: that there is an 'isomorphism between good sociology and radical sociology' (Becker and Horowitz 1972: 50). 'Isomorphism' is probably misleading here, since Becker and Horowitz do not argue that doing sociology is *the same* as engaging in radical political activity. But they do point to significant overlap, and a functional relationship, between the two activities.

The first step of this argument is recognition that because sociologists do not simply accept official views but subject them to scrutiny, they tend to be seen as a threat by those in power. Becker comments:

Elites, ruling classes, bosses, adults, men, Caucasians – superordinate groups generally – maintain their power as much by controlling how people define their world, its components, and its possibilities, as by the use of more primitive forms of control. They may use more primitive means to establish hegemony. But control based on the manipulation of definitions and labels works more smoothly and costs less; superordinates prefer it.

(Becker 1973: 204–5)

And, indeed, in 'Whose side are we on?', Becker argues that because officials are responsible for the running of institutions they 'usually have to lie':

> Officials must lie because things are seldom as they ought to be. For a great variety of reasons, well-known to sociologists, institutions are refractory. They do not perform as society would like them to. Hospitals do not cure people; prisons do not rehabilitate prisoners; schools do not educate students. Since they are supposed to, officials develop ways both of denying the failure of the institution to perform as it should and explaining those failures which cannot be hidden.
>
> (1967: 242–3)

Thus, it is not just that sociology's questioning of 'official realities' is *seen* by those in power as subversive, but that its effects *are* subversive: 'A sociology that is true to the world inevitably clarifies what has been confused, reveals the character of organisational secrets, and upsets the interests of powerful people and groups' (Becker and Horowitz 1972: 55). One aspect of this is that sociologists:

> violate society's hierarchy of credibility. They question the monopoly on the truth and the 'whole story' claimed by those in positions of power and authority. They suggest that we need to discover the truth about allegedly deviant phenomena for ourselves, instead of relying on the officially certified accounts which ought to be enough for any good citizen. They adopt a relativistic stance toward the accusations and definitions of deviance made by respectable people and constituted authority, treating them as the raw material of social science analysis rather than as statements of unquestioned moral truths.
>
> (Becker 1973: 207–8)

And if, in addition, sociological research confirms the validity of some of the views of subordinates who are critical of the way things are run, the offence of the sociologist is even greater.

However, most subversive of all is when, as in the case of labelling theory, the sociologist includes the activities of officials within the focus of his or her analysis, actually documenting their attempts to manipulate definitions, or to lie, so as to serve their own purposes. In doing this, the sociologist exposes the mechanisms of power and may thereby not only de-legitimate and destabilise the position of the powerful but also point up how it can be challenged.

In these ways, then, while Becker does not argue that sociological work should be directed towards achieving political goals, he regards its *effects* as politically radical, in that they threaten the dominant power structure. Of course, we might interpret this as no more than a *description* of what actually happens: that organisations and communities involve hierarchies, that those at the top maintain their position to a large extent by manipulating ideas and information, and that as a result sociological research may destabilise the organisation or community concerned. There is no *necessary* implication that this destabilising effect is politically desirable.[16] So, it is not just that the politically radical effects of sociological research will not be directly intended by the sociologist, but also that they will not always be seen as desirable from his or her point of view.

However, there is some evidence that Becker *does* regard these radical effects as politically progressive. He sees the sociologist who takes account of the views of underdogs, who disregards the dominant credibility hierarchy, and who documents the manipulative strategies used by those in power, as playing a role in a wider political movement to which all sociologists are effectively committed, whether they recognise it or not. Thus, Becker and Horowitz not only argue that sociological work that supports the status quo is typically of poor quality, and that good sociology tends to be radical in its consequences, but also imply that this radicalism is politically progressive. They outline the founding assumptions of radical politics as follows:

> where circumstances compel a choice between individual interests, self-expression and personal welfare, on the one hand, and social order, stability, and the collective good, on the other ... a radical politics acts for the person as against the collectivity. It acts to maximise the number and the variety of options people have open to them, at the expense of neatness, order, peace and system.
>
> (Becker and Horowitz 1972: 52)

In addition, the authors declare that 'radical sociology ... rests on a desire to change society in a way that will increase equality and maximise freedom, and it makes a distinctive contribution to the struggle for change' (1972: 52–3). The terms the authors employ here to describe radicalism are of a kind that imply its virtue. Moreover, they also state their own allegiance to this radical politics:

> We ourselves believe that every society and every set of social arrangements must be inspected for their potential inequalities and interferences with freedom, even those which seem to conform to one or another blueprint for a socialist utopia. ... While we look for the convergence of personal and public goals, when we are compelled to make a choice, it is on behalf of persons.
>
> (1972: 52)

It is also of significance that the authors see political radicalism as closely

---

16 Indeed, there are those who see it as undesirable and in need of restraint; see Shils 1980.

associated with 'a repudiation of all forms of mystical, theological and super-naturalist interpretations of events' (1972: 53). Here, in particular, there is a strong implication that pursuit of the true is closely related to achievement of the good society. Becker and Horowitz write: 'One task of a radical sociology is ... to persuade the oppressed and radical of the need for as total dedication to what is true as to what they may deem to be good' (1972: 54). Indeed, in a significant respect they see the sociologist as even more radical than the activist: 'the activist achieving his goals seeks to enjoy the fruits of his victory; the radical sociologist looks for new sources of inequality and privilege to under-stand, expose and uproot' (1972: 56).[17]

What this suggests, I think, is that while Becker regards science and progressive politics as distinct, and even recognises that they may occasionally come into conflict, he assumes that there is a fundamental affinity between them in the way they operate in the world. Moreover, I think this view is characteristic of what has come to be thought of as Chicago sociology (and of many other kinds of sociology too). As is well-known, in its early years, the Chicago Department of Sociology had a close relationship with practical efforts to deal with social problems in the city. These efforts arose out of Christian concern, both about the sinful ways of life that flourished in the new urban areas and about the poor living conditions of many inhabitants. Indeed, the two were treated as very closely related. Over time, however, a process of secularisation took place, with growing emphasis given to science as a basis for understanding the world, including social problems. Of course, many stressed the compatibility of religion and science, and to some extent what happened was a transmutation of a religious into a secular orientation, an orientation that appealed to science for its justification but went beyond it in its commitments.[18]

However, built into the growing influence of science was pressure towards the detachment of sociology from any immediate involvement in amelioration or reform. In fact, this was probably an essential requirement for acceptance of the subject as a legitimate scientific discipline in the university (Bulmer 1984; Harvey 1987). It is important to recognise, though, that this move involved a separation of sociology from practical concerns, rather than the abandonment of all interest in practical matters on the part of Chicago sociologists. To varying degrees, they retained a concern with urban problems and a belief in the value of sociology for illuminating and offering remedies for these problems. What changed was that they now increasingly assumed that scientific investigation must be independent of practical involvements if it is to be carried out in a rigorous fashion. It required a degree of detachment that would allow the

---

17 There may be doubts about the validity of my account of Becker's views here, arising from the dual authorship of the paper. However, it is worth noting that he reprinted it in a later collection; see Becker 1986. And he has confirmed the analysis in a personal communication. There is also an issue about the *nature* of the radicalism involved, but I will leave this on one side for the moment.

18 The career of John Dewey exemplifies this; see Ryan 1995.

questioning of taken-for-granted assumptions and the examination of social problems in a wider context. Hughes comments about Park:

> If he was ever tempted to become an 'expert' on some particular social problem, he was held back by his conviction that every event had a place somewhere in the universal human processes, that no situation can be understood until one finds in it those universal qualities which allow one to compare it with other situations – however near or distant in time, place and appearance.
>
> (Hughes 1971: 548)

Nevertheless, for Park, the function of sociology was still to facilitate the solution of social problems:

> Park came to believe, with Dewey and others, that the key lay in communication ... and public opinion. If only the reporting of events, large and small, were complete and the circulation of the news equally so, human progress would proceed apace.
>
> (1971: 544)

For Park, research amounted to 'bringing about reform by telling the news' (1971: 545).

The separation between sociology and practical concerns that began in the 1930s was extended in the 1940s and 1950s. A crucial event here was the shift from the social disorganisation paradigm towards cultural relativism (Carey 1975; Dubin 1983). In many ways, this relativism was the mirror image of the earlier Christian concern with sin and immorality. It built on the pragmatism that had undermined such moralistic thinking about social problems. From a pragmatist viewpoint, those problems were seen as failures in social adjustment, at most as pathological reactions to such failures. But the influence of anthropology, with its documentation of cultural diversity and implicit (if not explicit) condemnation of ethnocentrism, further encouraged detached sociological investigation. It stimulated sociologists to question not only conventional views about the causes of social problems and how they should be dealt with, but also the very conceptualisation of those problems – even what was, and was not, treated as a problem.

For Becker, another factor pushing in the same direction was Everett Hughes' encouragement of his students to study some occupation or institution of which they had personal experience. As a result, Becker, who was involved in the jazz scene as a pianist, did his masters thesis on the jazz musician. We can imagine that one of the effects of this would be to increase the tendency to take seriously the point of view of the people studied, rather than seeing these as simply a reflection of social disorganisation or of their social circumstances. At the risk of reification, we can say that in the early years of his career Becker lived in two social worlds: the hip world of the jazz musician, and of the other groups with which that occupation was involved, and the straight world of the sociologist. Moreover, he was marginal in academic terms, not having a teaching position and still considering music as a possible career (Debro 1970; Becker 1986).

What this suggests is that Becker's position would have enabled him to see the extent to which sociology, even Chicago sociology, was still shaped by the official views of mainstream society. This can be illustrated by the problems that arose in getting *The Fantastic Lodge* published, a life history that Becker collected in the course of studying heroin addicts (the author was the wife of a fellow musician) (Hughes 1961; Bennett 1981). The views that Janet expresses about her own situation, and especially about the role of law enforcement agencies in relation to addicts, may well have been close to those of Becker himself at the time, given that he moved in fairly similar circles to her. One of the sources of resistance to publication on the part of the Institute for Juvenile Research, based at Chicago and headed by Clifford Shaw, was concern about being associated with these views. In part this was motivated by fear of the effects on the funding of the Institute, but it also stemmed from a belief that her life history should be located in the context of the wider research project and subjected to analysis. And at the back of this, one suspects, was an antipathy to her radical views.

However, despite his commitment to the publication of Janet's life history without theoretical commentary, Becker did not see sociology as concerned simply with providing a voice for those on the margins. Instead, his view was that much current sociology was not living up to its own ideals, in that it failed to incorporate what could be learned from looking at the world from the viewpoint of those outside the mainstream. And, indeed, emphasis on the need for this was characteristic of the approach that he had learned from Hughes. This involved an insistence on treating everyone's behaviour in exactly the same manner, irrespective of who they were in terms of the conventional status hierarchy or the moral values of the wider society. A kind of scepticism is involved here, though one deriving from a commitment to scientific rigour rather than to epistemological doubt. It is not that what the powerful say must automatically be rejected, and what the powerless say automatically accepted, but that all views must be taken account of and subjected to careful scrutiny.

Nevertheless, the impression received by readers was often of radical critique. When applied to high-status groups this approach comes across to anyone reading it on the basis of conventional values as irreverent; while when it is applied to low status groups it seems to be validating the latter's 'unacceptable' views and forms of behaviour. So, given that most sociology had tended to accept the point of view of those higher up the status hierarchy, this orientation appeared critical of existing social arrangements. This was true even though it involved a *suspension* of conventional values, rather than the adoption of anti-conventional values as a foundation for sociological work.

As already noted, it seems likely that Becker's own political outlook involved radical criticism of the existing social order. And we can get some sense of this from another article that he wrote jointly with Horowitz, at around the same time as the one already discussed. In 'The culture of civility' they take San Francisco as providing a model of a city where an accommodation has been achieved between 'straight' society and law enforcement agencies, on the one hand, and deviant and ethnic minorities, on the other; so that considerable cultural diversity is allowed. The authors note that this involves each side giving up something in return for 'a tranquillity that permits one to go about his business unharmed that many will find attractive'. Thus, Becker and Horowitz comment that San Francisco's 'politicians and police can allow and live with activities that would freak out their opposite numbers elsewhere' (Becker and Horowitz 1970: 14). On the other side deviants 'curb their activities according to what they think the community will stand for' (1970: 17). So, the ultimate lesson of San Francisco is that 'the price of civilisation, civility and living together peacefully is not getting everything you want' (1970: 17).

The authors emphasise that this tolerant social order cannot be imposed from above by federal, state or city bureaucracies. Indeed, the policies of these agencies generally inhibit local accommodation, and thereby make things worse. Rather, the culture of civility is the outcome of a 'myriad of separate local bargains [which] respect and reflect what most of the involved parties want or are willing to settle for'. And the authors contrast what had happened in San Francisco with attempts at rational urban planning:

> Too often, the search for 'model cities' implies not so much a model as an ideology – a rationalistic vision of human interaction that implies a people whose consistency of behavior can nowhere be found. ... To design a city in conformity to 'community standards' – which turn out to be little more than the prejudices of building inspectors, housing designers and absentee landlords – only reinforces patterns of frustration, violence and antagonism that now characterise so many of America's large cities.
>
> (1970: 18–19)

What we have here is a kind of radical liberalism (or, if one prefers, a moderate libertarianism), and it is not difficult to see an elective affinity between this and the detached sociological attitude encouraged by Hughes. Just as sociology requires us to suspend some of our own cognitive assumptions and moral evaluations in order to understand the perspectives and behaviour of others, so too this political stance demands a recognition that others have different views, and that only by accepting their right to act on these (within limits) will we ourselves be free to live in our own way (within limits).

It is also worth noting the state of American sociology at the time that 'Whose side are we on?' was written. In the late 1950s and 1960s, the dominance of functionalist sociology and survey research was challenged from several directions. Significant here was the growing influence of critics like C. Wright Mills, the sudden publication of labelling theory in 1962, in which Becker himself played a key role as editor of *Social Problems* (Spector 1976), and

Gouldner's savaging of the commitment to value neutrality (Gouldner 1962). This was also a time of increasing political radicalism on the part of students. In many ways, we can see Becker as aligned with the radicals in their reaction against the dominant forms of sociological work. At the same time, as we have seen, he sought to resist demands that sociology should serve radical political action in a direct way, and to counter the rejection of social scientific work in radical political circles as impossible or pointless. There is a balancing act involved here, which is perhaps most evident in 'Radical politics and sociological research' (Becker and Horowitz 1972). And Becker's ability to keep his balance may have been enhanced by his combination of a professional commitment to a scientific sociology with a personal commitment to egalitarianism and libertarianism. In other words, in the circumstances of the time, the ambiguities generated by these commitments may have been functional for him, and for the kind of sociological work he wished to promote. In the late 1960s there was no pressure for this ambiguity to be addressed, and addressing it would have raised doubts about the radicalism of his position. By 1972 there may have been more pressure for clarification, which Becker and Horowitz provide to some extent; though some ambiguities remain.

There is evidence to suggest, then, that at the time he wrote 'Whose side are we on?' Becker may not only have believed that sociology is politically radical in its effects but also that this radicalism is desirable. But it is important to remember that the central message of Becker and Horowitz's article is that political radicalism requires good sociology, and that this involves adherence to traditional methodological requirements. These authors explicitly warn against tailoring sociological work to suit political demands. Indeed, at one point they comment that 'the radical sociologist will ... find that his scientific "conservatism" – in the sense of being unwilling to draw conclusions on the basis of insufficient evidence – creates tensions with radical activists' (1972: 55). We can summarise what these authors say as follows: by resisting taking sides, in the sense of trying to be impartial and scientific, the sociologist will nevertheless serve the struggle of the underdogs against the powerful, and thereby further the pursuit of freedom and equality. Indeed, a scientific sociology will be more effective in political terms than one that is biased in a radical direction. Sociological work necessarily erodes the power of those at the top by undermining their control of knowledge, and in doing so it facilitates the emergence of organisations, communities and societies in which power differences are abolished or at least reduced.

If it is correct to ascribe this 'Enlightenment' view of the social role of research to Becker, it is something he shares with Gouldner. At the same time, Gouldner is correct to draw a distinction between their positions. The difference stems from the conceptions of the larger society to which each writer is committed. Where Gouldner adopts a view much like that of Mills, Becker's perspective reflects the influence of Hughes; both in terms of recognising the complexity of forms of social organisation as well as what we might call the urbane political scepticism to which that recognition leads (see Chapoulie 1996: 22–5). For example, Becker's emphasis on the relativity of subordination and super-ordination undermines any simple view of society as consisting of the powerful and the powerless. And there is evidence in his work of a pluralism whereby who is in power varies across communities and organisations, rather than being consolidated into a single power élite.[19] Moreover, Becker's political outlook seems to be liberal rather than socialist, and it is resolutely anti-Utopian. If San Francisco in the late 1960s was the good society, it was one in which freedom of the individual was maximised in practical terms, but where the freedom of everyone was nevertheless curtailed somewhat so that all could live in peace. By contrast, under the influence of Marxism, Gouldner holds out the prospect of a new society in which complete freedom and equality can be realised.[20]

What emerges from this discussion is that 'Whose side are we on?' does not call for partisan research in the sense of research designed to serve the interests of one side rather than another in society. For Becker, any political radicalism that sociological work has is necessarily a by-product of a sound scientific approach. And in this respect his article is sharply at odds with much recent advocacy of researcher partisanship, some of which appeals to the radical reading of his article for support.[21]

Epistemological radicalism

In many respects, the discussion in the previous section has resolved not just the question of whether or not 'Whose side are we on?' advocates political partisanship but also its epistemological ambiguity. It is clear that what Becker meant by the inevitability of taking sides was that researchers could not avoid the risk of being accused of bias, avoid having sympathies for some people rather than others, or take into account the views of everyone. There is no clear evidence that he was arguing that there are conflicting factual views of the world, all equally valid. Indeed, he holds out the possibility of getting the whole picture by putting many partial studies together. And he insists on the importance of trying to prevent both official pressure and personal sympathies distorting research, and on the need for the sociologist to be committed to the scientific pursuit of objective knowledge. Confirming this, in his reply to Riley's claim that his article advocates a relativistic position, he describes his main focus as having been on accusations of bias, not on actual bias. In other words, what he offered was a sociological analysis of bias, not a philosophical or a methodological one.[22] The discussion of actual bias and how it can be combated constitutes only a small part of the article, and Becker probably

---

19 It should be noted, though, that Lemert ascribes neglect of this pluralism to labelling theory, and to Becker. See Lemert 1974.
20 On Gouldner's views, see Chapter 4.
21 See, for instance, Mac an Ghaill 1991 and Troyna 1995.
22 It is perhaps of significance that Riley is a philosopher by training.

regarded it as voicing fairly obvious methodological principles that needed no more than a mention. In the sociological context in which he was writing, these principles were neither novel nor contentious. The distinctive contribution of the article, from the point of view of its author, clearly lay in his application of a moderate sociology of knowledge perspective to the work of sociologists themselves, thereby illuminating some of the problems they face, notably the negative reactions of others to their work.[23]

Furthermore, this interpretation fits with the clarification of his approach to the sociology of deviance that Becker provided in response to criticism (Becker 1973). There, he acknowledges the contradiction between the idea that deviance is what is so labelled, on the one hand, and references to secret deviance and false accusations, on the other. And, as we saw, he sought to resolve it by reformulating the distinction between rule-breaking and obedient behaviour as that between actions which are open to labelling as deviant in terms of a particular set of rules and those which are not. In this manner he adopts what I have been calling a realist rather than a constructionist approach. Moreover, it is one that is non-evaluative: there is no implication that any particular set of rules is morally justified (and there are only hints that current ones might not be). For Becker, the central features of labelling theory are that rules defining what is deviant vary across and within societies; that we cannot assume a direct correspondence between what *could be* labelled as deviant and what *is actually* so labelled; and, finally, that labelling can amplify rather than discourage deviance.

All this said, I think there is some residual ambiguity of an epistemological kind in 'Whose side are we on?', and this can be highlighted by looking more carefully at the parallel between Becker's treatment of bias and his work on deviance. Even in its reformulated version, Becker's approach to deviance treats that phenomenon as very much a social product, in the sense that what is deviant cannot be identified independently of some culturally variable set of rules for identifying it. In other words, although the acts labelled as deviant exist before and independently of the rules, their character as deviant does not. Above all, he insists that moral and legal rules do not identify intrinsic features of the acts that they pick out as deviant.

---

23 Much of the confusion in Riley's interpretation arises from his treatment of the sociology of knowledge in too monolithic and crude a manner, neglecting in particular that many of those working in this field have recognised the genetic fallacy. As Merton (1968: 515) comments:

> the perennial problem of the implications of existential influences upon knowledge for the epistemological status of that knowledge has been hotly debated from the outset. Solutions to this problem, which assume that a sociology of knowledge is necessarily a sociological theory of knowledge, range from the claim that the 'genesis of thought has no necessary relation to its validity' to the extreme relativist position that truth is 'merely' a function of a social or cultural basis, that it rests solely upon social consensus, and consequently that any culturally accepted theory of truth has a claim to validity equal to that of any other.

Now, if we were to apply this approach to the sociology of knowledge, what we would get is similar to the kind of sociology of science that has come to be referred to as the 'strong programme'.[24] This treats what is accepted as scientific knowledge at any particular time as socially defined, in much the same manner that Becker treats what counts as deviance as socially defined. It specifically renounces any concern with whether or not the 'knowledge' it focuses on is sound, treating this as irrelevant to the task of explaining how it came to be accepted as knowledge; just as for the most part Becker resists any temptation to pronounce on whether or not particular sets of moral or legal rules are justified, or particular acts are wrong. And for much of 'Whose side are we on?' he adopts the same attitude towards bias, focusing on the conditions that lead to the labelling of studies, or of particular knowledge claims, as biased. However, as we saw, at one point in that article he also addresses the issue of *actual* bias and how it can be avoided. In other words, when it comes to the sociologist's own methodological concern with bias, Becker abandons the sociology of knowledge: his focus becomes how sociologists can maximise their chances of producing valid conclusions. Here bias is not treated simply as what would be identified as bias in terms of some particular conception of science. It is now treated as a variable feature of the behaviour of the researcher. And in doing this Becker takes the nature of science, and the commitment of researchers to it, as given and proper.

What I am suggesting, then, is that ambiguity arises from the way in which Becker combines the sociology of knowledge and methodological arguments in the same article. The former is non-evaluative or value neutral in character, suspending judgement about whether or not the cognitive rules relevant to the field being studied are valid, just as labelling theory does not assume that particular actions are intrinsically right or wrong. By contrast, methodology is inherently normative: from its point of view conformity to or deviation from scientific method is an intrinsic feature of the behaviour of the researcher, not just a function of the labelling process. It is therefore a matter with which researchers *must* be concerned in their work. So, where Becker the sociologist of knowledge adopts a relativistic position, in the restricted sense of suspending judgement about the validity of accusations of bias, Becker the methodologist cannot, and does not, do this.

This interpretation of Becker's position carries some implications for his sociology of deviance. It suggests that his treatment of what is deviant as socially constituted may not be intended as an ontological claim about its true character, but rather as a methodological device designed to open up the whole field of deviance to sociological analysis.[25] Just as advocates of the strong programme

---

24 See Barnes 1974 and Bloor 1976. On subsequent developments in the social study of science, see Law and Lodge 1984 and Woolgar 1988.

25 Or, at least, while he may believe that actions are neither inherently good nor inherently bad, his sociological work does not necessarily depend on this assumption.

can argue that studying science sociologically does not involve denying that it produces knowledge of the natural world, so Becker could argue that sociology studies the way in which deviance is socially defined without denying that, for example, murder and theft are morally wrong. The question of whether they or other kinds of deviance are wrong is simply not the issue for a sociologist.[26]

In both cases, this suspension of the researcher's commitment to evaluative rules is a device that is designed to aid our understanding of the phenomenon concerned. It is assumed not only that the question of whether or not scientific knowledge is valid or deviance wrong is irrelevant to how one describes and explains it, but also that any concern with evaluation is likely to lead to error in the way we describe or explain these social phenomena. For example, it may encourage us to assume that the causal processes producing true and false beliefs, or good and bad behaviour, are fundamentally different in nature: that false scientific conclusions must be the product of deviation from what we currently take to be scientific method, and sound conclusions from adherence to it (Barnes 1974); or that bad behaviour must be caused by bad character or bad social conditions, while good behaviour must be caused by virtue or good circumstances (see Matza 1969).[27]

So, at least to some extent, what epistemological ambiguity there is in Becker's article stems from the fact that he carries out both sociological and methodological analysis side by side within it. While he makes explicit throughout his article the distinction between the sociology of knowledge and the concern with actual bias, by including both orientations within a single article he creates some potential for an epistemologically radical reading of it. And, of course, such radicalism *is* to be found both in some constructionist approaches to the study of social problems (Holstein and Miller 1993) and in later versions of the sociology of science (see, for example, Woolgar 1988).

However, I suspect that even this does not entirely dispose of the epistemological ambiguity in Becker's position. At one point in 'Whose side are we on?', he refers to the views of George Herbert Mead. He comments: 'The scientist who proposes to understand society must, as Mead long ago pointed out, get into the situation enough to have a perspective on it' (Becker 1967: 245), and Riley (1974a: 127) takes this as indicating Becker's commitment to a relativistic

---

26 This is the position explicitly adopted by Kitsuse; see Rains 1975.
27 Interestingly, there is a direct parallel here with Becker's later work on art (see Becker 1982). He insists that the difference between 'high culture' and 'popular culture' lies not 'in the nature of the work but in the process of honoring' (Becker 1986: 24–5). As with his approach to deviance, he defines art as what is labelled as art, rather than himself adopting any substantive view about that issue. And, here too, he has been interpreted as rejecting official definitions and wanting to validate as art much that is often excluded: photography, performance art, craft, etc. Moreover, Becker is explicit that his own 'anti-élitist' and 'democratic' preferences lead in this direction, as also does his artistic interest in photography. Yet, in part at least, what is involved in his approach is a suspension of concern about what is and is not truly art as outside the realm of sociological work, and indeed as detrimental to it.

epistemology. This has particular significance because there has been a long-running dispute about pragmatism as to whether it is a form of realism or idealism. The pragmatists' own answer to this, including that of Mead, was that it is neither; but for many commentators this simply leaves its epistemological position uncertain.

It is fundamental to Mead's philosophy that mind must be understood naturalistically as a product of evolution, and that as such its role is to bring about adaptation of organism to environment. Furthermore, it is out of the transaction between these that perspectives arise. This does not involve the organism in simply learning about objects whose character is fixed independently of it. Mead retained sufficient of the idealism he had learned from Royce and Hegel to see the transaction as two-way. He seems to regard the environment as in flux and as to a large extent unformed, so that even the structures that appear in an objective perspective (one that is shared by a group rather than being idiosyncratic) are relative to the human organism's capacities and needs (these also being subject to change). At the same time, the implication is not that these structures are arbitrary constructions on the part of the organism. Instead, we might see them as potentials inherent in the environment that are *realised* in the perspective as a result of human activity.

It should be said that there is little sign of the direct influence of these ideas in Becker's article. Instead, his reference to Mead seems to relate to one of the lessons drawn from Mead by Blumer: that close familiarity with the perspectives of the people whose behaviour one is trying to understand is required for social research. And elsewhere I have argued that Blumer's methodological arguments imply a form of realism, influenced as much by Cooley, Thomas and Park as by the 'objective relativism' or 'emergent realism' of Dewey and Mead (Hammersley 1989). Nevertheless, there is evidence in Becker's more recent work of the influence of this aspect of pragmatism, and I will end this section by examining it.

In the introduction to his collection of papers, *Doing Things Together*, Becker comments that: 'the papers in this collection don't so much argue as exemplify a position that accepts what seems to be a contradiction: that reality is socially constructed but that knowledge, while thus relative, is not wholly up for grabs' (Becker 1986: 3). And what he goes on to say illustrates this apparent contradiction. Thus, he describes himself as a 'confirmed relativist' (1986: 6) and insists that knowledge 'is what I can get other people to accept' (1986: 3). There are two aspects to what he means here. First, the researcher necessarily asks some questions and not others, and 'the selection of topics for investigation can never be justified logically or scientifically'. Secondly, just as selection of topics is based on 'the common practice of those who make such inquiries', so too is 'how to find an answer' and 'what constitutes an answer good enough for our purposes' (1986: 3). Here Becker appeals to the analogy with games, emphasising that the rules of a game often change over time. Further on, he emphasises that we always judge the validity of knowledge claims or ways of knowing from within a particular culture, and that cultures vary in the judgements they generate. All of this tends to imply a commitment to an epistemological relativism of some kind.

However, there are also places in this Introduction where Becker seems to adopt a realist perspective, hinting at the universality of truth even while emphasising the relativity of all justification. Much like Mead, he holds out the prospect of more universal perspectives, arguing that 'we can improve our knowledge and get more people to accept it by broadening the range of what we ask about, and of the kinds of acceptable answers' (1986: 5). He also indicates his rejection of some kinds of social constructionism on philosophical grounds:

> Some versions of phenomenological sociology (the ones that preface every noun with 'The Social Construction of ... ') seem to suggest that there is no reality, only interpretations, whose only warrant is that a lot of people accept them. In such a situation no one could ever be wrong; at worst they would simply have failed to persuade others that they were right. In such a situation there could be no science or scholarship, no logical proof or empirical confirmation of ideas and propositions.
>
> (1986: 2)

And, in discussing the clash between mainstream American culture today and the witchcraft beliefs of the Zapotec, he recognises that, because their views are integrated into a whole pattern of belief and behaviour, each side is unlikely to be persuaded by the arguments of the other. However, he believes that the Zapotec *are* likely to change their beliefs in the context of joint practical activity. Moreover, he sees asking a wider range of questions than our own culture would lead us to ask as increasing our chances of 'not being wrong' (1986: 6). This suggests that he is committed to some kind of realism – that the relativism that he espouses is cultural rather than epistemological. Where anthropologists had opposed ethnocentrism in the study of non-Western societies (see, for example, Herskovits 1972), Hughes and then Becker extended this attitude into the investigation of low-status cultures and subcultures *within* American society (see Chapoulie 1996: 22–3). This involved not just an emphasis on cultural diversity but also an insistence that the validity of the dominant views in any society must not be assumed.

Here again, then, we are faced with ambiguity, and this is not clarified by Becker's suggestion that his views are the same as those of the philosopher Richard Rorty. There are undoubtedly some similarities between the two. What Rorty is opposed to above all is abstract philosophical statements about the nature of truth, reality, morality, etc. *in general*. In his view, these amount to a claim on the part of philosophy to be a foundational discipline, and an important part of that claim is the idea that it provides access to knowledge whose validity is absolutely certain. Not only does Rorty argue that any such foundation is impossible, but also that it is unnecessary, and that attempts to achieve it have undesirable consequences. Rorty's attitude to philosophy, defined in this sense, is very similar to the attitude of Becker and other Chicagoans to influential kinds of sociology, especially to system theory. In both cases, the conclusions of Theory are contrasted unfavourably with what is obvious from a common-sense point of view. Instead, an unpretentious and pragmatic approach is recommended, according to which we cannot but start from where we are and work within the framework we have inherited. In addition, there is a resistance to abstract theorising in favour of more concrete and substantive arguments (see Rock 1979).

Nevertheless, there are some important differences between Becker and Rorty. While Becker describes himself as a relativist, Rorty denies that he is a relativist (just as much as he denies that he is a realist) (Rorty 1991). Like some other pragmatists before him Rorty claims to transcend, or perhaps to escape, the relativist–realist dichotomy. With Mead and Dewey, he dismisses those forms of realism that see perception and cognition as producing representations which correspond to external, independent objects whose character is fixed. But, for Rorty, presenting any alternative conception of reality and how we can know it is pointless. According to him, in claiming some statement to be true or some object to be real, we simply indicate to one another that these beliefs are good to believe. In addition, Rorty recognises that we will not easily be able to persuade everyone of what is and is not true in this sense, and he emphasises that our beliefs will inevitably be ethnocentric. Moreover, while, like Mead, he maintains a commitment to widening the group whose beliefs we share, he does so on grounds of the desirability of solidarity – not because he believes, as Becker and other pragmatists do, that the more widely a claim is accepted the more likely it is to be true (in some sense beyond being *accepted* as true). It is also central to Rorty's position that the distinction between the sciences and the humanities be erased: we must all become participants in a single conversation that is addressed to what is of general concern, rather than being seekers after specialised kinds of knowledge. Here too there seems to be a discrepancy, with Becker still committed to the value of disciplinary knowledge in the form of sociological research.

So, while Becker and Rorty share a similar orientation in certain respects, there are also significant contrasts; and these perhaps reflect the influence on Becker of older kinds of pragmatism. However, as I indicated, the latter are themselves not without epistemological ambiguity; and, even if Becker were to adopt Rorty's position consistently, I do not believe that this would eliminate the ambiguity. It is central to Rorty's argument that he has no epistemological position, and therefore is not a relativist. But the idea that we can escape all epistemological commitments is, surely, fallacious. Nor is the mixture of instrumentalism and relativism that he relies on stable. In effect, he oscillates between presenting an account of 'truth' in terms of what 'we' find it good to believe, and making claims – such as about what Dewey did and did not mean, and was right and wrong to believe, or about the failure of epistemology – that are certainly not presented simply as things that are good to believe, but rather as factual or moral truths of a more traditional kind.[28]

I think we must conclude, then, that Becker's position is not entirely free from epistemological ambiguity, but his attitude towards this is probably a phlegmatic one. He would argue, I suspect, that he has not claimed to resolve all the problems that attend sociology, even less those of philosophy. His approach is one that works in producing sociological knowledge, and he has not found it necessary to try to resolve the issue of if and how objective knowledge is possible. He assumes that it is, even while recognising cultural diversity. Such a response would reflect the kind of common-sense pragmatism that is quite closely related to many forms of philosophical pragmatism, including that of Rorty, and which is probably essential to any kind of research. However, it does leave some questions unanswered; and, given that Becker believes progress is made precisely by widening the range of questions we address, there must be a case for giving them further attention, even from his point of view.

Conclusion

In this paper I have argued against the radical reading of Becker's article, 'Whose side are we on?', which interprets it as implying that political partisanship is inevitable or desirable. I pointed to some ambiguities in the text: there are parts that support the radical reading, while there are others that run counter to it. I suggested that these ambiguities could be largely overcome by recognising the different senses in which Becker uses the term 'bias' or 'taking sides'. At the same time, I argued that he probably does view sound, scientific sociological research as having radical political consequences, and does believe that these contribute to the desirable goal of increasing equality and freedom. But it is clear that he regards this 'partisanship' as inadvertent, even though desirable: it is a by-product of objective research. I also suggested that the epistemological conflict between the constructionist understanding of bias provided by the radical reading and the realist view that seems to be implied in key sections of Becker's article could be resolved by distinguishing between the non-evaluative or value-neutral character of sociology and the necessarily evaluative character of methodology. Most of the epistemological ambiguity in 'Whose side are we on?' arises from the fact that it combines sociological and methodological analysis. I concluded, though, by suggesting that there is some residual ambiguity at quite a fundamental level in Becker's position, deriving from the influence of pragmatist philosophy.

As I made clear earlier, it is a presupposition of the approach I have adopted in trying to understand this article that writers aim to convey a coherent message. This is not true of all writers; most obviously, some kinds of poetry actively play on ambiguity (see Empson 1930; Wilson 1931). And, in recent

---

28 For pertinent criticisms of Rorty's position, see Warnke 1984, Triplett 1987 and Okrent 1993.

years, there have been calls for social science writing to adopt 'experimental' forms that subvert the authority claims built into conventional kinds of academic writing (Clifford and Marcus 1986). However, there is little evidence that Becker would support such a recommendation. His book on writing does not take this position (Becker 1986). He argues there that social science writing should be as clear and straightforward in its message as possible. And it seems very unlikely that his views would have been more 'constructionist' than this in 1967, the year when 'Whose side are we on?' was written. We can assume, I think, that the article was not written deliberately so as to be ambiguous.

So how are we to explain the ambiguities I have identified? In general terms the answer is obvious. No writer is in complete control of the writing process. This is the germ of truth in those points of view which portray writers as mere channels for some external or internal force; in our secular age no longer God, the Muse or even the Devil, but usually Discourse, Desire or Power. There are at least three aspects to this lack of control.

First, the language that we use in writing is not univocal: it carries multiple meanings, not all of which we will be aware of. As a result, the reader may pick up meanings that we did not intend, and would have wanted to eliminate. As noted earlier, in part at least, the problems with the reception of 'Whose side are we on?' have stemmed from the different interpretations that can be given to the term 'taking sides'.

Secondly, we draw on all manner of assumptions in our work, which carry implications that we may not be aware of but that may be inferred by a reader. And this is made more complex by the indeterminacy of implication: what is and is not implied depends on what auxiliary assumptions are adopted, so that what any text could be taken to imply is diverse. Writers seek to rule out some possible inferences on the part of readers, but they cannot anticipate all possible ones. In the case of Becker's article, I noted how his reliance on the Enlightenment assumption that the production of knowledge is politically progressive may have contributed to the misinterpretation of his message. Interestingly, it is unclear if one could reasonably claim that that assumption is implied by anything Becker says in the article, even though what he says elsewhere suggests that he is committed to it. What was perhaps more consequential was that many of his readers were committed to that assumption, and interpreted the article in light of it.

Third, a writer operates in a particular context. While he or she may be concerned to address a problem that has general relevance, as is indeed the case with Becker's article, to some extent it is contemporary audiences that are addressed – so that what is written will be shaped by the desire of the writer to position him or herself in relation to currently influential views on the matter in hand. I argued that we could gain a deeper understanding of Becker's article by seeing it both in the context of changes in 'Chicago sociology' and of the resurgence of that approach in the particular circumstances of the 1960s. I suggested that neither of these contexts forced the issue of objectivity to be addressed, and that this helps to explain why it was not examined and why epistemological ambiguity remained, over and above the inherent difficulty of the philosophical issues involved.

The ambiguity in Becker's article can be underlined by the fact that its message could be reformulated as a defence of the principle of value neutrality in the face of the failure of much sociology at the time to live up to that principle. Interestingly, this is precisely how Polsky presented his position, one that conforms closely to Becker's (Polsky 1967). Of course, had Becker written his article in this way, it probably would not have attracted much attention at all.[29] Certainly, it would not have been treated as the political challenge to conventional sociology that it has usually been taken to be. Yet, interpreted more accurately, it continues to have relevance for us today, not least in posing fundamental questions that still need answering.

29 There are no references in the Social Sciences Citation Index to Polsky's book in the period 1980–96.

4 Against Gouldner
On the fallacy of objective partisanship

Probably the most frequently cited source of arguments against the principle of value neutrality is Gouldner's article, 'Anti-minotaur: The myth of a value-free sociology' (Gouldner 1962). As its title indicates – complementing that of a subsequent and equally widely cited paper, 'The sociologist as partisan' (Gouldner 1968) – Gouldner rejects the principle of value neutrality in favour of partisanship, or of what he eventually came to label 'committed sociology'. In the book where these articles were reprinted, entitled *For Sociology*, Gouldner spells out his position in considerable detail, and responds to criticisms that had been made of it (Gouldner 1973a). His approach is a complex and distinctive one; and in this chapter I want to examine the critique of value neutrality he puts forward, and the case he presents for 'objective partisanship'.[1]

Gouldner's critique of value neutrality

In 'Anti-minotaur', Gouldner argues that value freedom is a 'group myth', 'rather than a carefully formulated and well validated belief appropriate to scientists' (Gouldner 1973a: 4). And he sets out to examine the way in which this myth has functioned and continues to function in the context of sociology as an occupation. He claims that it was invented by a 'magnificent minotaur', Max Weber, whose 'lair', 'although reached only by labyrinthine logic and visited only by a few who never return, is still regarded by many as a holy place' (1973a: 3). Gouldner argues that the role which value freedom played in Weber's day is different from that which it performs in post-war American sociology. For Weber it was essential in securing the autonomy of sociology from political control. By contrast, its latent function in mid-twentieth-century American sociology, according to Gouldner, is to serve the career interests of sociologists. It provides an excuse to some for 'pursuing their private impulses to the neglect of their public responsibilities': it is used by 'careerists' who 'live off

---

1 I will use the terms 'value freedom' and 'value neutrality' interchangeably in this article. Gouldner uses the former; but, for reasons that I will explain later, I think it is misleading. All references will be to Gouldner 1973a, since this is the most convenient source.

rather than for [sociology]' (1973a: 12), enabling them to 'sell their skills to the highest bidder'. This results in 'commercial debasement or narrow partisanship, rather than contributing to a truly public interest' (1973a: 13). In this way, the doctrine of value freedom has become 'a hollow catechism', 'a good excuse for no longer thinking seriously' (1973a: 6). It operates as a 'tranquilliser' and discourages academics from mobilising their political intelligence at a time when this is urgently required (1973a: 9). Thus, 'in refraining from social criticism, both the timorous and the venal may now claim the protection of high professional principle and, in so doing, can continue to hold themselves in decent regard' (1973a: 14). Gouldner insists that what is required is 'being an intellectual no less than a sociologist' (1973a: 16), rather than being a 'professional' who has accommodated him or herself to the powers that be. And he raises the spectre of 'a sociological atom bomb', or of sociologists serving in some equivalent to Auschwitz, as a possible result of them becoming 'narrow technicians who reject responsibility for the cultural and moral consequences of their work' (1973a: 26).

It is important to underline the character of Gouldner's critique of the principle of value neutrality. Early on in his article he comments:

> In the end, of course, we cannot disprove the existence of minotaurs who, after all, are thought to be sacred precisely because, being half man and half bull, they are so unlikely. The thing to see is that a belief in them is not so much untrue as it is absurd. Like Berkeley's argument for solipsism, Weber's brief for a value-free sociology is a tight one and, some say, logically unassailable. Yet it is also absurd. For both arguments appeal to reason but ignore experience.
>
> (Gouldner 1973a: 3–4)

And, a little later, he adds: 'I do not here wish to enter into an examination of the *logical* arguments involved, not because I regard them as incontrovertible but because I find them less interesting to me as a sociologist' (1973a: 4). For one reason or another, then, the task he sets himself is not to examine the case that has been put forward for value neutrality, but to apply sociological analysis to sociology itself: he will 'view the belief in a value-free sociology in the same manner that sociologists examine any element in ... the ideology of a working group ... from the standpoint of the sociology of occupations' (1973a: 4). What is intended, in short, is a reflexive application of the sociology of work to the work of sociology.

The background to Gouldner's argument

Myth and ideology

In considering the background to Gouldner's argument we must begin by noting the potential ambiguity in his claim that value freedom is a 'myth' or part of an 'ideology'. Each of those terms can be interpreted in two broadly parallel ways. Sometimes, they are used in a purely descriptive (and relatively uncontentious) fashion, to refer to a distinctive set of beliefs that a particular group of people hold.[2] But, often, they also carry an evaluative load: there is the implication that the beliefs are false, and/or that holding them has undesirable consequences.

These ambiguities are built into the history of the two concepts. The term 'myth' is derived from the Greek *mythos*, referring to 'a fable or story or tale', which was 'later contrasted with *logos* and *historia* to give the sense of "what would not really exist or have happened"' (Williams 1976: 176). Williams goes on to report that in the mid-nineteenth century the word came to mean not only a fable but also 'an untrustworthy or even deliberately deceptive invention' (1976: 177). This reflects the influence of the empiricism and rationalism of many Enlightenment thinkers, for whom myths and some (if not all) religions were the product of irrationality, and were seen as blocking the path to a rational reconstruction of human society that would increase happiness and bring about justice.

'Ideology' emerged in the wake of the French Revolution, and from the start was very much the product of Enlightenment attitudes. It was invented by the 'Idéologues', as their name for a discipline concerned with determining the validity of ideas by looking at how they had been formed. Central here was the assumption that knowledge comes from the senses, but that thought can be (and often is) distorted by the effects of what Bacon had referred to as 'idols' and what some of the *philosophes* called 'prejudices', most obviously self-interest. The task of ideology for the Idéologues was to analyse the operation of these prejudices, and thereby to open the way for an unprejudiced understanding of nature, including human nature, that would provide the basis for a rational social order.

However, the meaning of the term 'ideology' was soon transformed to refer to a set of ideas that is in some sense false, rather than to a discipline investigating the formation of false ideas. This transformation is usually attributed to Napoleon's rejection of his erstwhile supporters, the Idéologues, as metaphysicians who sought to establish government on the basis of abstract, and therefore unrealistic, ideas rather than on a 'knowledge of the human heart and of the lessons of human history' (Lichtheim 1967: 4–5; Williams 1976: 126–7). And, of course, applying the new meaning of 'ideology' to the work of the Idéologues themselves also transformed the meaning of 'ideologue'. However, this change in the meaning of 'ideology' by no means removed it from the context of Enlightenment assumptions. Indeed, it came to be virtually identical in meaning to the revised interpretation of 'myth', serving to reinforce extension

---

2 Even this usage is not entirely unproblematic; see Child 1944, Moerman 1968 and Sharrock 1974.

of the latter's meaning from patently fabulous tales to almost any kind of idea that misrepresents reality and/or misdirects action.

These Enlightenment senses of the terms 'myth' and 'ideology' are dominant today, although they have never gone entirely unchallenged.[3] In the case of 'myth', questions arose from an ambivalence in attitude towards the ideas of the past. The scientific revolution of the seventeenth century had led to an emphasis on the superiority of modern knowledge, yet reverence for the past was never completely extinguished, not least because of the continuing influence of humanist scholarship. Indeed, during and after the Enlightenment, the superiority of the modern was challenged by Rousseau, by the counter-Enlightenment, by the Romantics, and by Nietzsche. Similarly, there was reluctance on the part of some to reject the cultures of non-Western societies as simply irrational. It was often argued that what were strange ideas to modern European minds nevertheless made sense in other cultural contexts (Hazard 1964: 26; Hampson 1968: ch. 7). This kind of cultural relativism was to be found in its most developed form in the writings of Vico and Herder, and its influence extended throughout the nineteenth and twentieth centuries. Furthermore, this relativism or historicism was sometimes combined with Enlightenment notions of rational progress, notably in the work of Hegel, Saint-Simon, Comte and Marx. For them the ideas of the past, while from a modern perspective false, had nevertheless been essential to that very process of social development which had produced modernity. Moreover, Hegel reformulated the distinction between true and false in a dialectical manner, so as to transcend the conflict between universalism and historicism. For him, whether a set of ideas is true or false at any particular stage of history depends on its role in the development of Mind towards absolute truth; the latter constituting the unity of idea and reality.

There was another important aspect of these developments. Recognising the progressive role that 'false' ideas had played in the past was closely associated with the view that the factual validity of isolated items of knowledge is not sufficient for them to have socially progressive effects, and thereby be true in a larger sense. Thus, Hegel insisted on the need for a kind of science (or philosophy – the distinction was not clear) that would not only transcend natural science but also religion and art, and fulfil the functions that these had previously performed; functions that modern empirical science was incapable of serving. Similarly, both Saint-Simon and Comte came to believe that reason of a purely cognitive kind is not sufficient as a basis for social solidarity, hence their promotion of new religions designed to enable reason to fulfil the social functions demanded of it in the new age.

It was out of these developments that the two traditions arose on which Gouldner seems to draw most directly in his 'Anti-minotaur' article: functionalism and Marxism.

---

3 Interestingly, like 'ideology', 'myth' continued to be used occasionally in a positive sense. Here, Sorel's 'myth of the general strike' parallels Lenin's 'proletarian ideology'.

Gouldner's reliance on functionalism and Marxism

Gouldner's career was closely involved with the emergence of sociological functionalism (Merton 1982). The origins of this approach are to be found in the reaction of twentieth-century anthropologists and sociologists against the evolutionism of much nineteenth-century social theory, though it also draws on cultural relativist ideas going back to the Renaissance (Rowe 1965). Thus, as part of their work, Malinowski and Radcliffe-Brown and their students focused on the contemporary social functions that myths serve within 'primitive' societies. These were treated not as simply irrational but as conforming to a kind of unconscious social logic. In this context, then, the analysis of myth was primarily descriptive, but carried positive evaluative overtones, since social order was presented (at least implicitly) as of value, and myths were seen as playing an important role in holding societies together. Moreover, to a considerable extent, the desirability of preserving diverse forms of social life was an ethic that was constitutive of anthropological thought in the early twentieth century.

This did not mean that functionalist anthropologists treated myths as true; on the contrary, that they were false (even absurd) was largely taken for granted. Indeed, the distinctiveness of the functionalist message depended on the fact that, despite their apparently irrational character, myths perform positive social functions. This challenged a central Enlightenment idea – that false ideas have bad consequences. At the same time, functionalism did not represent a complete rejection of Enlightenment rationalism. As already noted, like positivism and Hegelianism, it pointed to an underlying rationality in social processes, this time of a synchronic rather than a diachronic kind. While the people being studied did not understand the true import of their own beliefs and practices, this was open to rational understanding by social anthropologists.

Closely related to this, functionalism not only suggested that positive consequences could arise from apparently irrational beliefs, it also implied that commitment to those beliefs arose from the social functions that they served: while the believers did not understand the functionality of their beliefs, it was because of this functionality that they had been led to adopt them, through a causal process operating 'behind their backs'. Sociological functionalists developed and extended this idea in the context of modern societies. Here, there was sometimes an implicit critique of conventional ideas, which was achieved by showing the underlying functions that apparently non-rational or even immoral practices served. The most striking examples of this are Merton's discussion of the 'boss system' in American politics, Bell's account of the functions of organised crime, and Davis's analysis of the functions of prostitution (Merton 1968; Bell 1960: chs 7 and 9; Davis 1937 and 1971: 341–51).[4] To take the first of these examples, Merton argued that the political boss system arises from the decentralised character of American politics, and persists because it serves the needs of less privileged groups for assistance and for opportunities to gain

---

4 For a discussion of this aspect of functionalism, see Matza 1969: 31–7.

upward social mobility, as well as the needs of local business for social stability and for the control of competition. This argument was put forward as an illustration of the distinction between manifest and latent functions: between the reasons people give for their actions and the social purposes which the sociologist can identify those actions as serving, and which generate them.[5]

In some respects, Gouldner's 'Anti-minotaur' article can be read as an application of functionalist analysis to sociology itself. This is signalled by his presentation of value neutrality as a myth, and his use of associated terms like 'minotaur', 'holy place', 'pilgrimage', 'dogma' and 'sacred'.[6] Of course, there is considerable irony in this. In applying a functionalist analysis to the beliefs of American sociologists, Gouldner is challenging their conception of themselves as engaged solely in the rational pursuit of knowledge. Indeed, he could be interpreted as suggesting that social scientists' claims to a rational approach towards their work should no more be taken at face value than other 'natives'' explanations for their myths. Sociologists' beliefs and practices too, it might be argued, have the form they do because of the social functions that they serve, functions of which they themselves may (or will necessarily?) be unaware. However, this is not quite the line of argument that Gouldner pursues, at least in this article.[7] In practice, he limits his functionalist analysis to just one aspect of the sociological belief system, the idea of value freedom, which he sees as reflecting a commitment to an unacceptable political liberalism.[8]

Of course, Gouldner breaks with the functionalist tradition in presenting the functions of value freedom in a negative rather than a neutral or positive light.[9]

---

5 Helm 1971 and Campbell 1982 have highlighted the ambiguities in Merton's, and others', use of the distinction between manifest and latent functions. Several different contrasts can be identified: between conscious intention and actual consequence (whether unintended subsequent consequences or collateral consequences of intended actions); between foreseen and unforeseen consequences; between common-sense knowledge and sociological understanding; between formal, official or avowed aims of organisations and their unofficial, secret or even illegal ones; and between appearance and underlying reality.

6 These all occur on the first page of his article, while subsequent pages contain repetitions of these as well as new words belonging to the same register.

7 The opening sentence of 'The sociologist as partisan' comes closer to this. There, Gouldner writes: 'Sociology begins by disenchanting the world, and it proceeds by disenchanting itself. Having insisted upon the non-rationality of those whom it studies, sociology comes, at length, to confess its own captivity' (Gouldner 1973a: 27). Of course, a question arises here about why we should accept the truth of this confession, and the tale of disenchantment on which it is based; since these presumably also serve latent functions.

8 There is a parallel with Weber here, who challenged the normative character of German historical economics to a large extent because he rejected the political assumptions on which it implicitly relied. The remedies proposed by these two writers are, however, diametrically opposed.

9 However, it should be noted that one of the functions (manifest or latent?) of the manifest/latent distinction was to identify a means by which sociology could generate 'news' (Merton 1968: 119–20), and showing the dysfunctions of high-status values presumably serves this purpose as effectively as showing the positive function of what is low status.

In this respect, and others, he was influenced by criticism of functionalism for justifying the status quo as the product of some underlying rationality. This criticism was inspired, to a considerable degree, by the influence of Marx and Marxism. Marxists, like functionalists, had long been concerned with how ideas can operate to preserve the existing social order. And there are respects in which Marx's own account of modern capitalism is functionalist (Cohen 1978).[10] However, Marxism assumes a close relationship between the truth or falsity of beliefs and the political functions they perform. In this respect, Marxism is an Enlightenment perspective, where anthropological and sociological functionalism are not.

So, we can see Gouldner drawing on Marxism as well as on functionalism in his analysis of value freedom: he argues that it is false or absurd and that, in the context of American sociology at least, it performs negative social functions. Indeed, there is a hint of a Hegelian-style argument to the effect that, while this principle had served positive functions in the past, in the context of Max Weber's Germany, it no longer does so and therefore must be abandoned if sociology is to play a progressive role in future social development. On this reading, value freedom is ideological in the dialectical sense of having exhausted its positive contribution to historical development.[11]

An assessment of Gouldner's argument against value freedom

In assessing Gouldner's argument, let me begin by looking at his initial claim that the notion of value freedom is absurd. In doing this, there are a couple of immediate problems. He complains that the meaning given to this idea by American sociologists varies widely, but he does not tell us what meaning or meanings he is assigning to it himself. He also does not spell out *why* he judges value neutrality to be absurd (other than that it is so in the light of 'experience') – relying instead on the use of 'myth', 'ideology' and associated language to convey this. We can, however, identify two arguments that *could* underlie this judgement, and these may assist us in understanding what sense he was giving to the term 'value freedom'. First, he might argue that it is obvious that sociological work will always be affected by the sociologist's values, so that 'in the real world' sociology can never be value free. And there is some evidence to suggest that he has this argument in mind. For example, at one point he comments that sociology is not free of all non-scientific assumptions, and that it cannot be made so (Gouldner 1973a: 4).[12] The second possible line of argument,

---

10 Furthermore, there were similarities between structural functionalism and 'official' Marxism within purportedly Marxist states. See Simirenko 1967 and Stojanovic 1973.

11 See also Gouldner 1970: 499–500. Interestingly, there is a hint of something similar in Weber, in the form of the idea that value neutrality was necessary in the context of 1913, where it had not been forty years earlier (Hennis 1987: 52). However, Weber would not have formulated this argument in terms of the dialectic.

12 This is an argument that is developed and illustrated further in Gouldner 1970.

by no means incompatible with the first, is that all sociological accounts, however much they may be intended to be purely descriptive, will have (or will be taken to have) evaluative implications. And Gouldner's conclusion that sociologists must accept responsibility for and take control of the consequences of their work would flow from this.

What seems to underlie these two arguments is the idea that the principle of value freedom requires sociology to be unaffected by values: that it should be carried out, and its findings interpreted, in ways that are uninfluenced by any values at all. If this is what Gouldner takes 'value freedom' to mean, then he is correct that it is absurd; but he is wrong to imply that this is what Weber – and, one suspects, most American sociologists – meant by it. Certainly, he does not supply any examples of statements supporting this interpretation, in either case. Nor are defenders of value neutrality forced to adopt this view in some logical sense. One can accept that sociological work is always potentially (and often actually) distorted by the sociologist's values, yet insist that it is possible and desirable to minimise the degree of distortion. Similarly, few would deny that descriptive accounts have implications for value judgements, and are often interpreted as supporting or undermining these. However, this is not incompatible with arguing that there is a fundamental distinction between factual inferences, on the one hand, and evaluative or prescriptive ones, on the other; and that the latter necessarily rely on value premises as well as on factual ones. So, while it is true that a literal interpretation of value freedom is absurd, there are other interpretations that may not be; and Gouldner does not establish that either Weber or any American sociologists hold to the literal view.

This is as far as we can go in assessing Gouldner's judgement that the principle of value neutrality is absurd; but we can conclude, I think, that his case in this respect is not convincing – as it relates to Weber and most other proponents of that principle. So, let me turn now to the functions that he believes the principle has served.

The case of Weber's Germany

Gouldner puts forward a range of ideas about the way in which the principle of value freedom operates within sociology. Some relate to Weber and the situation of German sociology at the beginning of the century. Central here are the claims that value freedom helped to maintain the internal cohesion, and the autonomy from external interference, of the modern university, particularly as regards the newer social science disciplines. Thus, Gouldner argues that 'one of the latent functions of the value-free doctrine is to bring peace to the academic house' (1973a: 7), by reducing competition among professors for students, or at least by restricting competition to the field of scholarship rather than of politics. In this way, Gouldner suggests, value freedom reduced political conflict within the university. Relatedly, it reduced the scope for professors to engage in political indoctrination of students, in a context where their influence was likely to be substantial. In this and other ways it served to protect the autonomy of universities from state intervention. Gouldner comments:

> Throughout his work, Weber's strategy is to safeguard the integrity and freedom of action of both the state, as the instrument of German national policy, and of the university, as the embodiment of a larger Western tradition of rationalism. He feared that the expression of political value judgements in the university would provoke the state into censoring the university and would imperil its autonomy.
>
> (1973a: 9)

On this view, value freedom amounts to a pact whereby the state would allow professors the freedom to pursue knowledge, and to teach their disciplines, so long as they did not openly preach political doctrines, especially those likely to threaten the state. Gouldner comments that 'there is little difficulty, at any rate, in demonstrating that these were among the motives originally inducing Max Weber to formulate the conception of a value-free sociology' (1973a: 6–7).

The first point to be made about this analysis is that it assumes that the principle of value neutrality was widely accepted and acted on in German universities in Weber's time. Yet Gouldner does not provide any evidence for this, and it does not seem to be true. The dominant tradition within the social sciences in Germany in the late nineteenth century was historical economics; indeed, that was the tradition in which Weber was himself trained. This was normative in orientation, not simply concerned with producing factual knowledge, and was directed towards serving policy-making and administration. And it was against this that Weber rebelled in putting forward the idea of value freedom. Moreover, the stormy reception given to his views suggests that they were far from widely shared or adopted (Lindenfeld 1997: 316–20; Hennis 1987: 52; Sharlin 1974: 350). Of course, it could be that Gouldner is arguing that the principle of value freedom *would have* functioned in this way *if* it had been widely accepted. This may be true; as he notes, some of the functions he ascribes *were* what Weber intended. But this is to analyse part of the case for the principle, rather than its functioning (or at least to examine its manifest rather than its latent function).

Given that here, to a large extent, Gouldner sees himself as simply repeating Weber's own arguments, we might consider how accurate his account of Weber's position is. This is not an easy question to answer, however. Interpreting Weber's methodological writings is not straightforward; despite Gouldner's implication to the contrary that 'a familiarity with Weber's work on these points would only be embarrassing to many who today affirm a value-free sociology in his name' (1973a: 6).[13] To a considerable extent, they take the form of

---

13 Weber's methodological writings are now virtually all available in English translation, but this was not the case when Gouldner wrote his article.

arguments against the views of nineteenth-century German economists whose work is largely unknown today, outside Germany at least. And Weber does not spell out the positions he is opposing, or his criticisms, very clearly. Partly as a result of this, there is substantial disagreement in the secondary literature about Weber's methodological position.[14]

However, despite the uncertainties of interpretation, there are elements of Gouldner's account of Weber that are of doubtful accuracy, on any reasonable reading of his work. One problem is that Gouldner fails to acknowledge, or at least underplays, distinctions – between science and politics, and between truth and practical values – that appear to have been fundamental for Weber; at least after his period of sustained methodological reflection. Thus, Gouldner's argument that Weber deemed 'the cautious expression of value judgements' permissible and believed them to be 'positively mandatory under certain circumstances' (1973a: 6), does not make clear whether this relates to a scientific or a political context. In arguing for value neutrality and value relevance, Weber's concern was with how practical value judgements should be handled in scientific contexts. He recognised that science necessarily depends on commitment to the value of truth, but argued that social scientists should not present practical value judgements as if these derived from research. He viewed the main task of research as producing factual conclusions, albeit value-relevant ones. And his motive for this seems to have been at least as much to protect politics from illicit scientific claims as to protect science from the influence of politics (Bruun 1972). Of course, in political contexts he certainly believed that the expression of value judgements was mandatory.

While in some respects Gouldner treats Weber's position as true for (as serving a positive function in) its time and place, in others he does not. He claims that Weber 'argues that professors are not entitled to freedom from state control in matters of values, since these do not rest on their specialised qualifications' and that this stemmed from the fact that he was not a liberal in the Anglo-American sense: he 'aimed not at the curtailing but at strengthening of the powers of the German state, thereby making it a more effective instrument of German nationalism' (1973a: 9). In response to this, Gouldner argues that it is at least as 'consistent' to argue that professors, like others, are 'entitled and perhaps required to express their values' (1973a: 10).

Now, it is true that Weber was politically committed to German nationalism.[15] However, he did not believe that furthering this was the goal of science or of the university, so that university professors were obliged to adopt the values of the state. Indeed, while he was a nationalist in his political

---

14 A good sense of the complexities of, and possible changes in, Weber's position is given in Sharlin 1974. See also the divergent interpretations of Oakes 1988, Hennis 1988 and Abraham 1993.

15 The classic text is his inaugural lecture; see Weber 1980. For an excellent summary of his position and of changes in it, see Bellamy 1992.

writings, he was also an outspoken critic of state policy in a number of areas, and of the influence of the Kaiser in particular. What he proposed in his methodological writings was restriction not of what professors believed or of what they said in political contexts, but of their expression of political views in the context of teaching and research.[16] In this sense he was a liberal, believing in the need for universities and science to have autonomy from the state, and indeed from other powerful political and religious interests. The commitment to value neutrality and value relevance was what was given in exchange for this autonomy (see Scott 1995).

Gouldner argues that:

> it appears that Weber was so intent on safeguarding the autonomy of the university from politics, that he was willing to pay almost any price to do so, even if this led the university to detach itself from one of the basic intellectual traditions of the west – the dialectical exploration of the fundamental purposes of human life.
>
> (1973a: 10)

As already noted, if anything, Weber was more concerned with protecting politics from the inroads of science than science from the influence of politics. A second important point is that Weber believed that there was very limited scope for the 'dialectical exploration of the fundamental purposes of human life', or at least for theoretical resolution of conflicts amongst those purposes. He denied that there was any *telos* built into the world, seeing values as matters of irrational commitment. For this reason, he saw no scope for science, in the general sense of scholarship, coming to conclusions about the purposes of human life. The only virtue that he seems to have believed it proper for the university to promote is integrity, by which he meant a commitment to clarity and consistency about both facts and values, and about their implications for action.

The case of American sociology

As already noted, Gouldner treats even those elements of Weber's case for value freedom that he views as sound as no longer functional in the context of mid-twentieth-century American sociology. He argues that there is no need to curb competition among professors in that context, and denies that they are in the influential position in relation to students that German professors were. He suggests that minimising political conflict is not desirable in a country where the political differences between the main parties are 'trivial', and where war is

---

16 There are, of course, problems in distinguishing between Weber's scientific and political writings, and this is made more difficult because his methodological position developed over time. See Sharlin 1974.

likely to be nuclear, so that success in it will not depend on national morale. He comments:

> Perhaps the need of the American university today, as of American society more generally, is for more commitment to politics and for more diversity of political views. It would seem that now the national need is to take the lid off, not to screw it on more tightly.
>
> (1973a: 9)

The best that can be said of these arguments is that they are interesting speculations. Gouldner provides no evidence for them, and they are open to question; at the very least on the grounds that they relate to differences in degree rather than of kind. For instance, that American professors in the 1950s had less influence on their students than German professors in the first decade of the twentieth century may be true, but it could be the case that their influence remained substantial so that political indoctrination was still a danger. It is also worth underlining that Weber believed in the need for political diversity, and did not see the principle of value neutrality as discouraging this. Quite the reverse. He feared that a failure to adhere to that principle would close down politics completely, turning it into scientific administration.

Perhaps the least convincing aspect of this part of Gouldner's argument is the idea that there is no longer any (or that there is now less) need for the autonomy of universities to be protected from state interference. This is surprising given that one of the criticisms made by radical sociologists in the 1960s and early 1970s concerned the extent to which, in the United States especially, the discipline had become dependent on Government funding and geared to serving its needs. Of course, Gouldner recognises this but sees the principle of value neutrality as implicated in this co-option, serving as an ideological disguise. Yet, it could be argued that what this points to is sociology's failure to live up to the principle of value neutrality, rather than the inadequacy of the principle itself. What Gouldner perhaps has in mind here is the argument that there has been a shift from sociologists choosing to investigate issues that they themselves believe to be of public importance to a situation where they investigate whatever sponsors will give them money to investigate. But, while this is an important issue, it is not one that need divide those who accept and those who reject the principle of value neutrality. One could accept that principle but also insist that universities must maintain autonomy, not just from the state but also from commercial interests, as regards decisions about what to investigate. And this would be very much in the spirit of Weber.

Clearly, it is true that there are differences between the two situations that Gouldner discusses. And some of these are relevant to the way in which the principle of value freedom functions. However, this does not show that the principle did not or could not serve a positive function in American universities. Nor does Gouldner provide support for his argument that there is a greater need for sociologists to play a political role in mid-century America than there was earlier in Germany.

It is worth noting that Gouldner not only argues that the principle of value freedom no longer serves a positive function in mid-twentieth-century America, but also criticises the *nature* of American sociologists' commitment to the principle. He contrasts Weber's 'agonizing expression of a highly personal faith', 'intensely felt and painstakingly argued' (1973a: 6), with the 'dogmatic' (1973a: 5) and ritualistic commitment of American sociologists to what is, in effect, a 'hollow catechism, a password, and a good excuse for no longer thinking seriously' (1973a: 6). Gouldner draws a contrast here in both cognitive and emotional terms: between thinking and unthinking acceptance, and between intense and superficial attachment to the principle. However, another way of putting this argument about the nature of the commitment involved is to say that American sociologists took the principle of value neutrality for granted and acted accordingly, without thinking carefully about exactly what it meant in abstract, whereas Weber could not do so. And we might ask what is wrong with their behaviour in this respect. There are two possible arguments against it. One is that the principle of value freedom is false, but then that is simply an assumption on Gouldner's part, or is part of what he is setting out to prove. The other argument is that sociologists ought to reflect on all of their assumptions. This might seem to be exactly what is demanded by the reflexive sociology that Gouldner recommends elsewhere (Gouldner 1970). Yet, taken literally, this recommendation is futile. One cannot continually reflect on all of one's assumptions, certainly not if one is actually to do any research. Any activity, including research, depends on much being taken for granted. Given this, once again, we come back to the question of *why* sociologists must not take the principle of value freedom for granted.

The answer to this could be that what had changed between turn of the century Germany and mid-twentieth-century America was not just the context but also the *content* of the principle of value neutrality. Gouldner hints at this when he refers to the embarrassment that would be produced if American sociologists recognised the true character of Weber's position. Once again, though, what seems to follow from this is not a challenge to the principle itself but to the way American sociologists interpreted it. And it may be true that the way in which it was operationalised in American sociology in the 1940s and 1950s was unsound, though Gouldner does not provide evidence for this. Moreover, even if his account of the motives of American sociologists were accurate, this would not in itself establish that the consequences of their commitment to that principle were undesirable. That actions can have latent positive functions was, after all, central to functionalism

Here again, then, as with his analysis of value freedom in Weber's Germany, Gouldner does not provide a convincing account. He offers a highly evaluative interpretation of the motives of American sociologists, and of the effects of their commitment to the principle of value freedom; yet he provides little evidential support for it. Furthermore, as we shall see, he does not begin to address the problems involved in identifying social functions of the kind he ascribes.

Summary: the ambiguity and inadequacy of Gouldner's case against value freedom

In effect, Gouldner's article straddles two different kinds of analysis: methodological and sociological. Yet, whichever of these points of view we assess it from, it is inadequate. As a methodological critique of the principle of value neutrality, the article fails because, as Gouldner himself admits, for the most part it does not address the 'logical' arguments in support of that principle. Furthermore, as we saw, his dismissal of value freedom as absurd relies on unsupported and probably inaccurate assumptions about how both Weber and mid-century American sociologists interpreted the principle. And, while he discusses some of Weber's arguments for it, he misinterprets them, especially in failing to observe Weber's distinction between scientific and political contexts. He also claims that whatever was true in Weber's time about the need for value neutrality no longer holds, but offers little evidence in support of this. Above all, there is none of the careful analysis of the meaning and validity of arguments about the role of values in research that one might reasonably expect of a methodological discussion of this issue.

Yet, the article also fails as a piece of empirical sociological analysis because, as we saw, it does not provide the evidence required for its claims about the commitment of Weber and of American sociologists to value neutrality; or about the effects that this commitment had. Gouldner does not appear to have carried out systematic research on sociology as an occupation, either in relation to Weber and his milieux or to American sociologists of the 1950s. Apart from relying on Gouldner's own experience as an American sociologist in the period concerned, the article presumably draws on Weber's writings and the secondary literature about him, and on the contemporary sociological literature; though no explicit references are made to these sources. Furthermore, there is little sign of the cautious consideration of alternative interpretations and explanations, and the tentative reaching of conclusions, that one might reasonably expect in sociological analysis. And this is very surprising, given Gouldner's reference at one point to the 'carefully formulated and well validated belief[s] appropriate to scientists' (1973a: 4), and against the background of the quality of his earlier empirical research (see, for example, Gouldner 1954). As an example of empirical sociological study too, then, Gouldner's article is very poor.[17]

---

17 One explanation for these defects may be that Gouldner's article began life as a presidential address to the Society for the Study of Social Problems: that is, it was originally designed for oral rather than written presentation. However, it was subsequently published in *Social Problems*, and Gouldner describes what is included in *For Sociology* as the 'full and unabridged version' (p. 463). Furthermore, as we shall see, much the same defects are to be found in his other work in this area.

A further problem lies in the functionalist character of Gouldner's analysis, a mode of argument that (as I noted) is to be found in both of the traditions on which he draws, not only sociological functionalism but also Marxism.[18] While this may be a legitimate form of explanation in principle, in practice it frequently operates in a way that is quite illegitimate, notably by encouraging speculative accounts: teleology is assumed rather than established. Very often, the existence of a pattern of action is explained by appeal to a *presumed* consequence of it that is *taken to be* in the interests of those involved. This is true of the examples that Merton uses in his article on 'manifest and latent functions', such as the Hopi rain dance and Veblen's analysis of conspicuous consumption (Campbell 1982). Gouldner's discussion of the functions of value freedom also fits this pattern. What is missing, first of all, is evidence that commitment to value freedom has had the effects that he claims. For instance, he argues that it has led to sociologists not engaging in public debate. Yet he does not document that there has been a decline in this; or that, if there has, commitment to value neutrality has caused it, rather than, say, increased specialisation. Secondly, there is no documentation of the mechanism by which commitment to value freedom was established. Here, he appeals to ulterior, unconscious or unofficial motives, but he does not begin to document the operation of these. Finally, perhaps the most fundamental problem with functional analysis is the status of the analytic judgement involved about the desirability or undesirability of the unintended or unofficial outcome (see Fallding 1963). Gouldner leaves no doubt about his negative evaluation of what he takes to be the motives for, and outcomes of, commitment to value freedom, but he does not provide the grounds for his evaluation. He seems to assume that these are obvious and compelling. Yet it is likely that those whom he is criticising would not find them so, and not all readers will do so either.

It is worth emphasising, furthermore, that even had Gouldner's sociological analysis of value freedom as a 'group myth' serving the political status quo been effective, it would not have validated his conclusion that the principle is methodologically unsound. This would be to assume that if commitment to a principle is adopted for bad reasons or has bad consequences the principle itself must be defective, and this conclusion does not necessarily follow. The right thing from a methodological (as from an ethical) point of view can be done for the wrong reasons, and vice versa. Moreover, in practice, motivation is usually complex, decisions often being overdetermined. Equally important, only an extreme consequentialist would argue that bad consequences automatically mean that the action taken was wrong. There are occasions when people feel, not unreasonably, that they must do what they believe to be right even though

---

18 For a discussion of the issues surrounding functional argument in the context of Marxism, see Halfpenny 1983. See also Cohen's (1982) distinction between consequence and functional explanation, and the debate between Elster, Cohen and others in the journal, *Theory and Society* 11(4), 1982.

undesirable consequences are likely to follow from it. As Weber remarks, quoting Luther, sometimes we must say 'Here I stand, I can do no other'. In addition, we must remember that *multiple* consequences flow from actions, not all of which may be undesirable, and they do not flow in a way that is entirely predictable. So, I suggest, Gouldner assumes too readily that what he takes to be bad motivation and consequences imply the invalidity or absurdity of the principle of value neutrality. In doing so he seems to rely on the Enlightenment idea that bad effects are caused by false beliefs. Yet, as we saw, this was not an assumption that was accepted by the functionalists, and with good reason (see Matza 1969).

I am not suggesting that there is nothing worthwhile in Gouldner's discussion of value neutrality. He is surely right that sociological analysis ought to be applied to the work of sociologists themselves. By turning American sociology back on itself he indicates that, despite its profession of faith in the principle of ethical neutrality, much of it was not *in fact* value neutral. Moreover, indirectly, he highlights the evaluative character of staple sociological concepts like 'myth' and 'ideology'. And the conflict between the use of these concepts and any commitment to value neutrality or objectivity has been noted by others. Thus, Geertz raises the question of 'what such an egregiously loaded concept [as 'ideology'] is doing among the analytic tools of a social science' that claims 'cold-blooded objectivity'. And he goes on to draw much the same parallel as Gouldner:

> If the critical power of the social sciences stems from their disinterestedness, is not this power compromised when the analysis of political thought is governed by such a concept, much as the analysis of religious thought would be (and, on occasion, has been) compromised when cast in terms of the study of 'superstition'?
>
> (Geertz 1964: 51)

However, as this quotation hints, Geertz draws a different lesson from the parallel with the analysis of religious beliefs. Instead of seeing it as undermining the principle of value neutrality or objectivity in the way that Gouldner does, he treats it as demonstrating that anthropologists and sociologists have not been sufficiently strongly, or consistently, committed to that principle. What this suggests is that the conclusion that ought to be drawn from Gouldner's sociological analysis of the principle of value freedom is not that there is something wrong with that principle, but rather that there are serious defects in the influential form of sociological analysis that he adopts.

In summary, then, Gouldner's argument does not provide a 'logical' case against the principle of value neutrality, nor in empirical terms does he supply convincing evidence for the functions he ascribes to American sociologists' belief in that principle. Furthermore, he relies on fallacious inference from those functions back to his conclusions about the value of the principle. Thus, his argument is weak in both methodological and sociological terms. To a considerable extent it relies for its force on an ironic appeal to Enlightenment rhetoric about the irrational and dysfunctional character of religion, rather than on substantive arguments.

It is also worth noting that in the 'Anti-minotaur' article Gouldner does not make clear the shape of the methodological approach he is recommending as an alternative to value neutrality. And this uncertainty about the position he is proposing is at first sight heightened in his later article on 'The sociologist as partisan', where he rejects what he interprets as Becker's advocacy of partisanship. After all, if he is in favour of neither value neutrality nor partisanship, what position is he adopting? But, as we shall see, his discussion of Becker's work leads to a clarification of his own approach.

The case for partisanship

'The sociologist as partisan' was written as a response to another article: 'Whose side are we on?', by Howard S. Becker. Gouldner reports that he was motivated by the fear that 'the once glib acceptance of the value-free doctrine is about to be superseded by a new but no less glib rejection of it' (Gouldner 1973a: 27). And he takes Becker as representing a growing body of sociologists who exemplify this. He notes that Becker never answers the question raised in his title. Indeed, Gouldner believes that from Becker's position 'neither strategic considerations, nor temperamental and moral considerations, can tell us "to which viewpoint we should subscribe"' (Gouldner 1973a: 29). But Gouldner argues that an answer to the question *is* to be found in Becker's other work; and this is that sociologists should adopt the perspective of the 'underdog'. Referring to the 'coterie' (1973a: 28) of sociologists to which Becker belongs, Gouldner comments:

> for them, orientation to the underworld has become the equivalent of the proletarian identifications felt by some intellectuals during the 1930s. For not only do they study it, but in a way they speak on its behalf, affirming the authenticity of its style of life
>
> (Gouldner 1973a: 29–30)

For Gouldner, Becker's failure explicitly to answer his own question in the article highlights the ambiguous, indeed ambivalent, character of his position. Another aspect of this is that while (according to Gouldner) Becker rejects the very possibility of value freedom, he argues that sociologists must avoid sentimentalism. Gouldner opposes this, arguing that passion and sentimentality 'may just as likely serve to enlighten, and to sensitize us to certain aspects of the social world' (1973a: 33–4). He complains that:

> while Becker invites partisanship, he rejects passionate or erect partisanship. In the very process of opposing the conventional myth of the

value-free social scientist, Becker ... creates a new myth, the myth of the *sentiment*-free social scientist.

(1973a: 33)

Here, Gouldner interprets sentiment as emotional commitment; and he complains about Becker's 'non-polemical and flaccid style' which he reads as 'oozing complacency' (1973a: 56), and sees as reflecting an 'unexamined and comfortable commitment to political liberalism' (1973a: 54).[19]

Gouldner offers a number of explanations for the ambiguity of Becker's article. One relates to a contradiction within Becker's perspective. This arises from the fact that his theory of deviance demands that it is rulemakers and enforcers who must be investigated, since it is they who define what is and is not deviant, while his symbolic interactionist approach requires him to adopt the perspective of the people being studied in order to understand them. This implies that Becker should take on the perspective of those in power, yet his own sentiments are clearly with those at the bottom of the hierarchy, especially those labelled as deviants. As a result, Gouldner suggests, Becker is pulled in opposing directions. Another explanation that Gouldner offers is that declaring his support for deviants would create practical problems for Becker in obtaining research funds and gaining access to research sites. Most fundamentally, though, Gouldner sees the ambiguity of Becker's article as stemming from his partisanship in support of 'one of the currently conflicting elites in the welfare establishment' (Gouldner 1973a: 32).

Gouldner portrays Becker's identification with the underdog as the result of a 'titillated attraction to the underdog's exotic difference ... the urban sociologist's equivalent of the anthropologist's (one-time) romantic appreciation of the noble savage' (1973a: 37). Furthermore, while Becker's work is an 'implicit critique of lower-middle-class ethnocentrism', at the same time it implies identification with liberal welfare élites who also reject the lower-middle-class perspective that dominates enforcement and welfare agencies. In this way Becker's position supports the view of those élites that deviants ought to be better managed, rather than seeing the causes of deviance as lying in the master institutions of the society. As a result, it does not express or encourage an active opposition to those institutions. What is involved is:

a sympathetic view of the underdog seen increasingly from the standpoint of the relatively benign, the well-educated, and the *highly* placed bureaucratic officialdom: of the American administrative class. What seems to be

---

19 In Chapter 3 I argue that Becker is indeed committed to a form of liberalism, but not of the kind that Gouldner implies here. Gouldner characterises liberalism as being no longer the 'conscientious code of isolated individuals' but 'the well-financed ideology of a loosely organized but coherent Establishment' (1973a: 55). There are strong echoes here of C. Wright Mills' analysis of American society in terms of a transformation from Jeffersonian to corporate liberalism. See Chapter 2.

> a rejection of the standpoint of the superior is ... actually only a rejection of the *middle-level* superior.
>
> (1973a: 39)

And Gouldner argues that there are careerist reasons why sociologists might adopt such an underdog perspective (1973a: 43). He summarises this argument as follows:

> The new underdog sociology propounded by Becker is, then, a standpoint that possesses a remarkably convenient combination of properties: it enables the sociologist to befriend the very small underdogs in local settings, to reject the standpoint of the 'middle dog' respectables and notables who manage local caretaking establishments, while, at the same time, to make and remain friends with the really top dogs in Washington agencies or New York foundations. While Becker adopts the posture as intrepid preacher of a new underdog sociology, he has really given birth to something rather different: to the first version of new Establishment sociology, to a sociology compatible with the new character of social reform in the United States today.
>
> (1973a: 49)[20]

As with his analysis in 'Anti-minotaur' of American sociologists' commitment to value freedom in the 1950s, Gouldner is concerned here with identifying the social functions of Becker's rejection of value freedom and his advocacy of underdog partisanship. And, once again, the account is highly speculative. As a piece of substantive sociology it is inadequate: at best it presents interesting hypotheses that require further investigation. Moreover, these are, again, very much functionalist hypotheses. Gouldner does not claim that he has accurately portrayed Becker's intentions, but rather the ideological functions of the position the latter has adopted: how it serves various interests, including Becker's own (1973a: 50). For the reasons outlined in the previous section, this is a form of analysis that is difficult to validate effectively. Moreover, to a large extent, the analysis is misdirected because it is based on a fundamental misreading of Becker's article. He was not recommending active partisanship, but rather highlighting the fact that accusations of bias are largely unavoidable for sociologists; however much they try to be, or even succeed in being, objective (see Chapter 3).

However, more than in 'Anti-minotaur', in this second article Gouldner engages with the 'logic' of the case that he is opposing. He rejects the idea that the sociologist ought to be partisan in the sense of simply adopting the perspective of the underdog. He directs two main arguments against this. First of all, he points out that there is a problem with how we identify underdogs. He notes

---

20 See the similar critique of Goffman in Gouldner 1970.

that Becker himself accepts that there is infinite regress in defining superordinates and subordinates, and the implication of this is that almost everyone is an overdog in some contexts and an underdog in others. In addition, Gouldner argues that there is no special virtue in those who lack power and authority, any more than in those who possess them. In particular, there is no reason to believe that the perspective of those placed at the bottom of society is more likely to be true than that of people at the top. Indeed, often, their perspective will simply be the dominant ideology internalised; in so far as the deviant and subordinate accept a role as passive victims rather than being rebels (1973a: 40). Here, he is rejecting any straightforward commitment to a standpoint epistemology.

In reaction against the kind of partisanship that he ascribes to Becker, Gouldner argues that what is required is *objective* partisanship. This requires a commitment to sociological analysis and to universal values, rather than to the perspective or interests of any particular group. Thus, Gouldner suggests that one of the central values that should guide the work of sociologists, apart from truth, is the elimination of unnecessary suffering. Inevitably, this will mean that the sociologist's work serves the interests of underdogs, but it does not mean that their perspective has been adopted.[21]

Objective partisanship is 'a partisanship that is set within the framework of a larger humanistic understanding', a 'reflective and tempered partisanship' that contrasts with 'the merely political partisanship of daily involvements'. What is required in this is the production of theories that are able to take account of the viewpoints of the various actors involved, and to locate them within the constraints exerted 'by institutions, by history, and indeed by biology' (1973a: 52). Where Becker may seem to deny the possibility of some overarching sociological perspective that can both understand and socially locate the views of the various groups of people involved in any institution, Gouldner insists that developing such an objective perspective is the proper task of sociologists. Moreover, on his account, this perspective does not simply provide us with factual understanding, but also allows objective evaluation of the social world, including evaluation of the views of the various participants. Gouldner seeks to clarify what is involved in this by elaborating on the concept of objectivity.

He considers three possible interpretations of this concept. The first is what he calls 'normative objectification'. This amounts to impartial judgement in terms of some moral value; but he emphasises that it may nevertheless be partisan in an important sense. To illustrate, Gouldner draws an analogy with judicial and medical judgements. He argues that rendering a judicial judgement does not imply an intention to mediate between contending parties: 'The function of a judge is not to bring parties together but is, quite simply, to do justice.' And, 'what makes a judgement possessed of justice is not the fact that it distributes costs and benefits equally between the parties but, rather, that the

---

21 Gouldner later formulates this in terms of a distinction between 'partisanship' and 'commitment' (1973a: 116). However, I will continue to use his earlier term of 'objective partisanship'.

allocation of benefits and costs is made in conformity with some stated norma-tive standard' (1973a: 57). So, objectivity can be partisan in that the judgement may come down entirely on one side rather than on the other. Gouldner rein-forces this point by switching to a medical analogy, noting that the physician is not regarded as less objective because he or she has made a partisan commit-ment to the health of the patient and against the germ.

What Gouldner means by 'objective partisanship', then, is commitment to a particular value, or set of values, rather than commitment to any particular social or political group, or even to the interests of that group. Here he is marking his position off not just from the one he ascribes to Becker but also from those interpretations of Marxism that subordinate intellectual analysis to the political needs of the working class or of the Party.

The second kind of objectivity that Gouldner discusses is what he calls 'personal authenticity'. What this entails is recognising that the world may not be how one believes it to be on the basis of one's political views. He describes this as 'the capacity to acknowledge "hostile information" – information which is discrepant with our purposes, hopes, wishes, or values' (1973a: 59). And he sees this too as central to objective partisanship. Indeed, it is in these terms that he interprets the concept of method, as follows:

> In the last analysis, method is an explication and objectification of the procedures the group believes are required before any item of belief may properly be certified (by members of the group) as true. 'Method', therefore, creates obstacles to the yea-saying impulses of our own conviviality, mutual affection or dependence, our personal biases and our movement loyalties or involvements. The essence of method is constraint, self-imposed constraint. Without it, it is unlikely that the individual can find his way to conclusions that will ever differ from those with which either he or his community began.
>
> (1973a: 100)

The third interpretation of objectivity Gouldner considers is that associated with the idea of sociology as a profession: producing knowledge by reliance on scientific method. Here objectivity amounts to 'transpersonal replicability', which requires that a researcher describe the procedures used in a study with sufficient explicitness for others to apply them. Conclusions are objective if this replication produces the same conclusions as the original study. Gouldner criti-cises this approach as amounting only to an operational definition of objectivity: 'it does not ... tell us very much about what objectivity *means* conceptually and connotatively'. Indeed, he argues that it does not capture all of what is normally meant by that term. He clarifies this as follows:

> it is quite possible ... that any limited empirical generalization can, by this standard, be held to be objective, however narrow, partial, or biased and prejudiced its net impact is, by reason of its selectivity. Thus, for example,

one might conduct research into the occupational-political distribution of Jews and come to the conclusion that a certain proportion of them are bankers and Communists. Given the replicability conception of objectivity, one might then simply claim that this (subsequently verified) finding is 'objective', and this claim could be made legitimately even though one never compared the proportions of bankers and Communists among Jews with those among Protestants and Catholics. It might be said that, without such a comparison among the three religions, one would never know whether the proportion of bankers and Communists among Jews was higher or lower than that among Protestants and Catholics. But this objection would simply indicate the technical statistical condition that must be met in order to justify a statement concerning the Jewish *differential*. Insofar as one happens not to be interested in making or justifying a statement about this, the objectivity of the original statement remains defensible in terms of the technical conception of objectivity as replicability. Thus it would seem that the replicability criterion falls far short of what is commonly implied by objectivity.

(1973a: 61–2)

What this comment suggests is that Gouldner sees an intimate connection between universal values other than truth and what would count as objective findings. The latter are not simply factual statements that are accurate; they must also provide a 'true' picture of the social world in broader value terms. Thus, the statement that a certain proportion of American Jews are bankers or Communists may be valid in itself, but as it stands it does not provide an objective account because it leaves open the possibility, and may be taken to suggest, that Jews belong to these groups disproportionately; thereby confirming anti-Semitic propaganda. So, for Gouldner, objectivity is more than validity, defined in terms of transpersonal replicability.

Gouldner sees those who regard sociology as a profession as interpreting objectivity in this narrow technical sense, and as thereby failing to provide the kind of objective knowledge, framed within a commitment to universal values, that he believes it is the duty of sociologists to supply. In pursuing this argument he returns to the issue of value neutrality, criticising Weber even more harshly than in his earlier article for emphasising the separation and discontinuity of facts and values. Weber is accused of inviting 'a fantasy that objectivity may, at some point, be surrendered entirely to the impersonal machinery of research' (1973a: 62), of seeking to 'overcome his experience of the world as grotesque' by formulating 'an incipient utopia in which the impure world is split into two pure worlds, science and morality'. Gouldner claims that Weber attempts to bridge the gap he has created by 'pasting these two purified worlds together, so that each is made sovereign in a different but adjacent period of time'; that is, in different phases of the research process. Here, Gouldner argues, 'the incongruity of the world has not so much been overcome as transcended in myth' (1973a: 63).

Gouldner's critique of Weber here suffers from the same faults as his earlier one. Moreover, while it is true that the latter sought to draw clear distinctions between factual and value claims, and between the activity of science and that of politics, it is not the case that he saw these as two entirely separate worlds.[22] Indeed, the concept of value relevance emphasises the connection between the two, both in terms of the selection of problems for study and of the contribution of research findings to political debate. Weber's distinction was between two vocations with different goals operating in the same world. And, indeed, the tension between them was at the centre of his own life. Furthermore, the important point that Gouldner makes about objectivity can also be made within a Weberian framework. If a study were designed to look at the role of Jews in American society, value relevance and value neutrality would *require* that a comparison be made with other groups. This point of view would also insist that value conclusions (negative or positive) cannot legitimately be drawn about ethnic groups solely from facts about their role in society, and should not be presented as if they can be.

A little later, Gouldner acknowledges the subtlety of Weber's position implicitly by suggesting that the latter recognised that 'the technical sphere would have to be brought into some sort of alignment with the value sphere', whereas the 'modern technical conception of objectivity ... regards the value problem and its relation to the technical as either negligible or dull', as well as assuming that 'somehow, social scientists will do the right thing' (1973a: 63). He also notes that professionalism can be corrupted, though he does not show that it *has* been in the case of American sociology. Here, again, he provides little or no evidence for his claims.

From this Gouldner goes on to consider the nature of the commitment to truth that Weber and others insist on. He argues that this cannot amount to the pursuit of truth for its own sake. The latter, he says, is 'always a tacit quest for something more than truth, for other values that may have been obscured, denied, and perhaps even forbidden, and some of which are expressed in the quest for "objectivity"'. He spells this out as follows:

> Objectivity expresses a lingering attachment to something more than the purely technical goods of science alone and for more than the valid-reliable bits of information it may produce. In this sense, 'truth for its own sake' is a crypto-ethic, a concealment of certain other substantive values through a strategy that, leaving them entirely in the open, diverts attention from them to another dramatically accentuated valuable: truth. The old Druidic sacred place is not destroyed; it is merely housed in an imposing new cathedral. In affirming that he only seeks the truth for its own sake, the scientist is therefore not so much lying as pledging allegiance to the flag of truth, while saying nothing about the country for which it stands.
>
> (1973a: 65)

---

22 He also drew a distinction between the political and the ethical (or religious) life.

And Gouldner goes on to identify the other values that 'lie obscured in the long shadows cast by the light of pure truth' as freedom, power, and what he calls 'wholeness'. About the last of these, he writes:

> one obvious implication of objectivity has commonly been to tell the 'whole' story. The longing here is to fit the partial and broken fragments together ... to overcome the multiplicity of shifting perspectives. Underlying the quest for objectivity, then, is the hope of dissolving the differences that divide and the distances that separate men by uniting them in a single, peace-bringing vision of the world.
>
> (1973a: 66)

Here, Gouldner underlines the point that objective partisanship is not a matter of attachment to the personal values of the researcher. At its heart is commitment to bring about a world in which universal values prevail and human beings are united in peace and justice. And this is, of course, a vision that was to a large extent shared by many Enlightenment thinkers of the eighteenth century, and by nineteenth-century writers like Saint-Simon, Comte and Marx. In these terms, the keystone of objective partisanship is that universal values are seen as forming an integrated whole, rather than being a collection of disparate commitments.

Yet this is a point of view that has been subjected to recurrent criticism during the nineteenth and twentieth centuries, not only from the Right but also from the Left.[23] Gouldner himself notes that it may be difficult for us to identify what our values are, and points to the fact that they may be in conflict, and not a matter of consensus (1973a: 58–9). And, indeed, those committed to universal values in the eighteenth, nineteenth, and twentieth centuries have often disagreed about the content of (and priority among) these values; in short, about the nature of the good society. There are important differences in this respect, for example, between Saint-Simon and Marx, two writers to whom Gouldner appeals.

This raises difficult questions about how sociologists are to set about attaining the objectively true value perspective from which Gouldner believes they must do their work. Put another way, this is the issue of why the particular complex of values that he identifies should be privileged, and of how conflicts among its elements can be resolved. But there are more fundamental problems as well. Gouldner notes that 'perhaps what has been most discrediting to the quest for human unity is that, since its classical formulation, its most gifted spokesmen have often had totalitarian proclivities'. This comment suggests that it is the 'spokesmen' rather than the ideal itself that is totalitarian in character. But a few lines later Gouldner writes:

---

23 On the Left, Herzen probably represents the most important nineteenth-century source; see Berlin 1981.

the plea for human unity has often, and *quite justifiably*, been interpreted as a demand for a tension-free society that was overseen by a close superintendence of men from nursery to graveyard, and was blanketed with a remorseless demand for conformity and consensus.

(1973a: 67, italics added).

And, of course, this resonates with the picture of the modernist project presented by some post-structuralists and postmodernists today, notably Foucault. Nevertheless, Gouldner remains committed to the possibility, 'despite difficulty', of extricating the 'larger hope' from the 'chilling' 'nightmare' (1973a: 67). What he does not explain, though, is how this is to be done, and why we should believe that it *can* be done. Of course, given that this is one of the most difficult problems in political philosophy, this omission is perhaps not very surprising. But the question remains: how is the kind of sociology he advocates to be pursued in the absence of a solution to this problem?

The great insight of Weber in this respect, it seems to me, is that sociologists can pursue their work and produce valuable (indeed objective) knowledge, *without having to resolve this political problem*. Even if one disagrees with Weber's post-Enlightenment assumptions about radical value conflict and the essentially irrational nature of value commitments, it is difficult to see what reasonable grounds there are for assuming that sociologists can overcome the value pluralism and conflict that are to be found in the modern world. And most sociologists today, even those who regard sociology as properly partisan, are probably closer to Weber than to Gouldner in this respect. They often treat values as matters of personal, political commitment; as a result, the kind of partisanship they advocate is very different from that of Gouldner (see Chapter 1).

In 'The sociologist as partisan', then, Gouldner outlines a distinctive view of the proper relationship between sociological research and practical or political values. He advocates objective partisanship instead of the kind of standpoint epistemology that he attributes to Becker. His position also differs from the objective partisanship that is characteristic of Leninist forms of Marxism, where intellectual work is subordinated to the demands of practical politics. Gouldner's is an approach in which the sociologist as intellectual plays a key role, serving the forces of progress by providing both knowledge of the social world and objective evaluation of it, and this may include criticism of the beliefs and actions of those engaged in political movements devoted to bringing about progressive social change. Gouldner believes that this kind of sociological work is in the long-term interests of humanity for a peaceful and just unity.

However, as we have seen, he does not mount an effective argument in support of this position. His account of the alternative points of view he criticises, such as that of Becker, is factually wrong in important respects, and relies on largely speculative analysis about motives and effects. Nor does he engage with the criticisms that have been made of the kind of objective partisanship he recommends. Above all, he does not address the issue of how the value position he adopts is to be justified, or how the reality of reasonable disagreement, if not of value pluralism, is to be overcome. And this despite the fact that his approach makes resolution of that problem a precondition for doing sociological work.

The revolutionary role of sociology

In later parts of *For Sociology*, where Gouldner responds to criticism of *The Coming Crisis of Western Sociology*, he clarifies his conception of the kind of partisanship or commitment that he favours. Central here is the argument that the transformation of sociology is intimately connected with the transformation of society – towards what he calls 'human self-emancipation'. And he sees this relationship as having three aspects. First, as already noted, he believes sociology to be *necessary* for bringing about progressive social change; indeed, in many ways, he treats sociologists as the advance guard in this process. Second, and equally important, is the reciprocal argument that progressive social change is essential for the creation of an adequate sociology. Certainly, he suggests that: 'the renewal of sociology is something that not only entails a change of ideas. It also requires a reconstruction of how sociologists live as well as of how they work'. Finally, Gouldner claims that attaining a true understanding of society is itself one of the goals at which societal reconstruction is directed:

> Clearly, we cannot have a reconstructed society without a critical revamping of our established ways of thinking about society. At the same time, I shall also argue that one of the reasons why we want a new society is that men may better live in it without lies, illusions and false consciousness. The new society we want is, among other things, a society that will enable men better to see *what is* and say *what is* about themselves and their social world. In other words, the very purpose of the new society is, in *some* part, to create a new sociology. A sociology then is not simply an instrument for creating a new society. It *is* that, vitally and importantly that, but that only in *part*. A sociology that says *what is* about man and society is also worth having in its own right and for its own sake, because it is in the nature of man to hunger after truth and to want to know who and what he is.
>
> (1973a: 82)[24]

Gouldner elaborates further on this argument, spelling out its practical implications. He emphasises the way in which conventional sociological work depends on a social infrastructure, including a set of domain assumptions that is

---

24 One of the respects in which Gouldner seems to depart from Marxism is that the latter implies the withering away of social science once communism has been achieved (Cohen 1972). By contrast, Gouldner sees the social transformation he desires as necessary for the full realisation of sociology. Unlike Althusser, though, he provides no rationale for why social science will still be necessary; see Elliott 1987: 172–85.

largely taken for granted. And he calls for a reflexive sociology in which these assumptions are subjected to scrutiny. However, this reflexivity is not simply a matter of theoretical reflection but also of action. It is necessary both to discover *and to institute* 'the human and social conditions for the restriction of irrational and ideological components of discourse, for the control and exposure of false consciousness' (1973a: 78–9).

Gouldner argues that what is required is the construction of new 'theoretical communities' or 'collectives' of sociologists. Indeed, he suggests that: 'It is precisely on this organisational level that social theory attains its fullest reflexivity' (1973a: 80). The work of these communities has both negative and positive elements. On the one hand, they would challenge the ideas and institutions of the wider society: 'there is a need to *create* tension, conflict, criticism and struggle against conventional definitions of social reality, to extricate oneself from them, and to undermine their existential foundations by struggling against the social conditions and institutions that sustain them'. This is the 'oppositional, polemical, critical, isolating and combative side of the process' (1973a: 96). On the other hand, the positive work of these communities is to establish the conditions in which rational discourse is possible: 'within whatever liberated social space is carved out, we begin at once to design and create new communities that support rational discourse in sociology and social theory.' (1973a: 96). Central to this positive task is application of the developing theoretical knowledge produced by sociologists to construct and reconstruct their own communities, a process through which the validity of sociological knowledge is also tested. Thus, Gouldner regards the unity of theory and practice as central to reflexive sociology, and it is largely within these new sociological communities that this unity is to be forged.

Gouldner's argument for 'theoretical collectives' reflects his view that universities have failed in their task:

> The university's central problem is its failure as a *community* in which rational discourse about *social* worlds is possible. This is partly because rational discourse as such ceased to be its dominant value and was superseded by a quest for knowledge *products* and information *products* that could be sold or promised for funding, prestige and power – rewards bestowed by the state and the larger society that is most bent upon subverting rational discourse about itself.
>
> (1973a: 79)

He argues that the new sociological communities (in part, at least) should be made up of sociologists who:

> come together not to pursue careers but to foster rational discourse aimed at understanding their society as a totality. ... [What is sought is] the cultivation of a *practical reason* that contributes to the emancipation of man. ... [These sociologists are] not technicians hierarchically linked in a bureau-

cratic chain of command, with each working in isolation at his own specialised bit of the research. They are, rather, scholars in open and intense contact ... each working on problems of his own choosing and as he pleases, but within the common commitment to understand the concrete totality of modern society.

(1973a: 114)

Gouldner sees the proposed new sociological communities as running in parallel with and assisting other organisations more directly involved in political action, but at the same time he emphasises the need for their autonomy. He argues that practising sociologists should not play leadership roles in political movements (1973a: 121). Nor should they become mere service-providers for these:

> Sociologists should under no conditions become the market researchers of the Revolution, helping Movement people or socialists realise any goals they might wish. Instead, I believe that sociologists should help the Movement and socialists only to the extent that they are judged as contributing to *human emancipation* and to the extent that they pursue this goal with *awareness* of the difficulties and dangers of possible costs and unanticipated consequences.

(1973a: 107)

Summarising, what Gouldner puts forward here is a conception of sociological work as properly in the vanguard of social change, but as needing to transform itself in order to fulfil this task; this transformation also representing a move towards the ideal society at which social change is directed. He recommends the establishment of communities of sociologists who organise their lives collectively on the basis of their work and in such a way as to facilitate that work. These will critique the surrounding society, thereby clearing the way for emancipatory change, and themselves apply the theoretical knowledge they have produced in organising their communities. In doing so, and in resisting and seeking to undermine dominant institutions, they subject that knowledge to practical test and provide the basis for reformulating it and for further practical application. In this manner, they rationalise the conditions in which they operate and generate further theoretical progress and social change. As Gouldner remarks: 'knowledge about society cannot be established without *recreating at once* a part of society and ... what we learn about re-creating that one part of society has implications for all of society' (1973a: 98). Furthermore, these theoretical communities complement and further the activities of emancipatory political movements, but at the same time maintain autonomy from those movements. Gouldner describes his position as a 're-invention' of the Frankfurt 'Critical School of Theory', produced by tracing out the organisational implications of Lukács' 'call for the study of the social totality' (1973a: 114).

Of course, Gouldner's views here reflect the optimism of many sociologists on the Left in the late 1960s and early 1970s. Not surprisingly, examined from near the end of the century, some severe problems stand out. One of these concerns the assumption that the validity or adequacy of sociological work depends on the social conditions under which it is produced. If this were true, and given that the conditions in universities when Gouldner was writing were not such as to support an adequate sociology in his view, how could his own work be a sound basis for the proposals he makes, especially when these are of such a radical character? Within Marxism this problem was 'solved' by the argument that scientific socialism is based on the true consciousness of the working class, this claim being underpinned by a philosophical meta-narrative about the path of socio-historical development towards the realisation of humanity's species-specific being and its aspiration for true knowledge. In the twentieth century, this meta-narrative has been subjected to devastating criticism, and has now been largely abandoned, even on the Left. This has occurred under the theoretical influence of structuralism and post-structuralism, and under the practical influence of feminism, anti-racism and the collapse of Soviet communism. Given his reference to Lukács, Gouldner seems to be committed to this meta-narrative, but he offers no explicit account of or justification for it. Furthermore, in some places he appeals to alternative positions: both to the positivism of Saint-Simon and Comte, and to the critical theory of Habermas. Yet these are incompatible, and are themselves problematic.[25]

A second, related, issue concerns the very close connection that Gouldner assumes between theory and practice: the idea is that sociological work can make discoveries that will provide the basis for social reconstruction, and that the success or failure of attempts at reconstruction will confirm or refute the theory concerned. This ambitious model begs many questions about what research can produce (and over what time-scale), and about what practice needs and can achieve.[26] We can get a sense of the scale of the demands he makes on social research from the following:

> It is a function of the emancipatory social sciences to liberate man's reason from any force, in or out of himself, symbolic or not, in the psyche and in the society, that cripples and confuses reason. It is the special function of these social sciences continuously to dissolve man's opaqueness to himself; to help him understand those forces that act upon him that he ordinarily finds unintelligible; and to help him transform these natural forces that use him as an object into humanly controllable forces under his control.
>
> (1973a: 102)

There are serious doubts about whether, even in the long term, sociological

---

25 As regards Habermas, see the criticisms to be found in Lukes 1982 (Habermas replied to these in Habermas 1982). For a discussion of the various meta-narratives underlying critical social research, see Hammersley 1995a: ch. 2.

26 In the terms I have used elsewhere, it is a strong enlightenment view of the relationship between research and practice. See Hammersley 1998c.

research can provide the knowledge required for this programme to be realised. The implicit model seems to be the control that the natural sciences have delivered. Yet, while that has been significant, it has fallen short of the total control that was sometimes promised or expected.[27] Moreover, this modernist dream of control has increasingly been questioned, not just in terms of the costs of attempting to realise it, but also the possibility *and the desirability* of achieving it. Ironically, these doubts can be found in the Frankfurt School of critical theory to which Gouldner himself appeals, notably in Horkheimer and Adorno's *Dialectic of Enlightenment* (Adorno and Horkheimer 1973).

At a more mundane level, there are problems with the role that Gouldner assigns to practice in testing theoretical ideas. To the extent that the success of practices depends on more than the theory on which they are based (and who would deny that this is so?), outcomes do not provide a strong indicator of the validity of the theory concerned. Practical failure does not necessarily imply error, nor does success imply truth. For this reason, there are doubts about the possibility of integrating theoretical and practical reason in the way that Gouldner proposes. Furthermore, he seems to assume that only one set of practical recommendations can be drawn logically from any theory, whereas there is always scope for competing practical inferences; both because there is a plurality of values, and because each value is open to different interpretations.[28]

Another problem with Gouldner's proposed theoretical collectives is that they seek to combine features of traditional academic communities with some of those from both revolutionary political parties and Utopian communities. As a result, fundamental dilemmas are likely to arise, not only between the demands of research and those of politics, but also between the tasks of community-building and of engaging in action designed to undermine conventional social institutions. For example, Gouldner sees individual sociologists as 'each working on problems of his own choosing and as he pleases' (1973a: 114), but it is difficult to understand how this could be sustained in a community directed towards undermining the social order. In this connection, there are interesting, but unaddressed, questions about the proper treatment by these communities of those members who deviate from the internal theoretical consensus in ways that are judged to be politically unacceptable.

There are also issues about the external relations of the proposed sociological collectives. While Gouldner insists that sociologists must be free to criticise the political movements with which they are associated, he also argues that they 'must not arrogate to themselves the right to set goals for the Movement, or to set themselves above the Movement as a new elite and, in effect, use their posi-

---

27 Medicine is a good illustration of both the gains made and the futility of attempts at total control; see Porter 1997: ch. XXII. Porter's pessimistic summary of one aspect of this is: 'longer life means more time to be ill' (p. 716).

28 Much depends here on what Gouldner means by 'theory', but he provides no clarification of this. For an outline of the scope for different interpretations of values, focused on the example of justice or equity in education, see Hammersley 1997.

tion as a way of acquiring power for themselves' (1973a: 107–8). Yet, while not incompatible, these different requirements are not easily reconciled. It seems inevitable that there would be considerable disagreement even within the socio-logical collectivities themselves about what is and is not legitimate criticism of current political strategies, and even more so between sociologists and non-sociologists belonging to the relevant political movements. Such tensions have been endemic within Marxism, and they are exemplified by the career of Lukács, whose work Gouldner claims as the basis for his own (see Lichtheim 1970). Moreover, Gouldner's separation of sociological communities from polit-ical organisations seems to be at odds with his assumption of a dialectical relationship between theory and practice, and with some aspects of the 'nega-tive' function he assigns to those communities: notably, 'struggling against the social conditions and institutions' that sustain 'conventional definitions of social reality' (1973a: 96).[29]

Finally, there is also potential conflict among different political goals. Gouldner assumes these to be in harmony, but it is important to recognise that they may come into conflict. This can be illustrated by another of the traditions that Gouldner appeals to. It is no accident that Saint-Simon, Comte and their followers were accused of being anti-democratic. This stemmed from their belief that social reconstruction should take place on the basis of science, of which they saw themselves as custodians. They believed that this role for science was essential if society were to be based on reason and its developmental potential realised. But this conflicted with influential interpretations of democracy (see Simon 1963: 34). Gouldner faces the same dilemma, and one suspects that he would have been even more sensitive to criticism on this score than were many of the Saint-Simonians and positivists. While Gouldner recognises that intel-lectuals have special interests (1973a: 120), he does not seem to doubt that there is a close connection between their concern with 'furthering culture' and pursuing the other goals to which radical political movements are committed.[30]

Conclusion

In this chapter I have examined Gouldner's critique of the principle of value neutrality and his arguments for sociological partisanship. As I noted, his work in this area continues to be influential: it is a standard reference. However, the details of his argument and of the position he develops are rarely addressed. Indeed, one reason that his work is important is that it makes explicit what today seems to be largely taken for granted. Also valuable is the encouragement

---

29 A useful comparison is with those Marxists who see the proper role of intellectuals as to operate *within* a political party. See the discussion of Gramsci and Althusser in Chapter 2. Like Althusser, Gouldner seems to prioritise *intellectual* over *political* practice.

30 This is one illustration of the way in which many twentieth-century intellectuals have attached themselves to populist political movements in the belief that those movements were destined to create a society fit for intellectuals to live in.

he gives to the application of sociological analysis to sociological work itself. As he comments in *The Coming Crisis of Western Sociology*, 'a Reflexive sociology ... implies that sociologists must surrender the assumption, as wrong-headed as it is human, that others believe out of need while we believe – only or primarily – because of the dictates of logic and evidence' (Gouldner 1970: 490). At the same time, I have shown that Gouldner's arguments against value neutrality and for partisanship are unsound, in both methodological and socio-logical terms. Indeed, what his work demonstrates is not that the principle of value neutrality is false and that what is required is a 'moral sociology' (Gouldner 1970: 491), but rather that the kind of sociological analysis he employs, relying on a speculative functionalism embodied in concepts like 'myth' and 'ideology', is defective. In other words, what we learn from his reflexive application of sociology to itself is that it has failed to live up to its own principles, not that those principles are defunct.

Moreover, it follows from this that the kind of objective partisanship that Gouldner recommends represents a potential source of bias in sociological enquiry. To some extent, he seems to recognise this himself: in advocating 'personal authenticity' – the capacity to recognise 'hostile information' – as an important aspect of objectivity. Yet to think of information as either hostile or friendly is already to operate within a political rather than a scholarly frame-work (see Gouldner 1970: 494). And this is reinforced by Gouldner's insistence that judgements about the objectivity of research findings must go beyond truth to take other values into account, in the form of what he calls 'normative objec-tification'. He seems to assume that any conflict amongst the values that he sees as underlying sociological objectivity is necessarily temporary, that in the long term they will be in harmony: so that the 'whole picture' produced by socio-logical analysis will not only be true but will also promote justice, human freedom, unity and peace. Yet, while it is true that there is a difference between judging according to personal preference – that is, subjectively – and judging in terms of some stated value principle (see Kaufmann 1949), there will often be little chance of consensus – even among sociologists – about *which* objective value is to be given priority in any particular situation. Gouldner himself notes that different judgements about what is and is not desirable, and about what should be done, will be generated by different values: for instance, by a concern with social reconciliation as opposed to an emphasis on justice. Equally, there may be conflict between judgements based on these practical values and those concerned with truth (interpreted in the mundane sense of empirical validity). In other words, there is no guarantee that discovering and publishing the truth about some situation will have desirable consequences. And, to the extent that conflicts among universal values are endemic, the sociologist cannot meet Gouldner's ideal and will have to trade off one value against another.

By contrast with this, Weber's position was post-Enlightenment in character. He recognised the inevitability of value conflict and argued that the sociologist is duty-bound to give priority to truth. For Weber, objectivity as personal authenticity was paramount. Furthermore, he took the view that while sociologists have reasonable grounds for claiming some authority about factual matters, there is no reason why their value judgements should be given any more weight than those of others. And he saw the principle of value neutrality as a way of protecting against this.

While Gouldner maintains a distinction between the role of the sociologist and that of the political activist, in effect the direction of his argument is towards a reduction (if not the complete erasure) of that distinction (see Gouldner 1970: 497–500). He is right to emphasise that the sociologist is always a person who plays other roles and that this will affect his or her sociological work; *and* that the effect may be positive, not necessarily negative. However, what he fails to accept is what was central, indeed agonising, for Weber: that social science and politics are different occupations, in the sense of being directed towards goals that are not consistently in harmony. We can choose to be political activists or to be scientists; both are valuable professions. Indeed, as individuals, to some extent we can do both kinds of work, as Weber himself did. But we should not pretend that we can do the two simultaneously; even less that we can, or inevitably will, do the one through doing the other. Yet this is precisely what is involved in Gouldner's proposal of theoretical communities that unify theory and practice.[31]

On the basis of his assumption of harmony among universal values, what Gouldner seems to propose is a kind of secular priesthood of sociologists. Indeed, at one point he notes that what he has in mind is the project of nineteenth-century positivism, and that it may involve 'an illicit yearning that links science to religion' (1973a: 66). What this implies, I suggest, is a position which positively encourages the adoption of those interpretations of the world that seem most likely to promote desirable political goals, rather than those that are true; in other words, it encourages bias (see Chapter 6). And this is confirmed, I suggest, by the character of Gouldner's own argument in the articles I have been discussing. I pointed out the defects of his treatment of Becker's 'Whose side are we on?', and the speculative character of much of his discussion of the functions of value freedom. More than this, though, in effect what he does is to construct sociological accounts that *explain away* the positions of those with whom he disagrees, and this often more by allusion than by argument. At most, the persuasiveness of his criticisms is superficial, deriving from the use of language that portrays those who take a different view as operating under the influence of superstition and/or of venal motives. Most of the time, he does not engage with evidence or with the 'logic' of competing points of view in order to establish his conclusions. The mode of writing he employs assumes the validity of his own position – as the true religion, if you like – rather than seeking to make a case that is designed to convince those who do not share his starting assumptions. It is a mode of writing which echoes that of

31 For a discussion of the senses in which research is, and is not, necessarily political, see Hammersley 1995a: ch. 6.

Marx, Lenin and Mills – to list some of those whose influence he acknowledges – and one that has had considerable influence subsequently. In many ways, this has been the most influential, and the most unfortunate, aspect of Gouldner's legacy.

Of course, Gouldner is surely right to recognise that there are powerful forces operating within societies that constrain the autonomy of sociologists, not just externally but also internally. However, he fails to see that the proper defence against these can only be an insistence on the principle of value neutrality. To argue, as he does, that sociologists should promote universal values is to plunge them into a role that they have neither the resources nor the authority to navigate.

5 Methodological purism
Anatomy of a critique

Applying labels to the arguments of other people is not uncommon in academic discussions. These may be labels that are already in use or they may be new. In this chapter I want to consider an example of the coining of a new label: 'methodological purism'. This term was applied in a recent dispute about racism among teachers in English schools. I participated in this dispute, and was accused of methodological purism in the course of it, along with others (see Troyna 1993; Gillborn and Drew 1993; Gillborn 1995: ch. 3; Troyna 1995). The dispute arose in the context of a series of mainly qualitative studies of the education of ethnic minority children in England, which claimed to be able to document school process in a way that larger-scale quantitative studies could not, and which reported systematic teacher racism at both organisational and classroom levels.[1] However, a qualitative study by Peter Foster, a doctoral student of mine, ran counter to this trend, claiming that there was not widespread racism on the part of teachers in the school he studied (Foster 1989 and 1990a). And the predominant response to his book was to criticise him for overlooking what the critics saw as clear evidence of teacher racism (Blair 1993; Connolly 1992; Gillborn and Drew 1992). But Foster went on to challenge the findings of many of the other studies in the field, arguing that the evidence which they supplied for their conclusions was inadequate (Foster 1990b, 1991, 1992, 1993a, 1993b, 1993c). The response to his criticisms was to dismiss them as based on a fallacious approach (Wright 1991; Connolly 1992; Gillborn and Drew 1992; Gillborn 1995). Following this, a colleague and I entered the debate by questioning some of the claims made for qualitative research in this area, and addressing the criticisms which had been directed at Foster (Hammersley 1992b; Gomm 1993 and 1995; Hammersley 1993; Hammersley and Gomm 1993); and it was at this point that the accusation of methodological purism arose.[2] In this chapter, without claiming neutrality, I want to try to step

---

1 For discussions of and references to this literature, see Troyna 1991, Gillborn 1995 and Gillborn and Gipps 1996.
2 For earlier discussions of this charge, see Hammersley 1993, Foster 1993d and Hammersley 1997.

back a little from this dispute in order to examine its character and implications. I will begin by looking at the term 'methodological purism' itself.[3]

The meaning of 'methodological purism'

Labels for others' positions can serve a variety of functions. They may do little more than provide a short-hand means of reference to a particular type of argument. Equally, though, they can hint at a larger context that is intended to clarify the presuppositions or ramifications of the views concerned, or they may point to an analogy which shows those views in a different light from that in which they have conventionally been understood.[4] Of course, labelling may also function as a vehicle for negative evaluations. And this was certainly the case with 'methodological purism'.[5] What this phrase seems to refer to is an excessive preoccupation with methodological as against substantive matters, and an overly severe approach to assessing the possible invalidity of research findings. However, there is also the strong implication in some of the discussions that a sinister political function (albeit perhaps unconscious) underlies methodological purism: a *denial* of racism, an unwillingness to accept *any* evidence of teacher racism (Gillborn 1995: 51).

Some evaluative labels used in critiques operate as no more than a means of summary dismissal, having been emptied of virtually all cognitive meaning. A notorious example is the term 'positivist'. However, new formulations like 'methodological purism', which put together existing words, cannot but carry some content. And, on the face of it, this phrase might seem ill-suited to be a vehicle for negative evaluation. According to the dictionary, 'purism' refers to an insistence on purity: on the need to avoid mixing things that do not go together, and especially mixing the morally doubtful with the virtuous. In these terms, *methodological* purism might be interpreted as an emphasis on the need to meet high methodological standards, and a resistance to deviation from those standards for reasons of personal preference, expediency, social pressure, etc. And this might appear to be an attitude that ought to be encouraged among researchers. Indeed, I believe that it is. However, as we shall see, both 'purism' and 'methodology' also carry some negative connotations.

We can capture the negative implications of 'purism' by thinking about it against the background of modern political philosophy. By contrast with most ancient and medieval views, modernism in this context is often presented as having a 'down-to-earth' rather than an 'idealistic' orientation, involving a

---

3 For convenience, throughout the paper I will use the phrases 'methodological purists' and 'the critics of methodological purism' to identify the two sides. However, it needs to be remembered that, contrary to what has sometimes been implied (see, for instance, Drew and Gillborn 1996), both sides are qualitative researchers, rather than one side being 'mere methodologists'. Moreover, both sides have been critics of the other's research.

4 See, for example, the use of labels in Gellner 1974.

5 This is not surprising given that the term was coined as a response to criticism.

rejection of pure (and necessarily unattainable) ideals in favour of a commitment to practicable goals. And, closely associated, is a 'realism' about what motivates people to do what they do. From this point of view, purism may be interpreted as a refusal to take account of 'reality', or a failure to recognise the need for 'dirty work' if ideals are to be even approximated.[6]

Moreover, there is also sometimes the implication that purism is a front, and that it hides impure motivation; in other words that it is an ideology which furthers the interests of those who promote it, or of those whom they serve. For instance, purism may be regarded as a pose that implies superiority over those who are compromised by their practical engagement in worldly activity, especially politics. It amounts to 'claiming the moral high ground' (Gillborn 1998: 50), a phrase which nicely conveys the impurity of purism through its military connotations. Purism may also be viewed as obstructing practical improvements in people's lives through spurious appeal to allegedly more important matters, to do with transcendental values like truth, beauty or nobility.

This identification of impure motivation behind purportedly pure commitment to ideals derives from a central element of modernist political philosophy and social science: a tendency to rely on a vocabulary of motives that emphasises the pursuit of interests, rather than explaining actions in terms of commitment to ideals. This reflects the influence of a 'hermeneutics of suspicion', whereby appearances are interrogated to discover what it is that has produced them and, especially, what it is that they disguise.[7] Of course, modernism is far from unequivocal in this respect. After all, some modern political philosophers have argued that the pursuit of self-interest leads to the maximisation of benefits for all.[8] Furthermore, some forms of Enlightenment modernism explicitly identify themselves with ideals – with the 'rights of man' (and later of women), with liberty, equality and fraternity, etc. And, of course, 'anti-racism' – to which the critics of methodological purism are committed – partakes of this. Nevertheless, a predominant theme of modern politics is the appeal to self-interest and a distrust of declarations of principle, this distrust being based on a recognition that interests are often disguised by such declarations. And it is this that seems to underlie the use of 'methodological purism' as a vehicle for criticism. The gist of the argument is that, while methodological purism may appear to be

---

6 The key figure here is, of course, Machiavelli. For a critical account of modernism in this sense, see Strauss 1975.

7 Marx and Nietzsche are the most influential sources for this. On 'the hermeneutics of suspicion', see Ricoeur 1970.

8 In a curious way, this is true not only of Mandeville, Smith and Bentham but even of Marx. He argues that the pursuit of its own interests by the bourgeoisie destroys feudalism and subsequently develops capitalism right through to the point of collapse. Similarly, the proletariat's pursuit of its own interests results in the emancipation of everyone because it is the universal class. In this respect, there is no more room in the framework of Marx for idealism, in the sense of a belief in ideals that are separate from reality, than there was in that of Hegel; see Wood 1991.

concerned with principles – indeed with *methodological* principles – in fact it serves particular political interests, albeit in a disguised way.[9]

There is another context in which a negative evaluation of 'purism' can be generated, and one that is even closer to the field in which the methodological purism dispute arose. This is the concept of 'racial purity' that is promoted by some racists. They see races as distinct in their characteristics, as forming a hierarchy, and therefore as not to be defiled by intermarriage or other kinds of close contact. By resonating with this discredited notion of purity, the term 'methodological purism' hints in an entirely connotational way at the racist character of the orientation it is used to criticise. Moreover, the apparent remoteness from one another of these two concepts in terms of substantive content may, far from counting against the connection, actually reinforce it. After all, dissimulation is often seen as a central feature of all ideologies.

There are, then, ample resources within the historically sedimented meaning of 'purism' to generate negative as well as positive evaluations. And further potential ambiguity is introduced by the term 'methodological'. On the face of it the meaning of this word also carries a positive, or at least a neutral, evaluative load. But, here again, negative connotations are present as well. Thus, we can find a sustained attack on the role of methodological thinking in the writings of those who reject the very idea of social *science*. An example is the work of Gadamer, who argues that the assumption that understanding social phenomena can be achieved by following a *method* betrays a fundamental misconception of what is involved in understanding the social world. Whereas a scientistic orientation assumes that we can and must rid ourselves of all preconceptions and simply follow rigorous procedures, in fact understanding necessarily depends on 'prejudices', in the sense of presuppositions; and these are enabling as well as restricting. What is required, then, according to Gadamer, is an openness in dialogue with other perspectives, a willingness to topicalise and reconsider the prejudices on which our current understandings are based. The model of enquiry is that of listening and learning, rather than probing and analysing. What is needed is a receptiveness to what can be revealed to us, not the following of some predefined 'correct' method (see Warnke 1987).[10]

The idea that all understanding reflects the background assumptions and socio-historical location of the researcher has come to be widely accepted, and is sometimes used against the claim of methodology to offer a means by which objective knowledge can be produced. Thus, in his critique of methodological purism, Gillborn emphasises the way in which both research findings and

---

9 Of course, there is scope for modernists to apply the complex, not to say contradictory, resources available to them in a selective fashion; along the lines of 'We act on the basis of principle; you act so as to serve your own or the system's interests.'

10 Despite Derrida's disagreements with Gadamer (Michelfelder and Palmer 1989), a similar opposition to method can be found in his work; and in this respect he is representative of most post-structuralism and postmodernism. For a recent critique of method in the context of educational research, from yet another point of view, see Carr 1997.

evaluations of their validity 'may reflect particular political, methodological, class-based, gendered and racialized assumptions'. And he questions any claim to escape from the effect of such assumptions (Gillborn 1995: 53).[11]

There are also less philosophically abstract sources of negative meaning surrounding the term 'methodological'. One of these is a rejection of what is seen as the preoccupation of quantitative researchers with technique, and specifically their privileging of quantitative method and dismissal as unreliable of research that does not match its requirements. The complaints of Mills about the fetishism of method (Mills 1959b: 224), and of Gouldner about 'method-olatry' (Gouldner 1967) seem to fall into this category.

A development of this critique is to be found in some justifications for research biographies or natural histories of social research projects, where what researchers actually do is contrasted with the prescriptions to be found in methods texts. What might be interpreted from the point of view of those texts as failure to meet the relevant requirements – as sloppiness, bias, etc. – is some-times presented instead as showing the impracticality of the prescriptions. The implication is that if researchers were to try to follow these methodological rules to the letter, little or no knowledge would be produced.[12] Indeed, one commen-tator has dismissed textbook accounts as 'technicist conceptions of research', on the grounds that 'in their determination to lay bare the allegedly logical and sequential phases of the conception, execution and dissemination of social research … [they] help to sanction and reproduce "the myth of objectivity"'. What is required instead, it is suggested, is 'a perspective in which research is not construed as something pristine but as something "carried out by flesh and blood figures who are engaged in real life activities"' (Troyna 1994: 5). Here we have a direct line of contact with modernist political criticisms of purism as failing to take account of the practical demands of reality. It is presumably against this background that repetition of the claim that 'methodology is too important to be left to the methodologists' by some of the critics of methodo-logical purism is to be understood (Gillborn 1995 and 1998; Drew and Gillborn 1996).[13]

Of course, such criticism of prescriptive or technicist methodology need not amount to a dismissal of methodology *in toto*. We might reject the textbook accounts but insist on the importance of researchers engaging in reflection

---

11 Where Gadamer outlines an alternative approach to the production of knowledge, much usage of this idea in the social sciences, including that of Gillborn, does not. It hints that objectivity is not possible while nevertheless making claims about the world that are apparently to be taken as uncompromised by the writer's own background assumptions and socio-historical situa-tion (see Hammersley 1998e).

12 See, for example, Bell and Newby 1977. It is worth noting that these authors also expressed concern about the methodological 'anomie' that sociology was suffering.

13 The source of the phrase is Becker 1970: ch. 1, though the sentiment is also to be found in the work of C. Wright Mills (Mills 1959a and b). For a discussion of Gillborn's use of this phrase in comparison with that of Becker, see Hammersley 1998d.

about how they do their work.[14] However, even methodology in this form is open to possible negative evaluation. Thus, Troyna questions if such reflection has much significance, suggesting that research biographies often present no more accurate a picture of research than do methods texts. Indeed, following Denzin, he raises the question of whether these biographies do not effectively *constitute* the realities they describe rather than merely documenting them.[15]

Methods texts and research biographies may also be criticised for privileging methodological over substantive considerations. This relates to the question of the goals of research, of the extent to which these are restricted to the production of knowledge or are extended to include other concerns: for example, assisting professional groups in achieving their aims (such as promoting education), or pursuing political goals (such as emancipating women, empowering clients, or fighting racism). On the basis of an extended conception of the purposes of research, assessment of research findings should not be concerned predominantly with methodological matters, such as validity and reliability, but must give equal or greater weight to practical, ethical and/or political considerations. Here, the criticism implied by application of the term 'methodological purism' to assessments of research on teacher racism would seem to be that they were too narrow in focus, neglecting the wider goals of this research – for example its role in the project of anti-racist political education.[16]

So, the term 'methodological purism' has a considerable capacity for mobilising negative evaluation. And some of the implications I have discussed are to be found in explicit form in the specific arguments that its critics deploy. As we shall see, it is argued that the methodological criteria that the purists apply are so severe as to be impractical, thereby undercutting all research on racism in education, and perhaps qualitative research in other areas too. It is also suggested that 'impure' interests lie behind methodological purism. One version of this is that the methodological purists are concerned with defending schoolteachers against criticism. Thus, Gillborn claims that 'the defence of teachers ... is given a central place in the [methodological purists'] project'

---

14 This is the position of Bell and Newby (1977) .

15 There are two additional points he makes. First, he suggests that, because it is qualitative researchers who generally produce reflexive biographies, this form of research is opened up to scrutiny in a way that quantitative work is not; thereby consolidating the common prejudice that qualitative research is the weaker of the two. Secondly, he argues that the requirement that research be reflexive results in younger researchers being exposed to intrusive surveillance by those who occupy positions of power within the research community and outside. On this last point, see Paechter 1996.

16 Of course, where postmodernist scepticism about the possibility of knowledge is entertained, these other goals may become the *exclusive* concern. There are hints of this scepticism in Troyna (1995), despite the fact that he also rejected some features of postmodernism; see Vincent 1998: 21–2. Similar equivocation is to be found in the work of Gillborn; see Hammersley 1998e. Marcus (1994) has argued that ambivalence is characteristic of attitudes towards postmodernism.

(Gillborn 1995: 56; see also Gillborn 1993: 7–9).[17] But, of course, the most serious accusation of this kind is that methodological purism is racist. Gillborn argues that it 'goes too far'; that, effectively, it is a form of the 'new racism' (Barker 1981). He claims that it privileges 'the values, expectations and assumptions of the dominant ethnic group', and in doing so 'may defend processes that systematically serve to disadvantage minority groups' (Gillborn 1995: 63). In this way, 'the new racist political discourse is … reworked using the language of scientific neutrality' (Gillborn 1995: 61). Thus, methodological purism is judged to be 'fundamentally racist' 'in its basic assumptions and presentation of minority students' (Gillborn 1998: 34).

In part, what is involved here is the accusation that the work of the methodological purists is biased; indeed, 'racially' biased. And this creates an interesting symmetry, since bias (this time in the form of a systematic tendency towards claims of racism) is a feature that the methodological purists identified in the research they criticised (Foster *et al.* 1996). This raises fundamental questions about the nature of the relationship between the contrasting points of view adopted by the methodological purists and their critics.

Clarifying the character of the conflict

At the most superficial level, what we are faced with in this dispute is a disagreement about factual matters. On one side, there is research claiming to document endemic racism in particular schools, and to show that it is widespread: in the form of indirect (and sometimes direct) discrimination, both in selection decisions (allocation to bands, sets and courses) and in the treatment of children in the classroom (Gillborn 1995: 45–7; Gillborn and Gipps 1996). On the other side, the methodological purists argue that often the evidence offered to document racism in the particular cases studied is not convincing, and that there is currently no strong evidence showing widespread racism among teachers, according to most interpretations of that term. In other words, they treat claims that there *is* widespread teacher racism as of uncertain validity (Foster *et al.* 1996).[18]

---

17   There has been a long-running debate within the sociology of education about the effect of its 'critical' approach on teachers (see Simon 1975 and Young 1973).

18   Some of the criticisms of methodological purism refer to racism in schools generally. However, it is teacher racism, rather than pupil racism, with which those labelled methodological purists have been concerned. Another area of possible misunderstanding is worth noting at this point as well. It is easy to overlook the distinction between suspending judgement about the validity of a claim and *denying* the validity of the claim. One reason for this is that 'validity' is often interpreted as warranted assertibility, in terms of which the above distinction seems to disappear. That distinction also tends to get obscured where the focus is on implications for action, or on the effects on action, of knowledge claims and counter-claims. In these terms, too, questioning the validity of a claim and denying its validity may tend to be confused. It is important to recognise, however, that the methodological purists do not assert that teacher racism is rare. Their argument is that currently we do not have sufficiently strong evidence to conclude that it is widespread, *on most definitions of the term, and judged by research criteria* (see Hammersley 1995a: ch. 4).

However, in various ways, the dispute goes beyond this disagreement about factual matters. As I noted, both sides have accused the other of bias. These accusations can be interpreted in different ways. They may be complaints about the inconsistent application of agreed methodological rules. And, in part, this seems to be the case. Thus, the critics of methodological purism sometimes hint that it involves raising the standard of validation for claims about racism by comparison with other claims. Gillborn argues that methodological purists are 'especially damning of researchers who claim to identify school-based processes that disadvantage members of one or more ethnic minority groups' (Gillborn 1998: 53). And, in response, the methodological purists accuse their critics of applying lower standards of assessment to work that claims to discover inequality and racism than they do to research that does not (Foster *et al.* 1996: ch. 7). Of course, identifying deviation from the proper application of methodological standards is not a straightforward matter. It *would* be relatively straightforward if there were some foundation of indubitable evidence in terms of which the validity of knowledge claims could be adjudicated. However, neither side defends this sort of foundationalism. And, without a foundation of brute facts, the scope for reasonable disagreement about what is convincing evidence is considerable. The methodological purists have explicitly outlined an alternative, non-foundationalist, approach to assessing validity. According to this, what is convincing evidence depends on judgements about plausibility and credibility: about the degree of compatibility of the knowledge claim with what is currently taken to be established knowledge; and about the likelihood of error in the process by which the claim or the evidence for it was produced. And it is recognised that these judgements are unlikely to be consensual, especially in a contentious area like racism in education.

However, the disagreement between methodological purists and their critics does not seem to lie simply in discrepant judgements about validity within a common framework of methodological assumptions. The critics explicitly reject the approach to the assessment of knowledge claims put forward by the methodological purists. One aspect of their critique is the charge that this approach sets the criteria for validation too high *in general*, with the result that social and educational research, or at least qualitative work, effectively becomes impossible. What is involved here is the argument that, like foundationalism, the approach of the methodological purists assumes that social research involves, or can involve, the provision of sufficient evidence for the claims presented to be accepted as true. And it is this that the critics appear to reject. For example, Gillborn criticises what he takes to be the methodological purists' assumption that it is possible to identify 'a critical mass of evidence, beyond which a case should be accepted as proven, but where anything less is rejected' (Gillborn 1995: 52). Elsewhere, he insists that 'there is no single standard, no "significance test", for qualitative inquiry' (Gillborn and Drew 1993: 355). And the conclusion that seems to be drawn from this is that a more lenient approach needs to be adopted in judging the validity of research findings about racism, recognising that there will inevitably be different views.

This criticism points to a very difficult problem, one that is analogous to that concerning the proper relationship between ideals and practical feasibility in social and political life more generally: at what point, if any, is it justifiable to trade ideals off against expediency? When, if ever, should ideals be abandoned on practical grounds, or scaled down to make their pursuit more practicable? It is probably true that the position taken by the methodological purists is deflationary: if generally accepted it would reduce the knowledge that social scientists can justifiably claim to have produced in some areas; and it may make the task of validating knowledge more difficult in the future. But, of course, this does not necessarily count against it, because such a re-evaluation might simply bring current practice into line with what is proper. Yet the problem is precisely to determine what *is* an adequate level of evidence that must be reached before knowledge claims can be accepted as valid. It is tempting to think of the threshold of cogency set within science as fixed in some absolute and external way. This, indeed, is implied by foundationalism. But once we give up that epistemological view, no fixed threshold can be assumed. Thus, on the basis of the alternative account put forward by the methodological purists, where knowledge claims are judged on the basis of plausibility and credibility, it seems likely that research communities operating in different fields will set their thresholds of cogency at different levels.[19]

Several factors may affect these thresholds. One consideration is that relaxing the standards beyond a certain point simply erases any distinction, in terms of probable validity, between the findings of research and lay interpretations of the same phenomena, and thereby undermines researchers' claims to expertise.[20] However, what threshold is feasible in any area will also depend on the difficulties currently faced by those working there. These may be diverse in character, relating not only to obstacles (including both ethical restrictions, for example on the kinds of experimentation that can be done with human beings, and practical restrictions, for instance on the length of interviews) but also to assessments of the extent to which appearances could be deceptive (for example in terms of the reliability of inferences from experimental findings to the 'real world', or from what people *say* they do to what they actually *do*). To the extent that such difficulties vary in severity across fields, one would expect there to be variation in cogency thresholds.[21]

---

19 Of course, there are problems with comparing cogency thresholds across disciplines, or even across sub-disciplines, to the extent that these involve different types of knowledge.

20 While there are researchers who advocate such an erasure, they rarely embrace the logical conclusion that follows from this: that there is no justification for public funding of research, or for the whole apparatus of research publishing.

21 A commonly used contrast is that between archaeologists' attempts to reconstruct forms of social life in prehistoric societies and those of historians working on more recent periods. The argument goes that there is much less evidence available to the former, so that what is acceptable in archaeology would be dismissed as speculative by historians. Nevertheless, many would wish to argue that it is important to maintain a distinction between what is required for a conclusion to be drawn legitimately, and what evidence is currently available. The recognition that many questions cannot currently be answered is of crucial importance in most areas of research. See Hammersley 1993.

The dispute between the methodological purists and their critics can perhaps be seen in these terms, in part: as a difference in view about what is the appropriate cogency threshold in social research. It can be formulated as follows: methodological purists claim that in some social science research there is too little difference in methodological status between what are presented as research findings and lay knowledge claims; whereas the critics insist that there is sufficient difference, and that the level of validation demanded by methodological purists is unrealistic, given the difficulties faced by researchers in the field concerned.

Detailed argument about what level of evidence is possible and necessary in social and educational research would be required to resolve this aspect of the dispute. However, not only do the critics of methodological purism not offer this, but (as noted earlier) in places they seem to reject the very notion of a cogency threshold. And this seems to imply that social research can be no more than a matter of putting forward interpretations that are generated by diverse, value-laden points of view. This could represent a form of relativism, a rejection of the traditional view of science as capable of generating substantial rational consensus about factual matters (and perhaps also of the idea of truth as correspondence with, or accurate representation of, phenomena); or at least of the applicability of this scientific approach to the field of social research.

If this *is* the basis for the critics' rejection of the attempt to operate a communal cogency threshold, some clarification of and justification for the enterprise in which they are engaged is required. For example, what would be the basis for their own claims to expertise as educational researchers? Furthermore, if this relativistic position were adopted, it would render the methodological purism dispute no more than a conflict between incommensurable paradigms, and thereby would undercut the critics' own charge of bias against the methodological purists. Yet, they clearly believe that they are correct and the purists wrong; and so rely on some sense of the concept of validity that extends beyond their own perspective.

So, this disagreement about the possibility of a cogency threshold clearly does not capture the core of the dispute. The critics' position cannot be a relativistic one. This conclusion is reinforced by another element of the way they question the methodological framework adopted by the purists. As already noted, one feature of that framework is a reliance on the plausibility of knowledge claims, in other words on the degree to which these are implied by, or not in conflict with, what is currently taken by researchers to be sound knowledge. And it has been argued by the critics that this represents a source of conservative bias: that it involves accepting dominant ideological views as valid, and represents a failure to exercise the critical attitude that is an obligation of social scientists (Troyna 1995). On these grounds, they have sometimes explicitly contrasted their own 'critical' stance with what they see as the 'uncritical' approach of the methodological purists (Gillborn 1995: ch. 3). What they have not done, however, is to make clear what 'critical' means in this context. In the next section, then, I will sketch what this position appears to involve, comparing it with what I will call the 'analytic' approach that motivates methodological purism.[22]

Critical and analytic approaches

Outlining the critical approach first, this assumes that society is characterised by deep-seated inequality between dominant and subordinate groups, and as a result by a clash of interests and potential conflict between these groups. Equally important, it assumes that the social system functions to maintain the hierarchy, both through the direct exercise of power and through the role of ideology in persuading people of its legitimacy. It is argued that, in this context, the central task of the researcher is to expose inequalities and injustices, to document them and their sources. Equally important is ideology critique: criticism of the conventional wisdom that covers over inequality or seeks to legitimate it or explain it away. This is opposed both on the grounds that it is false in epistemic terms and that it serves to block progressive social change, these two features being taken as closely related.

Central to what it means for research to be 'critical', then, is that it evaluates current social arrangements according to some value principle (notably, equity or social justice), and challenges them where they do not realise that principle. On this basis, ideas that are seen as supporting social injustice are criticised. Of course, judgements about what is inequitable, and about what inequities exist, are not straightforward. Thus, even the judgements of self-declared critical researchers about these matters will not necessarily be in agreement or be sound, since they are themselves part of society, and so are subject not only to material constraints but also to ideological ones. As already noted, it is a key assumption of the critical approach that dominant groups maintain their position to a considerable extent through their control over ideas. And social science may play a role in this process of cultural reproduction, albeit often inadvertently. So, without being aware of it, researchers may produce research that is guided by assumptions that are false and politically conservative in their implications or consequences. Given this, it is demanded of researchers that they be reflexive or self-critical, in the sense of continually examining their working assumptions for the effects of the dominant ideology.

One way in which ideology can infect research is through the researcher giving more credence to information deriving from dominant groups, or their representatives, than to that from subordinate groups. It is essential from a 'critical' point of view, therefore, that researchers reject the conventional hierarchy

22 What are presented here are ideal types, specifically designed to illuminate the methodological purism dispute. However, they necessarily have more general relevance. The distinction drawn here is similar to Whitty's account of analytic and possibilitarian orientations in the new sociology of education (Whitty 1977; see also Foster *et al.* 1996: ch. 1). There are also parallels between the debate discussed here and one that has taken place in the sociology of deviance; see Downes and Rock 1979.

of credibility.[23] 'Official' views are to be challenged, in terms of both their validity and their function. And the taken-for-granted assumptions of researchers themselves must be interrogated, since these may reflect their role in the social infrastructure; which, in effect, is often as a 'servant of power'. Complementary here are arguments that those who are marginalised by the social system have superior insight into its operation. It is claimed that, since they have no commitment to preserving the status quo, they are less likely to be deceived by the dominant ideology. Moreover, they have direct experience of its oppressive operation, from which other members of society, including many researchers, are cushioned.[24] In summary, then, hermeneutic suspicion must be directed at the dominant views in a society, and towards research that seems to reinforce them. By contrast, the perspectives of those on the social margins should be valorised, though even these may be distorted by ideology in some respects, and should therefore be open to critique.[25]

The body of research that the methodological purists criticised conforms, more or less, to this 'critical' approach. It had challenged the conventional view that there is little racism in the education system, and that what there is amounts, among teachers, to a few prejudiced individuals. It expanded the scope of the meaning of 'racism' beyond prejudice-based direct discrimination, this narrow definition being rejected as ideological. It reported widespread teacher racism of various kinds, explaining this in terms of the racist character of dominant social structures in English society.

From a 'critical' point of view, the methodological purists' questioning of the findings of this body of research stems from their having taken over common-sense assumptions. First of all, it is claimed, they have tended to employ the conventional, narrow definition of racism, which hides the ways in which the operation of schooling disadvantages black pupils. Secondly, it is implied that the reason why the methodological purists demand further evidence of teacher racism is because they begin from the common-sense assumption that most teachers are not racist. In effect, they are resistant to the discovery of teacher racism, and this reflects their own backgrounds and the resulting tendency to believe official accounts rather than the accounts of ethnic minority students.[26]

In short, the methodological purists are charged with failing to question (or even to recognise) ideological assumptions. Indeed, as we have seen, the critics argue that this tendency is enshrined in methodological purists' use of

---

23 On the concept of 'hierarchy of credibility', see Becker 1967. See also Troyna 1995 and Hammersley 1998a. The article by Becker in which this concept is introduced was discussed in Chapter 3.

24 Researchers who originate from, or have some special relationship with, one or more marginal categories of person – in terms of social class, sex, 'race', disability, sexual orientation, etc. – can of course promote their views by appealing to these arguments.

25 For an exemplification of this approach see Mac an Ghaill 1988, and the commentary on it in Hammersley 1998a.

26 Methodological purists do not accept the validity of these criticisms, of course.

plausibility as a criterion of assessment. Closely related is the claim that the methodological purists fail to recognise the implications and consequences of their own work: the fact that, because they operate on the basis of ideological assumptions inherited from the society they are studying, their work reinforces those assumptions by giving them apparent scientific warrant. In this way, so the argument goes, methodological purism serves to reinforce the status quo, and is itself racist (Gillborn 1998: 34): to fail to challenge the inequalities that lie 'both *within* and beyond the research process' (Troyna 1995: 397) is to be party to an unjust society.

This, then, is the 'critical' approach within which the critics of methodological purism seem to operate. By contrast, the methodological purists are committed to what I will call the analytic approach. Significantly, this also places great emphasis on the role of criticism. However, what analytic researchers mean by 'being critical' is different from what is meant in 'critical' research. For them the focus for criticism is knowledge claims put forward by other researchers, rather than the social arrangements referred to in those claims. Analytic researchers see the critical assessment of arguments and evidence as central to the process by which scientific knowledge is produced, and they regard the production of such knowledge as the sole task of research. It is argued that only by meeting the challenge of collegial criticism will the results of research have a greater likelihood of validity than competing claims to knowledge about the same issues generated by other means. So, in an analytic context, being critical means assessing arguments and assumptions in terms of logic and evidence, and being prepared to suspend judgement about matters if there is not convincing evidence to support or reject a particular knowledge claim.

This approach requires researchers to limit the presuppositions from which they start to those that are generally accepted as beyond reasonable doubt within the relevant research community; a community that ought to assess knowledge claims in such a way as to err on the side of rejecting the true as unproven rather than accepting the false as true. Analytic research necessarily starts from appearances – from informants' accounts, from what seems to be happening on the basis of observation, etc. However, these *are* only a starting point; they are not taken to be self-revelatory and their validity may be rejected during the course of investigation. Indeed, the aim is to move beyond them, since this is necessary in order to generate news (Gomm 1976). But this news must be supported by evidence that ought to be found convincing by other researchers, whatever their political convictions or theoretical preferences; and if it is not found convincing by most colleagues then further evidence must be supplied in order to try to achieve a consensus.

On the basis of this view of the role of criticism in the production of research-based knowledge, analytic researchers criticise the critical approach as *insufficiently* critical: as placing excessive reliance on prior assumptions about the nature of the social totality, assumptions that are neither common-sense nor well-established on the basis of empirical research. It is argued that the very concept of criticism on which critical researchers rely rests on a whole host of assumptions about the true nature of the society being studied and the forms of deception it involves. And the complaint is that these assumptions are treated, in effect, as articles of faith: 'critical' researchers defend them by explaining away other views as the product of ulterior motives or ignorance. Central here is illegitimate use of the concept of ideology (see Sharrock and Anderson 1981). It is employed to cover over discrepancies between what critical theory says is the case and what some of the people studied themselves believe or do; thereby weakening the pressure on researchers to demonstrate that their account is more likely to be valid than common-sense beliefs. Equally, as we have seen, the concept of ideology can also be used to explain away conflicting arguments on the part of fellow researchers – as conservative, racist, etc. – without having to produce evidence designed to convince anyone who does not already share 'critical' researchers' starting assumptions.[27] Closely associated is a functionalist mode of argument, characteristic of system and reproduction theories, whereby whatever occurs can be assumed to serve the status quo; in fact, the more benign a feature appears to be in superficial terms, the more open it is to func-tionalist explanation – on the grounds that the disguise conceals its conservative function all the more effectively. Analytic researchers argue that these argumentative devices are self-serving; and that they close 'critical' research off from criticism to a degree that may undermine its capacity to produce sound knowledge. The danger is that it becomes a form of dogmatism.

So, analytic researchers do not accept most of the substantive assumptions about the nature of society on which the critical approach is premised. However they do not *reject* those assumptions either; treating them instead, along with others, as hypotheses to be investigated. While analytic researchers recognise the existence of widespread inequalities and social conflicts in modern societies, they do not assume that these are always between just two sides, oppressed and oppressors, or that all inequality and conflict derive from a single fundamental source, or even from a small number of sources. Nor do they assume that these sources are different in kind from those that generate equality and harmony. Above all, analytic research does not *presuppose* the existence of a single social system that operates in such a way as to reproduce inequities, and to disguise its role in this.

More fundamentally, analytic researchers are sceptical about the idea that any situation studied is part of a single social totality whose essential character can be known. In other words, they question the premise – built into the crit-ical approach – that there is a single, all-purpose theoretical perspective that grasps the nature of social reality exhaustively. They also reject the spurious teleology introduced into conceptualisation of the social world by critical researchers' functionalist modes of argument; a teleology operating not at the level of the individual, the group, or the organisation but at that of social

---

27 For documentation of this in relation to one of the critics of methodological purism, see Hammersley 1998e.

classes, genders, 'racial' groups, or social systems; where the agent of last resort seems to be Capitalism, Patriarchy, or Racism. Thus, methodological purists have criticised critical, anti-racist researchers for treating racism in the same way that many Marxists have conceptualised capitalism – as an agency that structures the social world in a manner designed to ensure its own reproduction (Foster *et al.* 1996: 165–70).

While analytic researchers do not necessarily reject macro models of society, they insist that these cannot exhaust the character of social reality; that they must *not* be of a kind that attributes false teleology; and that they can only be validated on the basis of substantial aggregate level analysis *and* micro investigation of local social situations that does not presuppose their validity.[28] While analytic sociologists are aware that appearances may be misleading and even deceptive, they argue that whether and how this is so must be *discovered*, not presupposed. From their point of view, the critical approach tends to reduce research to filling in the details of how the system is assumed to reproduce itself; with the nature of that system and its reproductive capacities being taken for granted. All that is left open for investigation by that approach, they suggest, is how these manifest themselves in particular contexts. Thus, analytic sociologists criticise the tendency of critical researchers to assume that deception, ideology, etc. come from only one direction: from above. They see this as overlooking the *range* of forms bias can take and the *diversity* of interests it may serve.[29]

As part of this, they question the one-dimensional status and power structures that critical researchers often assume, insisting on the diversity of social positions (without implying that these have equal power) and the varying insights and biases these positions may generate. Thus, they argue that the credibility hierarchies to be found within a society, organisation or community are often based on multiple, and dissonant, criteria; and are subject to negotiation. Furthermore, it is assumed that people at the bottom of them may not only have insights but also blindnesses, perhaps even reason to lie or to deceive themselves – that *their* social position can lead to misconceptions just as much as can that of people at the top.[30] Conversely, those at the top may be able to supply useful and accurate information, despite the interests and assumptions

---

28   There are sociologists who do adopt an analytic approach, notably some interactionists, who *do* seem to reject macro theory; see, for example, Rock 1979: ch. 7.

29   This stems from their abandonment of two ideas that were central to much Enlightenment thinking, and that have been influential in the social sciences throughout the nineteenth and twentieth centuries: that the good and the true are closely related to one another; and that there is a single harmonious conception of the good. Thus, they do not assume that sources of bias are necessarily bad in moral or political terms.

30   It is interesting to find this latter argument in the work of Gouldner (1973a: 40), who is often (and rightly) treated as a key figure in the development of the critical approach in sociology. He deploys this argument against what he sees as Becker's advocacy of partisanship. However, like other critical researchers he can only recognise bias on the part of subordinate groups as arising from distortion of their views by the dominant ideology.

that shape what they say. On this basis, analytic sociologists argue that the reports of all informants must be assessed in terms of potential sources of error, including both interests and limitations on access to information (these limitations being potentially as serious for all types of informant, and varying relative to the topic being investigated). In summary, whoever's account of the world is being analysed, the starting assumption must be that their beliefs and behaviour have some recognisable internal logic or intelligibility (this is often referred to as the principle of charity); but equally, as a source of information, the data they provide must be scrutinised for threats to validity (Hammersley 1998a).

Of course, the analytic approach also recognises the danger that researchers may be deceived by their own background assumptions. This is precisely the reason why there is an effort to minimise questionable initial presuppositions. So, they too advocate researcher reflexivity (see Hammersley and Atkinson 1995). However, the concern here is exclusively with the likely validity of assumptions, not with their political implications or effects; nor is the putative social origin of assumptions regarded as conclusive in assessing their validity, for reasons already explained. It is believed that through the critical assessment of assumptions error can be minimised and progress made towards sound knowledge. But this depends, to a considerable degree, on researchers working within a community that subjects knowledge claims to assessment, and does so solely on the basis of their cognitive validity and through appeal to what is currently accepted as knowledge (itself always open to challenge) and/or to evidence that is judged unlikely to be in error (this also being open to potential challenge).

There is another feature of the critical approach that analytic researchers dispute. This is the way in which it blends fact and value. Terms like 'equality', 'inequality', 'discrimination', and 'racism' are used by that approach in ways which imply that they refer to features of the world that are inherently good or bad. Analytic researchers reject this value-loaded approach because it suggests that evaluations and prescriptions can be derived directly from social science evidence. This is not to deny that there is a great deal wrong with the world, or that inequity and racism are wrong – indeed, on most interpretations, they are wrong by definition. But what *counts* as inequitable depends on judgements that rely on value as well as on factual assumptions. And analytic researchers emphasise that there are very often reasonable disagreements about such matters, and that social research cannot resolve these definitively. All it can do is to provide factual evidence that bears on these judgements and disagreements.[31] So, analytic researchers regard the way in which critical research rests on evaluative assumptions about society, and evaluates social arrangements, as misrepresenting the capabilities of research; and as likely to have unacceptable

---

31 Of course, factual evidence can throw doubt on a value perspective through raising questions about factual assumptions on which it depends; but facts alone cannot validate a value judgement. It might be added here that analytic researchers regard methodology as properly evaluative in character, unlike the social research it is designed to serve. The evaluative criteria it depends on are those appropriate to the pursuit of knowledge in the most effective manner.

consequences for all concerned. It oversteps the legitimate boundaries that constrain the authority of researchers (Foster *et al.* 1996: ch. 7).[32]

Up to now I have focused on differences between the two approaches in their theoretical and methodological assumptions. But it is important to note that what generates these differences, to a large extent, is a divergence in view about the *purpose* of research. The critical approach is committed to the unity of theory and practice, in one form or another. In other words it takes as at least one of its goals the bringing about of social change of particular kinds. The production of knowledge is treated as a means to that end, even if the good society is also defined as one in which true knowledge of the world finally becomes available.[33]

There can, of course, be a range of different views about the relationship between knowledge production and other goals. There are at least three main possibilities here:

1   The goal is to bring about political change, with research seen as of value solely as a means to this end, and pursued in any way which serves that end. Indeed, its value may be taken as lying simply in the legitimacy it can confer, which can be used to promote particular policies. Here, knowledge production is subordinated to political goals, and the value of particular findings is judged entirely in terms of their political usefulness (which may depend on their validity, but need not).

2   The ultimate goal is to bring about political change, but the immediate goal is to produce knowledge relevant to this. Here, validity is an important consideration in its own right, but research – interpreted as concerned with the pursuit of valid knowledge – is only engaged in to the extent that it seems to have direct and positive instrumental value in political or practical terms.

3   The immediate goal is to produce knowledge, but it is hoped that this will contribute to desirable political change. Here, the primary concern is with the validity of knowledge claims, and interest in the political or practical contribution of research is suspended during the course of enquiry.

What varies here is the relative priority given, on the one hand, to the production of valid knowledge and, on the other, to political or practical goals. While much Marxist academic work in the past has, in effect, treated science or

---

32   This does not imply that values are matters of irrational commitment, only that researchers have no specialised expertise as regards value conclusions, and that claims to such expertise distort the democratic process. In fact, the analytic approach does not even assume that researchers have exclusive access to sound factual knowledge of the world since, by contrast with critical researchers, they deny that common-sense is necessarily ideological.

33   The most elaborate version of this argument about the good society 'realising' truth is in Hegel, but it can be found elsewhere; see, for example, Gouldner 1973a: 82. Gouldner's argument is discussed in Chapter 4.

scholarship as properly autonomous, and has therefore largely restricted itself to the task of knowledge production, many critical researchers today reject both the possibility and the desirability of such autonomy, arguing for a strong interpretation of the union of theory and practice (Stavenhagen 1971; Kemmis 1988) and/or for explicit partisanship (Gitlin *et al.* 1989; Troyna and Carrington 1989; Mac an Ghaill 1991; Mies 1991; Gitlin 1994; Humphries and Truman 1994; Siraj-Blatchford 1994).[34] This often implies a redefinition of the concept of validity to incorporate political implications or consequences, for example along the lines of what Lather refers to as 'catalytic validity' (Lather 1986a and 1986b). At the very least, it may be argued that where assessments of validity are uncertain we should ensure that we err on the side that will do least damage from some political point of view (see Gillborn 1995: 60).

The significance of this change in orientation has been obscured by continuing commitment to the Enlightenment idea that the true and the good have a close affinity, so that pursuing one is a means of pursuing the other. What has happened is that previously researchers pursued knowledge, judged in terms of cognitive validity, in the belief that by doing so they were contributing to the improvement of society, whereas now some critical researchers judge validity in terms of whether or not the assumptions involved or findings reached serve desirable political goals.

By contrast, analytic research distinguishes not just between research and politics as two different kinds of activity, with different goals, but also between academic and practical research (Hammersley 1995a: ch. 6; Foster *et al.* 1996: 32–4; Hammersley 1999b). The goal of academic research is to contribute to a developing body of knowledge whose likely validity is greater than that of lay ideas. For this to be possible, contributions have to be assessed by fellow researchers primarily in terms of validity, these assessments being motivated by an organised, though limited, scepticism (see Merton 1973: chs 12 and 13).

---

34 There seem to be differences in view about this among the critics of methodological purism. Troyna advocated partisanship; see, for example, Troyna 1995. However, Gillborn's position is less clear. He states that '"partisan" is a poor descriptor for critical research' (Gillborn 1998: 50–1). He also denies that critical research must involve 'an overt political struggle against oppressive social structures'. He comments that 'although sociological research offers the potential to contribute to such struggles, there are obvious limitations in attempting to build this overtly into every project' (Gillborn 1995: 197–8). This leaves open the possibility that he sees such a contribution as the *covert* goal of research. At the same time, he defines critical research as 'work that challenges received wisdom in the best traditions of the sociological imagination'. This is a much weaker definition. Indeed, as it stands, it could imply that even the work of the methodological purists is 'critical', since they are challenging what is currently the dominant view in the field of research on 'race' and education. Gillborn clearly does not accept this, which indicates that there is an implicit restriction on what would and would not count for him as received wisdom; one shaped by what I have identified as the guiding assumptions of 'critical' research. This is supported by the fact that his reference to 'the sociological imagination' is an allusion to C. Wright Mills's position, which draws a distinction between the pursuit of politics and of research but also assumes the 'progressive' political character of the latter. See Chapter 2.

While the knowledge produced must be value relevant, in the sense of having some potential interest to outsiders, this need only be indirect and remote. By its very nature, academic research is not directed towards satisfying specific needs for information. Instead, it provides general resources that *may* be useful for practical purposes, but even then usually only in combination with information from other sources and on the basis of experience and judgement. Moreover, the knowledge will often be usable by those on different sides of political struggles. No close affinity is assumed between the true and the good. Indeed, as noted earlier, the good is regarded as frequently open to different, equally reasonable, judgements; with research unable to play any role in adjudicating among these, beyond providing evidence about the factual assumptions built into them.

From an analytic point of view, practical research shares the same restriction to a proper concern with factual knowledge. However, it operates within the framework of the practical activity it is intended to serve. It seeks to meet the information needs of that activity, and in doing so takes over some factual assumptions that would be treated as of uncertain validity in an academic context. One reason for this is that whereas in academic research validity is assessed solely in terms of degree of cogency, in practical research assessments must also take into account the likely costs of different kinds of error, with those costs being judged in the terms used by the relevant practitioner group(s). These differences between academic and practical research arise from a trade-off – between maximising the likely validity of the findings and maximising their direct relevance to practitioners. In these terms, the two forms of research are incompatible; though both are of value, and each may provide resources for the other.

From an analytic point of view, the 'critical' approach can be regarded as a form of practical research that is tied to a particular political project, but which seeks to present itself not only as serving universal interests but also as meeting the requirements of academic research, when it does not and cannot do this. Indeed, it transgresses even the proper limits of practical research in its conflation of fact and value.

Accusations of bias

In light of the conflict in approach that I have outlined, it is useful to look again at the accusations of bias that each side in the methodological purism debate has directed at the other. Bias is best conceptualised as systematic deviation from what would be the most effective route to one goal because of commitment to another (see Chapter 6). So, what is bias from the point of view of one goal is not necessarily bias from that of another. As we have seen, for analytic sociologists the sole immediate purpose of research is the production of knowledge, and they believe that critical research is biased because it takes for granted factual presuppositions which are open to genuine question, and because it defends these by means of practical value judgements. It also judges findings in terms of their implications or anticipated consequences, and this risks accepting as true what is in fact false. Analytic sociologists regard these features of the critical approach as arising from commitment to other goals, and as ill-suited to the production of sound academic knowledge, as likely to intro-duce, and to protect, error.

In part, the ascription of bias by critical researchers to analytic sociology is framed in similar terms. From their point of view, analytic research is biased because it is believed to take over common-sense assumptions that are ideolog-ical; assumptions that are false, and are widely believed only because they serve the interests of dominant groups. It is argued that this bias stems from analytic researchers' 'failure' to recognise the true character of the society they are studying. The assumption here is of an existential choice: one either adopts the perspective of common-sense or adopts that of critical theory; and this choice determines whether or not the findings of one's research are ideological. Common-sense is regarded as ideologically closed, as incapable of overcoming the errors built into it without external, theoretical correction; even though those errors may be the truth in distorted form. So, analytic sociology is seen as treating evidence – how the social world presents itself – in an insufficiently crit-ical way: it fails to recognise that systematic deception is involved; that the social system generates a false image of itself. It is argued that the evidence provided by appearances can only serve as a means of gaining knowledge if this deception is recognised, and the evidence interrogated for what it conceals; in other words, on the basis of a theoretical perspective giving knowledge about the social system behind this deception. Rather than simply documenting appearances, research must look for telling signs of underlying processes that systematically disguise themselves. In terms of this kind of analysis, what is required is a 'symptomatic' rather than a 'literal' reading of evidence; and analytic researchers are biased because they treat as knowledge what is ideological, as a result of their failure to exercise a proper reflexivity based on critical theory.

At the same time, the conception of bias employed by critical researchers is broader than this concern with threats to the cognitive validity of knowledge claims. And this stems from the fact that critical research is directed towards the goal of bringing about progressive social change as well as producing know-ledge. Just as knowledge claims are to be judged in terms of political criteria, so bias is constituted by deviation from those criteria. Since social and educational research is part of society, it must be judged according to the same values as any other institutional sector: for example in terms of the extent to which it sustains inequality or promotes equality. It is in these terms that methodological purists are accused of discriminating against black pupils by not accepting their accounts of racism (see Connolly 1992; see also Troyna and Carrington 1989); and by doing work that is not geared to countering racism, indeed which may even make that political task more difficult (Gillborn 1995).

These two aspects of bias are seen by some critical researchers not simply as compatible but as two sides of the same coin; reflecting their commitment to the assumption that there is a close affinity if not an identity between the true and the good.

Conclusion

In this chapter I have examined a recent dispute in the field of research on racism in education, seeking to clarify the sources of disagreement. I have made explicit my own commitment to one side of this dispute, but I have tried to understand the arguments on the other side as well as I can. While on the face of it this disagreement was about the strength of the evidence supporting the claim that there is widespread racism on the part of teachers in English schools, I have suggested that what lies at its root is a more fundamental disagreement about the nature of social and educational research. Thus, the critics of methodological purism assume that research takes place within a society that is racist in character, and they see it as a central part of the researcher's role to combat that racism. On this basis, the arguments of the methodological purists are criticised, in effect, for a failure to accept this commitment; and as a result are themselves treated as racist. Here, to a large extent, the critics draw on what has come to be referred to as a 'critical' approach to social research. This relies on a conception of society as characterised by inequality and conflict between dominant and subordinate groups, and as systematically operating in such a way as to maintain that inequality, through both coercive and ideological means. Thus, critical research is based on substantial factual assumptions, and is explicitly value-laden, both in its presuppositions and in its findings; its goal is not simply the production of knowledge but also the pursuit of political goals. In short, it is partisan.

By contrast, those labelled 'methodological purists' argue that it is an obligation of social scientists to adopt as their sole immediate task the production of knowledge. While they may do academic research for a variety of reasons, it should not be pursued in a way that is designed to support any particular practical or political project, however laudable. Indeed, precautions must be taken to avoid any concerns external to the pursuit of knowledge introducing error. One such precaution is to minimise reliance on presuppositions about society that are not generally accepted as empirically well-established amongst researchers; and to remain open to any questioning of those presuppositions, in the spirit of organised scepticism. Also required is a suspension of commitment to evaluations of what is being studied, relying on the use of practical values other than truth solely as a basis for identifying value-relevant phenomena for investigation. I labelled this the analytic perspective.[35]

The obvious question that arises from all this is whether or not the methodological purism dispute is resolvable, even in principle. To start with, it is worth

35 This perspective sees practical research as non-partisan in the sense that it is primarily concerned with producing sound knowledge, but as partisan in that it is designed to serve the information needs of a particular group. Thus, from an analytic point of view, it is necessary to make a sharp distinction between academic and practical research, and to be clear about which type is being conducted in any particular case (see Foster *et al.* 1996: 32–4). Furthermore, while the analytic perspective does not deny the value of practical research, academic enquiry is regarded as the core task for those working in universities.

noting that agreement might be possible about the extent of racism among teachers in English schools, under certain conditions. For the methodological purists, 'racism' would have to be interpreted as a value-relevant descriptor rather than as an evaluative term; and it would have to be clearly defined according to some standard of equity, by means of which potential inequalities in treatment and outcome could be identified.[36] If on this basis research findings were produced that showed widespread teacher racism, and these were cogent in the evidential terms specified by the methodological purists, there could be agreement between the two sides about the factual issues that were the initial stimulus for the dispute. There is nothing built into the approach of either the methodological purists or their critics that would prevent such agreement; though the difficulties that would be faced in resolving the dispute in this way should not be underestimated.[37]

There may also be some scope for agreement in methodological terms. Both sides are committed to at least some role for evidence in judging claims about the *way in which* racism could operate in the education system. And the kinds of evidence on which they rely are very similar, even if the way they use these varies somewhat (see Hammersley 1998a). This overlap reflects the fact that the critical tradition has been shaped by some of the same epistemological stances – not just positivism, but also neo-Kantianism, phenomenology and structuralism – that have also informed the analytic approach.

However, if my analysis of the dispute is correct, any agreement of this kind would be only superficial. Underlying the dispute are fundamental differences in view about the purpose of social and educational research. Moreover, in the case of the critical approach, this is closely bound up with a set of theoretical presuppositions about the nature of society. This means that any agreement on particular issues, substantive or methodological, is likely to be very limited. Most of the time there is likely to be disagreement.

On this basis, it may be tempting to conclude that what we have here are incommensurable paradigms. Yet this is not a viable point of view for either side to adopt. Neither can be committed to the relativism that this implies: each believes that its view is superior to the other; and in general terms, not simply from its own perspective.[38] What this highlights is that, even without assuming epistemological relativism, we can recognise that there may be points of view that are hard to reconcile. Indeed, there is always the potential for intractable conflict among those operating under different guiding purposes. What this means is that while it may be difficult for either side in the methodological

---

36 This is the approach adopted in Foster *et al.* 1996; see also Hammersley 1997.
37 By contrast, it seems clear that the dispute could *not* be resolved by research showing convincingly that there was not widespread teacher racism. As I have argued, the existence of racism is a presupposition of 'critical' anti-racist research.
38 Of course, relativists also believe this about relativism; but therein lies the self-refuting character of their position.

purism dispute to persuade the other to change its views, this does not imply that there is no scope for rational discussion about what is at issue.

Such discussion could focus on at least two areas. One concerns the extent to which each side is correct in identifying bias on the part of the other; in the sense of a significant threat to the cognitive validity of research findings arising from the very nature of the other approach. For example, is it true, as the analytic sociologist argues, that critical research is likely to involve systematic error because it is concerned not just with producing knowledge but also with pursuing political goals? It is of significance here that critical researchers do not deny that practical goals can be a source of error. Indeed, they insist that this is the case where those goals are conservative, racist, etc. So, what they must defend is the idea that there is something about *their* goals which implies that pursuit of these through research is not a form of bias. Indeed, the critical approach often goes beyond this to claim that commitment to its political goals actually *facilitates* the production of knowledge; that those who do not accept the validity of the picture of society on which those goals are based are the prisoners of ideology. This is presumably what Horkheimer, one of the founders of critical theory, means when he says that 'right thinking depends as much on right willing as right willing on right thinking' (Horkheimer, quoted in Bottomore 1984: 16). However, it is difficult to see what cogent grounds there could be for believing this. And the critics of methodological purism certainly do not supply any.

On the other side we can ask: to what extent is it true, as the critical approach argues, that analytic research is committed to common-sense assumptions that lead it into systematic error? It is certainly true that analytic research cannot entirely avoid reliance on common-sense assumptions, even if it minimises controversial assumptions. Moreover, what is and is not controversial is socially determined and is likely to be generated by other considerations than a concern with truth. It may very well derive from a hierarchy of credibility that reflects the power structure of the society.[39]

The response that analytic researchers can make to this argument has three closely related components. First, reliance on common-sense cannot be avoided by anyone: no research can start from scratch. The belief that it can relies on

39 Under the influence of post-structuralist and postmodernist ideas, some critical researchers give an epistemological twist to this, arguing that truth itself is socially constituted through the operation of power relations. There is a crucial ambiguity involved here, however. If the implication is simply that people's judgements about what is and is not true, and perhaps even some of their ideas about what is and is not good evidence, are shaped by their social context – including other concerns than validity – then this adds nothing to the point already made. However, if the argument is of a deeper epistemological kind, claiming that what is true (not just what is *taken* to be true) is socially constituted, in the sense of depending on the substantive and methodological assumptions prevalent at the time (or if the distinction between what is true and what is taken to be true is rejected), then a relativist position is being adopted that is self-undermining. It is self-undermining because if it were true its own claims would only be true under a particular regime of truth, and would be false under others.

some form of foundationalism. By contrast, as formulated here, analytic socio-logy draws on what is referred to in philosophical terms as contextualism (Williams 1991 and 1995). This is the epistemological view that justification always occurs against a background of beliefs whose validity cannot but be taken for granted until further notice. Any one or other of these background beliefs can subsequently be questioned, but it is not possible to question (and thereby to seek justification for) the whole of our beliefs all at once. Within this framework, most of the methods used by social researchers and many of the methodological ideas developed under foundationalism can be retained more or less intact. The aim is still to produce knowledge, conceived as representing relevant features of the phenomena to which it refers. And while there is no method that guarantees the production of knowledge, it is still assumed that there are better and worse routes to knowledge (see Hammersley 1998b; and also Chapter 6).

The second point follows on from this: that even critical researchers rely on common-sense assumptions. It is only *some* of those assumptions that they reject as ideological. For example, they do not usually deny the common-sense idea that there are power differences among individuals and groups, that what is supposed to go on in schools is education, or that money is a source of power. So, in practice, they accept *some* common-sense beliefs as true while treating others as false. Moreover, the common-sense assumptions they accept cannot but be implicated in their judgements about the validity of knowledge claims. What this underlines is that the analytic and critical approaches do not differ in their reliance on common-sense assumptions, though they do differ in *which* and *how many* assumptions are relied on.

The final defensive point that can be made by analytic researchers is that there is no reason to assume that common-sense is irredeemably erroneous and closed: it is possible to operate within a framework of common-sense assump-tions yet to discover and correct errors, and thereby to move towards the truth. Doubting that this is possible can only lead to complete scepticism: critical researchers must accept this third point, if they are to retain the idea that research can produce knowledge. What is at issue is how we can decide, ration-ally, what parts of common-sense are and are not likely to be true. As we have seen, for analytic researchers and for the methodological purists, this requires us to minimise questionable assumptions and to treat the remaining assumptions tentatively (rather than as undeniably true or false) until there is good evidence for or against them, even then rejecting or accepting them only until further notice. And the research community is regarded as playing a crucial role in assessing knowledge claims. By contrast, while critical researchers engage in such assessment of arguments and evidence, this is constrained by their treat-ment of some assumptions about the nature of society as indisputable; indeed, as a matter of moral and political commitment. From an analytic point of view this introduces potential bias into the research process.

While both analytic and critical sociology emphasise the role of criticism in social research, indeed each side accuses the other of failing to be sufficiently critical, neither adopts the position of epistemological scepticism – as we have seen, they could not do so and still make the substantive claims that they do. So, both depend on some means of stopping the process of critical questioning, which could, in principle, go on for ever.[40] In the case of analytic sociology, this is achieved by judgements, always open to revision, about what is beyond reasonable doubt; with acceptance of those judgements being a matter for the relevant research community. In the case of critical sociology, what serves this function is its founding assumptions. Only within the boundaries set by these does the critical assessment of evidence occur: what is outside those boundaries is not approached in order to assess its validity but rather to explain why people believe it despite its falsity. Moreover, while the research community may play a role within critical research in the assessment of evidence, its membership is limited to those who share a 'critical' approach. Furthermore, the views of some of those outside the research community – those who are deemed to suffer from, or to be engaged in resistance to, inequality – may be given a role in judging what is to be taken as well-established knowledge. The effect of this is to rein-force emphasis on the political implications or consequences of knowledge claims as against their validity, and to subvert the organised scepticism that from an analytic point of view should be at the centre of the critical assessment of evidence in academic research.[41]

The second main area where there may be scope for productive argument between the two approaches concerns the value of the pursuit of knowledge, as against other goals. From the point of view of the critical approach, knowledge is of value first and foremost for instrumental reasons; though, as we have seen, a true understanding of the world may also be regarded as an essential element of the good society.[42] In these terms, the primary aim of research should be to realise social ideals, such as 'equality'. Knowledge has no value in itself, apart from that political task. While this is sometimes combined with a conception of the good life framed in terms of democratic self-rule, with democracy modelled on intellectual discussion in pursuit of the truth, the search for knowledge sepa-rate from a direct concern with its contribution to the realisation of the good society tends to be seen as a form of alienation, or as simply ideological disguise for work that supports the status quo.

Underlying this 'critical' point of view is a unitary conception of what is valuable (see Hammersley 1995a: chs 2 and 7). By contrast, analytic sociology is committed to an acceptance of the plurality of values, with some conflict among these being inevitable. In these terms, the production of knowledge is of

---

40 In this context, Hegel's description of his approach in the *Phenomenology* as 'self-completing scepticism' is significant; see Forster 1989: 3–4 and *passim*.

41 This is not, of course, to say that one cannot adopt many of the theoretical ideas of critical or Marxist sociology as useful models for explaining social phenomena. Indeed, their value needs to be emphasised at the present time.

42 However, within Marxism this is seen as being achieved as much through social change itself as through progress in research; see Cohen 1972.

intrinsic value, and it is an expression of one aspect of human nature; though only one of many that should be valued.[43] This means that, engaging in enquiry, one necessarily foregoes other values – other aspects of human life – to some degree. But the same is true of all specialised occupations and activities, including politics. From this point of view, there is no single human ideal. Moreover, enquiry is of value however great or little use can be (or *is* made) of its findings in practical or political terms; so long as those findings relate in general terms to human beings' interest in their world. While analytic socio-logists must believe that it is better, other things being equal, to have knowledge rather than not to have it, they recognise that knowledge does not necessarily produce practical or political benefits; and that it may even have consequences that they judge undesirable (see Hammersley 1998c). And while the individual researcher may, on occasion, feel that he or she must abandon research in order to engage in some other activity that has greater priority, the analytic approach necessarily involves the assumption that the institution of academic research ought to be sustained, and must be protected from being misused for other purposes. Of course, there are important and difficult issues here which are open to genuine disagreement, but I suggest they are also open to rational exploration.

Despite their fundamental differences, then, there is some common ground, and there are some areas where those committed to critical and analytic approaches could engage in discussion.[44] Even so, the prospects of productive debate *actually taking place* between the methodological purists and their critics, or more generally between analytic and critical sociologists, do not seem good. This is because, as already noted, the critical approach is structured in such a way as to treat those who do not accept its fundamental assumptions as not just mistaken, and therefore as in need of persuasion, but rather as witting or unwit-ting agents of an unjust social system that must be resisted or overthrown. This is encouraged by its emphasis on the unity of theory and practice, which blurs or even erases the distinction between political struggle and academic discus-sion. This perhaps explains the fact that for the most part the critics of methodological purism have refused to engage with its arguments in any detail, preferring to denounce it as ideological, immoral, etc. For instance, one of the early responses to methodological purist criticism begins by complaining about

---

43 Not all aspects of human nature ought to be valued and developed, of course; but the argument is that those which are capable of providing benefit should be, even though developing them will involve costs and may sometimes have harmful consequences. In this respect, the analytic perspective relies on liberal political assumptions about valuing diversity and individual autonomy, though it does not assume that these should be valued in an unrestricted fashion. This kind of liberalism has been subjected to criticism by communitarians in recent times (see Sandel 1984), though the latter do not reject liberal values, and it seems unlikely that most critical researchers would do so either.

44 For a discussion of how fundamentally different views can nevertheless be assessed, see MacIntyre 1990.

the 'tediousness' of having to reply to criticism from this quarter (a complaint that has been tediously repeated!), and explicitly refuses to 'respond to each of the criticisms', on the grounds that this would allow the methodological purists 'to define what is important in relation to research on "race" and ethnicity' (Gillborn and Drew 1993: 354–5). This refusal to engage with the arguments of the other side undercuts the possibility of fruitful discussion. In this way, it seems to me, the critical approach disqualifies itself as a form of academic research: it turns sociology into a political morality play.

6   Bias in social research

with Roger Gomm

Accusations of bias are a recurrent event in the social and psychological sciences. Some of these have achieved the status of major public events, such as the attacks on hereditarian theories of intelligence, notably on the work of Cyril Burt (Kamin 1977; see also Mackintosh 1995); the response to the Glasgow University Media Group's books on television news (see Harrison 1985); and Derek Freeman's critique of Margaret Mead's *Coming of Age in Samoa* (Freeman 1983). And of course, in many cases, the reaction to an accusation of bias is a counter-charge, indicating that it is not just research itself but also evaluations of research that can be biased.[1]

However, despite the frequency with which it is used, the meaning of the term 'bias' has been given rather little attention in the methodological literature. And it is by no means unproblematic. For one thing, the term is ambiguous: it is used in several different ways. We will begin by outlining what seem to be its three main senses.

In the Preface to his book on the intellectual Left in post-war France, Sunil Khilnani announces that it is 'quite explicitly and in the original sense a *biased* book: it proposes a new angle of vision, one which brings certain significant patterns into clearer focus' (Khilnani 1993: vii). It should be said that the Oxford English Dictionary does not offer any evidence that this is the original meaning of the word; in fact, it does not mention this sense at all. Nevertheless, the idea that point of view can make a difference to how well one discerns significant patterns in a scene, or in a sequence of events, is a common-sense one. And it has been developed in a methodological context by Max Weber, in the form of his theory of ideal types. Weber defines an ideal type as: 'a conceptual pattern that brings together certain relationships and events of historical life into a complex that is conceived of as an internally consistent system'. Moreover, this is not a representation of reality 'as it is', but rather involves the 'one-sided accentuation' of aspects of reality in order to detect causal relationships (Weber 1949: 90).

---

1 For this counter-charge of bias in the case of Freeman's critique of Mead, see, for example, Ember 1985.

In Khilnani's terminology, ideal types are biased in such a way as to highlight what we otherwise might overlook. It is worth noting that here bias is seen as a *positive* feature, in the sense that it is illuminating: it reveals important aspects of phenomena that are hidden from other perspectives. At the same time, the possibility of negative bias remains, this presumably characterising a perspective that obscures more than it reveals. From this point of view, it seems that bias is an inevitable feature of any account, and its status as good or bad is left open for determination in particular cases.

This sense of the term 'bias' is sometimes used in the literature of social research methodology. Quantitative researchers occasionally employ it, notably in discussions of significance levels (see, for example, Levine 1993: 92). Qualitative researchers also use it. For example, it is often taken to be implied in Becker's influential argument that sociological analysis is always from *someone's* point of view, and is therefore partisan (Becker 1967: 245).[2] Moreover, the influence of relativist ideas, including those deriving from some of the French philosophers who are the focus of Khilnani's book, has encouraged this usage among qualitative researchers. The effect of this is evident, for instance, in the claim that 'the question is not whether the data are biased; the question is whose interests are served by the bias' (Gitlin *et al.* 1989: 245). Here, the recommendation is that research *should* be biased: in favour of serving one group rather than another.

Of course, this is not the predominant sense of the term 'bias' as it is used in the social sciences. Instead, bias is generally seen as a negative feature, as something that can and should be avoided. Often, the term refers to any systematic deviation from validity, or to some deformation of research practice that produces such deviation. Thus, quantitative researchers routinely refer to measurement or sampling bias, by which they mean systematic error in measurement or sampling procedures that produces erroneous results.[3] The contrast here is with random (or haphazard) error: where bias tends to produce spurious results, random error may obscure true conclusions.

The term 'bias' can also be employed in a more specific sense, to identify a particular source of systematic error. This is a tendency on the part of researchers to collect data, and/or to interpret and present them, in such a way as to favour false results that are in line with their pre-judgements and political or practical commitments. This may consist of a positive tendency towards a particular, but false, conclusion. Equally, it may involve the exclusion from consideration of some set of possible conclusions that happens to include the truth. This third interpretation of 'bias' will be our main focus.

Such bias can be produced in a variety of ways. The most commonly recognised source is commitments that are external to the research process, such as

---

2 For a discussion of the ambiguities of Becker's argument, see Chapter 3.
3 This usage of the term is the predominant one in many methodological texts. See, for example, Kidder and Judd 1986 and Babbie 1989.

religious or political attitudes, which discourage the discovery of uncomfortable facts and/or encourage the presentation of spurious 'findings'. But there are also sources of bias that stem from the research process itself. It has often been pointed out, for example, that once a particular interpretation, explanation or theory has been developed by a researcher he or she may tend to interpret data in terms of it, be on the look out for data that would confirm it, or even shape the data production process in ways that do this. This can arise in survey research through the questions asked in an interview, or as a result of the *way* they are asked (Oppenheim 1966). It is also a potential source of systematic error that has been recognised by experimental researchers, with various precautionary strategies being recommended (Rosenthal and Rosnow 1969; Rosenthal 1976). Nor does qualitative enquiry escape this kind of bias. Indeed, it is often thought to be particularly prone to it; not least because here, as is often said, 'the researcher is the research instrument'. Thus, one widely recognised danger in the context of ethnography is that if the researcher 'goes native' he or she will interpret events solely from the point of view of particular participants, taking over any biases that are built into their perspectives.

As will become manifest, even these three interpretations of 'bias' do not capture all of the distinctions that need to be made. Moreover, ambiguity is not the only, or the most serious, problem surrounding this term. We will argue that in the case of both quantitative and qualitative research it, and related concepts like truth and objectivity, have tended to be understood in terms of a foundationalist image of the research process. We are not suggesting that either quantitative or qualitative researchers wholly believe in this image, but it has long shaped their thinking – and its influence has not been entirely eradicated despite much explicit criticism.

Foundationalism and the conceptualisation of bias

All concepts form part of networks, and it is on the basis of their relationships with the other concepts involved in those networks that their sense depends. The usage of 'bias' that is our focus here relies on the concept of validity or truth. Bias represents a type or source of error, and in this respect it serves as an antonym of 'objectivity' (in one of that word's senses). These other concepts are, of course, themselves not uncontentious. 'Truth' is a term that is consciously avoided by many researchers, perhaps because it is so often taken to imply the possibility of absolute proof. But, even putting this on one side, the concept of truth or validity is open to competing interpretations.[4] Much the same is true of 'objectivity'. And, in recent years, especially under the influence of constructionism and postmodernism, there has been a growing amount of debate, especially among qualitative researchers, about the meaning of these

4 For diverse philosophical discussions of the concept, see White 1970, Kirkham 1992 and Allen 1993.

terms (Lather 1986a and 1993; Kvale 1989; Mishler 1990; Phillips 1990; Wolcott 1990; Harding 1992; Altheide and Johnson 1994; Lenzo 1995).

The dependence of conventional interpretations of these concepts on positivist assumptions is a central theme in the literature. And the same charge was directed many years ago at the concept of bias (McHugh *et al.* 1974: ch. 3). At the same time, 'positivism' is a much abused term; so much so that its meaning has become elastic. Moreover, the assumptions that are often criticised in discussions of validity and bias are not unique to positivism, in any meaningful sense of that word. For these reasons we will use the term 'foundationalism' to refer to a set of assumptions that seems to be implicated in much conventional usage of terms like 'validity', 'error', 'objectivity' and 'bias'.

In its most extreme form, foundationalism presents research, when it is properly executed, as producing conclusions whose validity follows automatically from the 'givenness' of the data on which they are based. This may be assumed to be achieved by the 'immediacy' of the conclusions or by methodological procedures that transmit validity from premises to conclusions. The sources of 'given data' appealed to by foundationalists are various. They include: innate ideas (Cartesian rationalism), perceptions (empiricism), physical objects (physicalism), observational consistencies (operationalism) and ideational essences (Husserlian phenomenology). The nature of the givenness varies, then, but in all cases the sources of data are treated as independent of, and as imposing themselves on, the researcher. Similarly, conceptions of the nature of any inference involved can vary; for example it may be deductive or inductive. But, whatever its form, it is taken to produce conclusions whose validity is certain, given the truth of the premises.[5]

On this foundationalist view, the course that enquiry should take is clearly defined and, as a result, deviation from it – whether caused by bias or by some other source of error – is also straightforwardly identifiable. Indeed, the research process is seen as self-contained: it relies on nothing outside of itself. The implication of this is that if erroneous conclusions occur they must result from the illegitimate intrusion of external factors, notably the subjectivity of the researcher or the influence of his or her social context. What is required to avoid error and bias is for researchers to be objective; in other words they must pursue the research in the way that 'anyone' would pursue it who was committed to discovering the truth, whatever their personal characteristics or social position.

To illustrate this kind of foundationalism, we can use an analogy with a rather bizarre game of bowls, where the position of the jack is fixed and the proper course of enquiry corresponds to a straight-line trajectory of the bowl bringing it into direct contact with its target. All other trajectories display the effects of error or bias. And the fact that one can hit or come close to the jack

---

5 It is perhaps important to emphasise that, as formulated here, foundationalism is a pure type. It does not even correspond to the position of the Vienna Circle positivists (see Uebel 1996).

by means of some of these other trajectories (as one would usually aim to do in a conventional game of bowls) simply indicates that one's conclusions can be correct for the wrong reasons as well as for the right ones.

The problems with foundationalist epistemology have long been recognised by philosophers. They have been explored both by those advancing such a view and by their critics.[6] Forms of empiricist foundationalism dominated Anglo-American philosophy of science from the 1930s to the 1950s, its problems being seen by many as merely technical and therefore as resolvable. However, the consensus amongst philosophers of science today is that foundationalism is indefensible. It is argued that there are no foundational data, and that the relationship between theory and evidence cannot be immediate or deductive, nor is there an 'inductive logic': the validity of theories is always underdetermined (Hanson 1958; Kuhn 1970; Gillies 1993). This collapse in support for foundationalism has led, most dramatically, to the emergence of sceptical and relativist views. These either abandon the concepts of truth and error completely, or reinterpret them in ways that are at odds not only with foundationalism but also with the everyday practical thinking of most scientific researchers. It should be noted, however, that much post-empiricist philosophy of science has pursued a more moderate line, exploring and trying to resolve the problems associated with realism (see Hammersley 1995a: ch. 1).

Methodological foundationalism was for a long time a guiding idea for quantitative researchers in the social sciences. And to some extent it continues to be. For example – perhaps as a result of the persistent, if largely implicit, influence of operationism – there is still a common tendency to treat the validity of numerical data as given, despite their constructed character and the sources of potential error built into them (Converse and Schuman 1974; Schuman 1982; Bateson 1984; Pawson 1989). Furthermore, statistical techniques are sometimes used as if they constituted a machine for transforming data into valid conclusions (Lieberson 1985; Oakes 1986; Ragin 1987; Levine 1993). This is certainly not to suggest that all quantitative researchers are naïve in these respects; but there is a strong tendency for simplistic methodological ideas to survive in practice long beyond the time that they have been consciously abandoned.

Even qualitative research has been influenced by a kind of foundationalism; despite explicit rejection of the validity of quantitative methodological canons, of positivism, and sometimes even of the model of natural science itself. At one time, virtually all qualitative researchers were explicitly committed to the idea that the aim of enquiry is to depict reality in its own terms, independently of the researcher and of the research process; and to the belief that this could only be achieved by close contact with it, for example through participant observation or life history interviewing (Hammersley 1989 and 1992a). This ethnographic 'realism' or 'naturalism' took for granted that there are facts about

---

6 See Suppe 1954 for an account of the collapse of what he calls 'the received view' and the arguments involved.

the world that can be apprehended by immediate experience, thereby providing a foundation for analysis; though the data were interpreted in pragmatist or phenomenological, rather than empiricist, ways.[7]

Given its influence in both areas, the collapse of foundationalism has much the same consequences for qualitative as for quantitative researchers: it threatens the justification for conventional research practice in both fields. So, the question arises: what response should social researchers make to the failure of foundationalism? And what implications does any response have for the concept of bias?

There has, of course, been a great deal of criticism of quantitative research for its commitment to positivism; and, in recent years, there has also been growing criticism of older forms of qualitative research for their reliance on realism. In place of the latter, many feminists, constructionists and post-modernists have opted for radical epistemological alternatives. This response has not always been unequivocal, but it is possible to identify two broad types of radical epistemology that have found some support: relativism and standpoint theory.[8] In the next section, we will examine the implications for the concept of bias of these alternatives to foundationalism.

Radical epistemologies and the concept of bias

A characteristic feature of much current methodological writing by qualitative researchers is the deployment of sceptical and relativist arguments. Thus, appeals to 'facts' (and not just to the 'brute facts' of foundationalism) and to 'findings' are sometimes met with accusations of positivism, and/or an insistence that there can be no grounds for claims to universal validity. To the extent that they continue to be used, such words are placed in scare quotes in order to distance the author from the foundationalism they are taken to imply (see Haack 1993: 16). It is argued that all accounts of the world reflect the social, ethnic, gendered, etc. position of the people who produced them. They are constructed on the basis of particular assumptions and purposes, and their truth or falsity can only be judged in terms of standards that are themselves social constructions, and therefore relative. Sometimes, what seems to be involved here is the accusation that accounts which claim universal validity are biased because, despite what they claim, their character reflects the social location of the researcher. But to formulate the claim that all accounts reflect their origins as 'all accounts are biased' is potentially misleading since, as we noted earlier, bias is a source or type of error, and 'error' only retains meaning by contrast with the possibility of truth.

The word 'truth' can, of course, be redefined in relativist terms, so that what

---

7 The philosophical differences involved here are not as great as is sometimes supposed. It is instructive that William James described his position as 'radical empiricism' (James 1912).
8 Instrumentalism is also sometimes appealed to. For a discussion, see Hammersley 1995a: 71–2.

is true becomes that which is taken to be true within some community whose members share a particular perspective. Returning to our bowls analogy, a relativist position seems to imply that the jack is wherever a group of bowls players agree to send their bowls. Here, 'error' and 'bias' represent deviations from the truth as consensually defined *within* a particular community. It is important to note, however, that such truths cannot be used to identify bias in the perspectives of members of *other* epistemic communities, at least not without self-contradiction. In this context, Kuhn's (1970) argument that different paradigms are *incommensurable* takes on its full meaning: it simply makes no sense, from a relativist point of view, for a member of one epistemic community to accuse members of another of being biased because their views deviate from what he or she takes to be true, rational, etc.[9]

According to relativists, we live in a world of multiple realities. But, of course, the argument that this is the nature of the world itself constitutes a claim to universal validity.[10] This self-undermining internal inconsistency of relativism has long been recognised, and one of its effects is that relativists tend to oscillate between undiscriminating tolerance and ideological dogmatism. At one level, in recognising multiple perspectives as each true in its own terms, relativism seems to be tolerant of everything. Indeed, there are no arguments within it that could exercise constraint on the proliferation of 'realities'; all that can be challenged are claims on the part of any perspective to *universal* truth. By contrast, *within* any community, relativism can be used to justify enforcement of the epistemic paradigm that is deemed appropriate to that community, allowing no scope for internal dissent about fundamentals. All challenges to the paradigm can be met by the response that this is what we as a community believe: 'if you do not believe it you are not one of us'. Indeed, given relativism, *there is no other possible response* to persistent dissent. And probably the most effective strategy for dissenters is to frame their disagreement in terms of the construction of a new paradigm, which then *itself* has immunity from external criticism; though its members are now barred from effective criticism of the epistemic community to which they previously belonged.[11]

Given these problems, it is rare for writers to stick consistently to relativism: other epistemological positions are frequently used to supplement it. One of the main ones is that which feminists refer to as standpoint epistemology. This

9 It might be possible to accuse them of bias in terms of the knowledge and procedures that prevail within their *own* communities, i.e. by internal critique; though such a challenge would always be open to the response that outsiders cannot understand the cultures of these communities.

10 *Epistemological relativism*, the idea that there are multiple realities, needs to be clearly distinguished from *cultural relativism*, the claim that there are multiple perspectives on, and in, the world. In these terms, we are cultural relativists: we believe that cultural and other kinds of diversity are an empirical fact of considerable importance. What we are rejecting is epistemological relativism.

11 For examples of arguments in favour of relativism in the context of social and educational research. see Smith 1989 and Guba 1992.

apparently provides a basis for retaining claims to universal validity while yet accepting the argument that the validity of all knowledge is relative to social location. This is achieved by arguing that one particular social location has unique access to the truth. Returning to our analogy with the game of bowls for the last time: according to standpoint epistemology, no straight-line route to the jack is possible, only a bowl with a certain kind of bias can make contact with the jack, given the configuration of obstacles surrounding it (these, of course, representing ideological barriers).

This standpoint approach is strongly modelled on Marxism and thereby on Hegelian philosophy. Hegel conceived of historical development as a process by which, through dialectical change, the distinction between subject and object, knower and known, was eventually overcome and true knowledge realised. And he claimed that, because the historical process had reached its final stage of development in his lifetime, he was in a position to achieve absolute knowledge of the world, in a way that no previous philosopher had been. At the same time, in his *Phenomenology*, discussing the dialectic between master and slave, he also provided a distinctive version of this philosophy of history whereby oppressed groups have insight into the nature of the world that is not available to their oppressors. Marx developed these ideas into a conception of the development of history as not yet complete, but which could be brought to completion by a proletarian revolution. He argued that since the working class suffer the most intense form of alienation under capitalism, they have a unique capacity to understand it and thereby to overthrow it. Feminists have adopted a similar position, but of course with women treated as the oppressed group occupying a standpoint that provides epistemologically privileged knowledge (Smith 1974 and 1987; Hartsock 1983; Harding 1983; Flax 1983).

Within standpoint epistemology there is scope for claims not just about truth but also about bias. However, these can be formulated in different ways. Bias could be seen as an inevitable feature only of the beliefs of those who *do not* occupy the standpoint position: their views of the world being necessarily ideological. Meanwhile, those who *do* occupy the standpoint would be viewed as not subject to bias, by virtue of their social location. Alternatively, along the lines of our formulation of the bowls analogy, it might be argued that the difference between those who do and do not have the right standpoint is the nature of the bias that their position supplies. Either way, both true and false standpoints are seen as social products, so that whether a knowledge claim is true or not is determined not by *if* it has been shaped by the personal and social characteristics of the researcher but by the *nature* of those characteristics.

This is an argument whose deficiencies were explored many years ago in the sociology of knowledge, where it was labelled 'the genetic fallacy' (see, for example, Hartung 1952 and Popper 1966: ch. 23). While standpoint epistemology appears both to allow recognition of the way in which the validity of all accounts of the world is determined by the socio-historical locations of those who produce them *and* to be able to justify claims to universal truth, this is an illusion. Indeed, the most developed version of this position, Hegelian epistemology, shares the same failing as relativism: to the extent that all accounts of the world are socio-historically located and are true or false in virtue of their location, the same must also be true of Hegel's own claim to stand at the end of History. There is no historically neutral or independent criterion by which the validity of his philosophy of history can be established. And it was precisely this feature that left open the possibility of others using the same historicist argument to claim that History would be realised at some different point in its development and in a different way, as in the case of both Marxists and feminists. But, of course, *their* arguments are also open to precisely the same challenge.

Put another way, the key question is: how is one to judge the validity of statements about the source of a knowledge claim? This cannot be done in terms of *their* sources without infinite regress. Both Hegel and Marx sought to avoid this by an appeal to logic or science. And, while not usually making *this* kind of appeal today, many critical researchers and feminists try to avoid the problem by adopting a weaker version of standpoint epistemology, one which allows for the possibility that the working class can be misled by the dominant ideology, or that some women may suffer from false consciousness. Indeed, the standpoint is sometimes treated as consciously adopted rather than as a perspective that is inherited from one's social position. In these weaker terms, no social position is seen as in itself providing access to valid knowledge; it only offers a *potential* for such knowledge. But, of course, this move effectively undercuts the standpoint argument because knowledge claims are no longer to be judged primarily in terms of their source but according to other considerations. The distinctiveness of standpoint epistemology as an alternative to foundationalism has disappeared. Like all other non-foundationalist positions, it now faces the problem of how to determine what is true and what is false. And bias, in its original sense, once again becomes a threat to validity that is universal, not restricted to those occupying the wrong standpoint.

As we have indicated, relativism and standpoint epistemology are rarely adopted in pure form. Indeed, what often happens is that they are used in an instrumental way. Sceptical or relativist arguments are applied selectively in order to critique some phenomenon or some view while other phenomena or views are kept safe from their corrosive effects. Similarly, standpoint epistemology is used to protect particular views through its capacity to disqualify critics on the grounds of their social characteristics. The intended aim of this instrumentalism is often to expose biases arising from the power of dominant groups in society. However, as we have tried to show, neither of these radical epistemological views can sustain a coherent conception of bias. And their selective use amounts to ontological gerrymandering (Woolgar and Pawluch 1985; Foster *et al.* 1996: ch. 1).

For the reasons outlined above, we take it that neither of the currently influential epistemological alternatives to foundationalism provides an adequate basis for reconstructing the concept of bias. So, how is the problem to be solved?

A non-foundationalist interpretation of 'bias'

Given the failure of foundationalism, and the weaknesses of radical alternatives to it, it is necessary to rethink the issues surrounding truth, objectivity and bias as these relate to social research. The remainder of our paper is intended to contribute to this as regards the last of these concepts. We noted earlier that while the failure of foundationalism had led to the adoption of radical epistemological views on the part of some philosophers of science, many adopted a more moderate approach, seeking to construct a position centred on a form of realism that avoids the problems affecting foundationalism. This is the sort of epistemological position that we will assume in attempting to make sense of the concept of bias.

We can only sketch that position here.[12] A first assumption is that the distinction between accounts and the phenomena they purport to represent is a viable one; in other words that researchers do not simply constitute or construct phenomena in the very activity of representing them, in the strong sense that phenomena have no existence independently of accounts of them. However, in formulating this distinction between accounts and the things they refer to, it is important not to think in terms of a contrast between language and reality. Rather, the distinction operates *within* reality, between particular signs and their referents. Language is part of reality, and so too are the authors of accounts: they cannot stand outside it. A second point is that researchers do not have direct contact with the character of the phenomena they seek to describe and explain. Their accounts are not simply impressions left on them by the world, nor are they logically derived from such impressions. So, in a weaker sense, researchers *do* constitute or construct the phenomena they describe, but under the constraint of not producing an account that is at odds with the evidence available. Furthermore, their accounts do not *reproduce* phenomena in linguistic terms. Rather, they represent them from one or another point of view, defined in terms of particular relevances.[13] The third point is that because we do not have direct contact with the nature of phenomena, we have to make *judgements* about the plausibility and credibility of evidence: about the extent to which it is compatible with, or implied by, what we currently take to be established knowledge; and the likelihood of error involved in its production. The final point is that, in academic research, the community of researchers plays a crucial role in subjecting knowledge claims to assessment on the basis of criteria of plausibility and credibility that are generally more sceptical than those operating in other areas of social life; in the sense that they err on the side of avoiding accepting as true what is in fact false.

An essential element of this communal assessment is consideration of potential threats to validity, that is of sources and types of error. This points to the

---

12 For fuller discussions of this realism and its implications for assessment of the validity of research findings, see Foster *et al.* 1996 and Hammersley 1998b and c.

13 This is not a form of relativism because what is presented from the different perspectives must be non-contradictory.

performative character of the concept of error. Its use involves a calling to account; or, to put it another way, a labelling of deviance. In common with the other terms in the network to which they belong, 'error' and 'bias' form part of an accountability system. Since the community of researchers have a responsibility to do their utmost to find and keep to the path that leads towards knowledge rather than error, the possibility that deviation from it has occurred is a continual preoccupation; the potential for deviation is endemic.

As we saw, for the extreme foundationalist, bias is a straightforward matter. It is systematic error produced by the influence of presuppositions whose validity is not given, and therefore is not known with certainty. And its elimination depends on avoiding all such presuppositions. It follows from this that hardly any distinction needs to be drawn between error in the process of research (dependence on false premises etc.) and erroneous findings. The first almost inevitably leads to the second; and the second kind of error is an absolutely reliable indicator of the first. Given this, both the findings of research and the behaviour of researchers can be described as biased without this causing confusion. Moreover, systematic error is seen as always a culpable matter, given that it is easily recognised and avoided.

The influence of foundationalism has also meant that a clear distinction is not always drawn between, on the one hand, a researcher having relevant commitments, for example particular political views, and, on the other, these commitments impacting negatively on the research process. Thus, researchers are sometimes described as biased simply because they have commitments pertaining to the field in which research is being carried out. This follows from the foundationalist idea that the researcher must strip away all his or her assumptions until bedrock is reached, and then build up true knowledge from that foundation solely by logical means.[14]

Once we abandon foundationalism, error becomes a much more difficult and complicated matter. Most obviously, where before we had a procedure by which it could in principle be identified easily and with certainty, this is now no longer the case: judgements about the appropriateness of methods and about the validity of conclusions must be recognised as fallible. Moreover, it is no longer simply a question of whether or not methodological rules have been followed. For the most part, such rules can be no more than guidelines, and considerable judgement is involved in applying them; for example in coming to conclusions about the cogency of the evidence for particular research claims. We also have to recognise that the link between procedural and outcome error is not as tight as foundationalism assumes. Above all, outcome error is not necessarily the product of culpable procedural error.

14 The original model here is, of course, Descartes, but this idea can be found across most kinds of foundationalism. For example, in the context of qualitative research methodology, see the recommendation of Glaser and Strauss (1967: 37) that researchers should not read the literature relevant to their research before they begin the process of analysis. This was abandoned in some later accounts of grounded theorising; see for instance Strauss 1987.

All this forces us to make a whole range of distinctions that foundationalism ignores (see Figure 6.1).

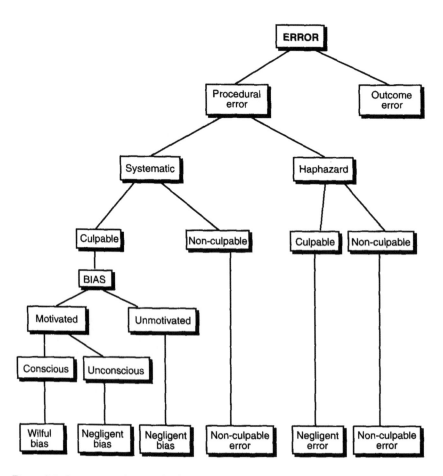

Figure 6.1 A conceptual network identifying types of error

In outlining this conceptual network, we concentrate on procedural rather than on outcome error; and we retain the distinction between systematic and haphazard error. However, the causation of systematic error is understood differently from foundationalism. Where for the foundationalist any reliance on presuppositions whose validity is not given must be avoided, such reliance is now seen as inevitable. In the course of enquiry about some matters, we necessarily take other matters for granted; and in the absence of a foundation of absolute givens these can only be matters about which we believe our knowledge to be sound but less than apodictic. If we did not make such assumptions, we would have no ground at all on which to stand, and we would lapse into a thoroughgoing scepticism.[15]

However, this procedural reliance on presuppositions whose validity is open to potential doubt does not necessarily lead to outcome error. Sometimes it will take us towards the truth rather than away from it. Judgements have to be made, then, about the validity of presuppositions, but in the absence of any prospect of absolute proof. As a result, the accountability system operating within research communities takes on an even more important role than it does under foundationalism.[16] Moreover, where previously procedural error was a matter of logic, it now becomes deviance from communal judgements about what is and is not reasonable behaviour in pursuit of knowledge in the relevant context, with these judgements being open to dispute and to subsequent revision.

As we saw, the distinction between culpable and non-culpable systematic error does not apply within foundationalism. However, it becomes very significant once we abandon that view. Given that all research necessarily relies on presuppositions, none of which can be established as valid beyond all possible doubt, we can never know for sure that a presupposition is leading us towards truth rather than away from it.[17] Colleagues can legitimately disagree, and any researcher may come to change his or her own assessment of the matter. Even more strikingly, what we know *now* often enables us to see how researchers of the past went wrong, *yet without necessarily implying that they should have known better*. And in the future others may have this advantage over us, even rejecting our judgements of our predecessors. The idea of the fully reflexive researcher is a myth. Indeed, it is of course the classic Cartesian myth: the idea that the truth, indeed the whole truth, is available to us here and now if only we can think clearly and logically. But, as we noted, it is not possible to question *all* one's assumptions at once, and questioning assumptions always involves costs as well as potential gains.

So, given that judgements must be made about which presuppositions are and are not reliable, both by researchers and by commentators on research, and that these judgements will change over time in light of evaluations of the progress of enquiry, we must recognise that there is always the potential for systematic error. Furthermore, some of that error will be non-culpable, in the sense that the researcher could not have known that what was being relied on

---

15 This is the gist of anti-Cartesian arguments, for example those developed by Peirce and Wittgenstein.

16 This has led one philosopher of science to argue that 'it is a mistake to assume that the objectivity of a science depends upon the objectivity of the scientist' (Popper 1976: 95). This is an exaggeration, it seems to us, since the operation of the research community in enforcing objectivity depends on the commitment of individual scientists to that ideal. Nevertheless, like Popper, we see the role of the research community as essential.

17 We leave aside the issue of whether false presuppositions may sometimes be functional and true ones dysfunctional!

was erroneous or dysfunctional, so that he or she was acting reasonably in the circumstances – despite reaching false conclusions. At the same time, some systematic error *will* be culpable, in that researchers are judged to have been in a position to recognise that an assumption on which they were relying had an unacceptable chance of being wrong and might therefore lead them astray. In other words, they can be judged to be culpable on the grounds that they did not take proper methodological precautions to avoid error, for example by assessing the relative validity of alternative interpretations.

In short, then, while the abandonment of foundationalism requires us to recognise that research will inevitably be affected by the personal and social characteristics of the researcher, and that this can be of positive value as well as a source of systematic error, it does not require us to give up the guiding principle of objectivity. Indeed, what is essential to research, on this view, is that its exclusive immediate goal is the production of knowledge. Of course, there are all sorts of reasons why people become researchers and persist in this occupation (for instance, to make the world a better place, to earn a living, etc.). Such motives for doing research can be legitimate. But, from our point of view here, once researchers are engaged in their work they must be primarily concerned with producing knowledge, not with achieving these other things. While they need to take account of ethical considerations that relate to other values, truth is the only value that constitutes the goal of research. And it follows from this that one form of systematic error can be motivated by the pursuit of other goals than knowledge; since this may lead to the collection, analysis and/or presentation of evidence in such a way as to bolster a predetermined conclusion related to those goals. This is the basis for our distinction between motivated and unmotivated systematic, culpable error (see Figure 6.1).

Within this framework we could define 'bias' in several different ways. We might, for example, restrict its meaning to systematic, culpable, motivated error. Alternatively, we could treat this as simply one form of bias, using the term to refer to all kinds of culpable, systematic error, or even to all kinds of systematic error. There seems little advantage in defining it as all systematic error, since this involves a duplication of terms, and there are other important distinctions to be made. Our own preference is to define 'bias' as systematic and culpable error; systematic error that the researcher should have been able to recognise and minimise, as judged either by the researcher him or herself (in retrospect) or by others. This then allows us to distinguish between motivated and unmotivated bias, according to whether or not it stems from other goals than the pursuit of knowledge.

It is worth noting that even motivated bias can take different forms. It can be conscious or unconscious, in that the researcher may be more or less aware that he or she is tailoring the inquiry to produce findings designed to serve other goals than knowledge. Here we can distinguish, in principle at least, between wilful and negligent bias. We can also differentiate biased modes of operation in terms of how they handle evidence. At one extreme there is the out-and-out propagandist who will misuse and even invent evidence in order to support some cause. At the other extreme is the advocate or lawyer who uses genuine evidence to make the best case possible for a preconceived conclusion, but within strict guidelines. We should perhaps emphasise that we are not suggesting that advocacy, and perhaps even propagandising, are never legitimate. Our point is simply that these are not appropriate orientations for a researcher engaged in enquiry, and that the reason for this is that they do not maximise the chances of discovering the truth about the matter concerned, which is the primary responsibility of the researcher.[18]

Conclusion

In this paper we have sought to clarify usage of the term 'bias'. We outlined the ambiguities that surround it and argued that these arise in part from the fact that there has been reliance on a foundationalist epistemology that is inadequate. We also argued that radical epistemological alternatives, such as relativism and standpoint theory, do not provide us with a viable substitute. The conclusion we drew was that some sort of non-foundationalist realism is essential, and we sketched what a theory of bias might look like in this context. This involved us in distinguishing among a variety of forms of error, and reserving the term 'bias' for culpable systematic error. Furthermore, we drew particular attention to that form of bias which is motivated by an active commitment to some other goal than the production of knowledge.

We would like to end by emphasising that our preoccupation with clarifying the meaning of 'bias' is not an idle one. It seems to us that we live in dangerous times for research. There are attempts outside of research communities, on the part of funders (including governments), to define the goal of research in terms that subordinate the pursuit of knowledge to other concerns. In Britain, this can be seen in the increasing contractual restrictions on research financed by Government departments, which seem to be designed to ensure that published findings will support current policy (Pettigrew 1994; Norris 1995; Bridges 1998). Equally significant is the growing emphasis in the pronouncements of funding agencies, such as the Economic and Social Research Council, on the role of 'users' in all aspects of research. At the very least, this looks like the thin end of a wedge.

At the same time, there is also much pressure among researchers themselves, in many areas, to define their goal in practical or political terms. We see this in the demands of some commentators on educational research that it should be designed to serve educational purposes (see Stenhouse 1975 and Bassey 1995).

18 For this reason, we are in disagreement with those who see advocacy as a central element of social enquiry (see Paine 1985), and with all who recommend that the goal of research should be more, or other, than the production of value-relevant knowledge. Of course, legal advocacy is concerned with discovering the truth, as a basis for dispensing justice. But this operates within a strictly controlled environment, in which a judge and jury are to come to a conclusion. This is very different from the way in which research communities operate.

We also find it in those forms of social research that are committed to 'emancipatory' political projects, for example to the fight against discrimination on grounds of sex, 'race', ethnicity, sexual orientation or disability (see Cameron *et al.* 1992; Oliver 1992; Back and Solomos 1993; Gitlin 1994). The radical epistemologies we have discussed are, of course, often closely associated with these projects.

To the extent that such developments amount to redefining the goal of enquiry as the promotion of some practical or political cause, we see them as sources of motivated bias, and believe that they must be resisted. They threaten to destroy the proper operation of social research communities on which the pursuit of social scientific knowledge necessarily depends. However, in the absence of a convincing, post-foundationalist understanding of the nature of error and bias in social enquiry, there can be little or no defence against these threats. Our work here is intended to contribute to the construction of just such a defence.

Bibliography

Abraham, G. (1993) 'Context and prejudice in Max Weber's thought', *History of the Human Sciences* 6(3): 1–17.

Adams, L. (1977) *Walter Lippmann*, Boston: Twayne/G.K. Hall.

Adorno, T.W. and Horkheimer, M. (1973) *Dialectic of Enlightenment*, London: Allen Lane (first published in German in 1947).

Allen, B. (1993) *Truth in Philosophy*, Cambridge, MA: Harvard University Press.

Altheide, D.L. and Johnson, J.M. (1994) 'Criteria for assessing interpretive validity in qualitative research', in N.K. Denzin and Y.S. Lincoln (eds) *Handbook of Qualitative Research*, Thousand Oaks, CA: Sage.

Althusser, L. (1971) *Lenin and Philosophy and Other Essays*, London: New Left Books (first published in French in 1971).

—— (1969) *For Marx*, London: Allen Lane (first published in French in 1966).

Ansell-Pearson, K. (1994) *An Introduction to Nietzsche as Political Thinker*, Cambridge: Cambridge University Press.

Antonio, R.J. and Glassman, R.M. (eds) (1985) *A Weber-Marx Dialogue*, Lawrence, KS: University of Kansas Press.

Aptheker, H. (1960) *The World of C. Wright Mills*, New York: Marzani and Munsell.

Aron, R. (1983) *The Committed Observer*, Chicago: Regnery.

—— (1969) *Marxism and the Existentialists*, New York: Harper & Row.

Avineri, S. (1968) *The Social and Political Thought of Karl Marx*, Cambridge: Cambridge University Press.

Babbie, E. (1989) *The Practice of Social Research* (fifth edition), Belmont, CA: Wadsworth.

Back, L. and Solomos, J. (1993) 'Doing research, writing politics, the dilemmas of political intervention in research on racism', *Economy and Society* 22(2): 178–99.

Ball, S. (1995) 'Intellectuals or technicians? The urgent role of theory in educational studies', *British Journal of Educational Studies* 43(3): 255–71.

Barker, M. (1981) *The New Racism*, London: Junction Books.

Barnes, B. (1974) *Scientific Knowledge and Sociological Theory*, London: Routledge.

Barone, T. (1994) 'On Kozol and Sartre and educational research as socially committed literature', *Review of Education/Pedagogy/Cultural Studies* 16(1): 93–102.

Bassey, M. (1995) *Creating Education through Research*, Newark: Kirklington Moor Press, in association with the British Educational Research Association.

Bateson, N. (1984) *Data Construction in Social Surveys*, London: Allen & Unwin.

Becker, H.S. (1994) 'Professional sociology: The case of C. Wright Mills', in R. Rist (ed.) *The Democratic Imagination: Dialogues on the Work of Irving Louis Horowitz*, New Brunswick, NJ: Transaction Books.

—— (1986) *Doing Things Together: Selected Papers*, Evanston, IL: Northwestern University Press.

—— (1982) *Art Worlds*, Berkeley: University of California Press.

—— (1974) 'Foreword', in H.A. Selby, *Zapotec Deviance: The Convergence of Folk and Modern Sociology*, Austin: University of Texas Press.

—— (1973) *Outsiders: Studies in the Sociology of Deviance* (second edition), New York: Free Press.

—— (1971) 'Reply to Riley's "Partisanship and objectivity"', *American Sociologist* 6, February, p. 13. Reprinted in G. Riley (ed.) (1974) *Values, Objectivity and the Social Sciences*, Reading, MA: Addison-Wesley.

—— (1970) *Sociological Work*, Chicago: Aldine.

—— (1967) 'Whose side are we on?', *Social Problems* 14: 239–47.

—— (1966) 'Introduction', in C.R. Shaw, *The Jack Roller* (Phoenix edition), Chicago, IL: University of Chicago Press.

—— (1964) 'Problems in the publication of field studies', in A.J. Vidich and M.R. Stein (eds) *Reflections on Community Studies*, New York: Wiley.

Becker, H.S. and Horowitz, I.L. (1972) 'Radical politics and sociological research: Observations on methodology and ideology', *American Journal of Sociology* 78(1): 48–66.

—— (1970) 'The culture of civility', *Transaction*, April, pp. 12–19.

Beetham, D. (1985) *Max Weber and the Theory of Modern Politics* (second edition), Cambridge: Polity Press.

Beiner, R.B. (1987) 'On the disunity of theory and practice', *Praxis International* 7(1): 25–34.

Bell, C. and Newby, H. (eds) (1977) *Doing Sociological Research*, London: Allen & Unwin.

Bell, D. (1980) *Sociological Journeys: Essays 1960–80*, London: Heinemann.

—— (1960) *The End of Ideology*, Glencoe, IL: Free Press.

Bellamy, R. (1992) 'Liberalism and nationalism in the thought of Max Weber', *History of European Ideas* 14(4): 499–507.

Ben-Tovim, G., Gabriel, J., Law, I. and Stredder, K. (1986) *The Local Politics of Race*, London: Macmillan.

Benda, J. (1927) *The Treason of the Intellectuals* (English translation, 1955), Boston, MA: Beacon Press.

Bennett, J. (1981) *Oral History and Delinquency: The Rhetoric of Criminology*, Chicago, IL: University of Chicago Press.

Berlin, I. (1990) *The Crooked Timber of Humanity*, London: John Murray.

—— (1981) 'Herzen and his memoirs', in *Against the Current: Essays in the History of Ideas*, Oxford: Oxford University Press.

—— (1969) *Four Essays on Liberty*, London: Oxford University Press.

Bernstein, R (1976) *The Restructuring of Social and Political Theory*, Oxford: Blackwell.

Blair, M. (1993) 'Review of Peter Foster: Policy and practice in multicultural and anti-racist education', *European Journal of Intercultural Studies* 2(3): 63–4.

Bloor, D. (1976) *Knowledge and Social Imagery*, London: Routledge.

Blum, A. (1970) 'The sociology of mental illness', in J.D. Douglas (ed.) (1970) *Deviance and Respectability*, New York: Basic Books.

Blumer, H. (1969) *Symbolic Interactionism*, Englewood Cliffs, NJ: Prentice Hall.

Bottomore, T.B. (1984) *The Frankfurt School*, London: Tavistock.
—— (1967) *Critics of Society*, London: Allen & Unwin.
Bottomore, T.B. and Rubel, M. (1956) *Karl Marx: Selected Writings on Sociology and Social Philosophy*, London: Watts.
Bridges, D. (1998) 'Research for sale: Moral market or moral maze', *British Educational Research Journal* 24(5): 593–607.
Brunton, R. (1996) 'The Hindmarsh Bridge: The credibility of Australian anthropology', *Anthropology Today* 12(4): 2–7.
Bruun, H.H. (1972) *Science, Values and Politics in Max Weber's Methodology*, Copenhagen: Munksgaard.
Bryant, C.G.A. (1985) *Positivism in Social Theory and Research*, London: Macmillan.
—— (1976) *Sociology in Action*, London: Allen & Unwin.
Bulmer, M. (1984) *The Chicago School of Sociology*, Chicago, IL: University of Chicago Press.
—— (1982) *The Uses of Social Research*, London: Allen & Unwin.
Cameron, D., Frazer, E., Harvey, P., Rampton, M and Richardson, K. (1992) *Researching Language: Issues of power and method*, London: Routledge.
Campbell, C. (1982) 'A dubious distinction? An inquiry into the value and use of Merton's concepts of manifest and latent function', *American Sociological Review* 47: 29–44.
Carey, J. (1975) *Sociology and Public Affairs: The Chicago School*, Beverly Hills, CA: Sage.
Carr, W. (1997) 'Philosophy and method in educational research', *Cambridge Journal of Education* 27(2): 203–9.
Carr, W. and Kemmis, S. (1986) *Becoming Critical*, London: Falmer.
Carr-Saunders, A.M. and Wilson, P.A. (1933) *The Professions*, Oxford: Oxford University Press.
Caute, D. (1970) *Fanon*, London: Fontana/Collins.
Chapoulie, J-M (1996) 'Everett Hughes and the Chicago tradition', *Sociological Theory* 14(1): 3–29.
Child, A. (1944) 'The problem of imputation resolved', *Ethics* LIV: 96–109.
Cleere, F. W. (1971) *The Intellectual as Change Agent in the Writings of C. Wright Mills*, unpub. Ph.D. thesis, University of Colorado.
Clifford, J. and Marcus, G. (eds) (1986) *Writing Culture*, Berkeley: University of California Press.
Cohen, G.A. (1982) 'Functional explanation, consequence explanation, and Marxism', *Inquiry* 25: 27–56.
—— (1978) *Karl Marx's Theory of History*, Oxford: Oxford University Press.
—— (1972) 'Karl Marx and the withering away of social science', *Philosophy and Public Affairs* 1(2): 182–203.
Coleman, J. (1972) *Policy Research in the Social Sciences*, Morrisstown, NJ: General Learning Press.
Collier, A. (1979) 'In defence of epistemology', in J. Mepham and D.-H. Ruben (eds) *Issues in Marxist Philosophy*, vol. III, Brighton: Harvester.
Condorcet, A-N de (1955) *Sketch for a Historical Picture of the Progress of the Human Mind* (English translation), New York: Noonday Press (first published in 1795).
Connolly, P. (1992) 'Playing it by the rules: The politics of research in "race" and education', *British Educational Research Journal* 18(2): 133–48.
Converse, J.M. and Schuman, H. (1974) *Conversations at Random: Survey Research as Interviewers See it*, New York: Wiley.

Conway, D. (1997) *Nietzsche and the Political*, London: Routledge.

Cooney, T. (1986) *The Rise of the New York Intellectuals*, Madison: University of Wisconsin Press.

Cressey, D. (1953) *Other People's Money*, New York: Free Press.

—— (1950) 'The criminal violation of financial trust', *American Sociological Review* 15: 738–43.

Curtis, J.E. and Petras, J.W. (eds) (1970) *The Sociology of Knowledge: A Reader*, London: Duckworth.

Dahrendorf, R. (1959) *Class and Class Conflict in Industrial Society*, London: Routledge & Kegan Paul.

Davies, M. (1995) *Childhood Sexual Abuse and the Construction of Identity: Healing Sylvia*, London: Taylor & Francis.

Davis, K. (1971) 'Sexual behavior', in R.K. Merton and R. Nisbet (eds) *Contemporary Social Problems*, third edition, New York: Harcourt Brace Jovanovich.

—— (1937) 'The sociology of prostitution', *American Sociological Review* 2: 744–55.

Debro, J. (1970) 'Interview with Howard S. Becker', *Issues in Criminology* 5(2): 159–79.

Denzin, N.K. (1990) 'Presidential address on "The Sociological Imagination"', *Sociological Quarterly* 31(1): 1–22.

—— (1989) *Interpretive Interactionism*, Newbury Park, CA: Sage.

Denzin, N.K. and Lincoln, Y.S. (1994) 'Introduction: Entering the field of qualitative research', in N.K. Denzin and Y.S. Lincoln (eds) *Handbook of Qualitative Research*, Thousand Oaks, CA: Sage.

Dewey, J. (1939) 'Theory of valuation', in O. Neurath, R. Carnap and C. Morris (eds) (1970) *Foundations of the Unity of Science: Towards an International Encyclopedia of Unified Science*, Vol. II, Chicago, IL: University of Chicago Press.

Dews, P. (1986) 'The *nouvelle philosophie* and Foucault', in M. Gane (ed.) *Towards a Critique of Foucault*, London: Routledge & Kegan Paul.

—— (1987) *Logics of Disintegration: Post-structuralist Thought and the Claims of Critical Theory*, London: Verso.

Dore, R.P. (1961) 'Function and cause', *American Sociological Review* 26: 843–53. Reprinted in N.J. Demerath and R.A. Peterson (eds) (1967) *System, Change, and Conflict*, New York: Free Press.

Douglas, J.D. (ed.) (1970) *Deviance and Respectability*, New York: Basic Books.

Douglass, R.B., Mara, G.R. and Richardson, H.S. (eds) (1988) *Liberalism and the Good*, New York: Routledge.

Downes, D. and Rock, P. (eds) (1979) *Deviant Interpretations*, Oxford: Martin Robertson.

Drew, D. and Gillborn, D. (1996) 'Hammersley and Gomm – A reply', *British Sociological Association Network Newsletter* 66, October, p.7.

Du Bois, B. (1983) 'Passionate scholarship: Notes on values, knowing, and method in feminist social science', in G. Bowles and R. Duelli-Klein (eds) *Theories of Women's Studies*, London: Routledge & Kegan Paul.

Dubin, S.C. (1983) 'The moral continuum of deviancy research: Chicago sociologists and the dance hall', *Urban Life* 12(1): 75–94.

Eden, R. (1987) 'Weber and Nietzsche: Questioning the liberation of social science from historicism', in W.J. Mommsen and J. Osterhammel (eds) *Max Weber and his Contemporaries*, London: Allen & Unwin.

Eisner, E. (1992) 'Objectivity in educational research', *Curriculum Inquiry* 22(1): 9–15.

Eldridge, J.T. (1983) *C. Wright Mills*, London: Tavistock.

Elliott, G. (1987) *Althusser: The Detour of Theory*, London: Verso.

Ember, M. (1985) 'Evidence and science in ethnography: Reflections on the Freeman-Mead controversy', *American Anthropologist* 87: 906–10.

Empson, W. (1930) *Seven Types of Ambiguity*, London: Chatto & Windus.

Erikson, K. T. (1966) *Wayward Puritans: a study in the sociology of deviance*, New York: Wiley.

—— (1964) 'Notes on the sociology of deviance', in H.S. Becker (ed.) *The Other Side*, New York: Free Press.

Factor, R. and Turner, S.P. (1977) 'The critique of positivist social science in Leo Strauss and Jürgen Habermas', *Sociological Analysis* VII(3): 185–206.

Fallding, H. (1963) 'Functional analysis in sociology', *American Sociological Review* 28: 5–13.

Fanon, F. (1965) *The Wretched of the Earth*, London: MacGibbon & Kee.

Fay, B. (1975) *Social Theory and Political Practice*, London: Allen & Unwin.

Fenton, N., Bryman, A., Deacon, D. with Birmingham, P. (1998) *Mediating Social Science*, London: Sage.

Finch, J. (1985) 'Social policy and education: Problems and possibilities of using qualitative research', in R.G. Burgess (ed.) *Issues in Educational Research: Qualitative Methods*, London: Falmer.

Fine, B. (1977) 'Labelling theory: An investigation into the sociological critique of deviance', *Economy and Society* 6: 166–93.

Fine, G.A. and Martin, D.D. (1990) 'A partisan view: Sarcasm, satire and irony as voices in Erving Goffman's *Asylums*', *Journal of Contemporary Ethnography* 19(1): 89–115.

Fine, M. (1994) 'Dis-stance and other stances: Negotiations of power inside feminist research', in A. Gitlin (ed.) (1994) *Power and Method: Political Activism in Educational Research*, New York: Routledge.

Fish, S. (1989) *Doing What Comes Naturally: Change, Rhetoric and the Practice of Theory in Literary and Legal Studies*, Oxford: Oxford University Press.

Flax, J. (1983) 'Political philosophy and the patriarchal unconscious: A psychoanalytic perspective on epistemology and metaphysics', in S. Harding and M.B. Hintikka (eds) *Discovering Reality: Feminist Perspectives on Epistemology, Metaphysics, Methodology and Philosophy of Science*, Dordrecht: Reidel.

Fleischmann, E. (1964) 'De Weber à Nietzsche', *Archives Européenes Sociologiques* V: 190–238.

Forster, M. (1989) *Hegel and Skepticism*, Cambridge, MA: Harvard University Press.

Foss, D. (1978) *The Value Controversy in Sociology*, San Francisco: Jossey-Bass.

Foster, P. (1993a) 'Teacher attitudes and Afro-Caribbean achievement', *Oxford Review of Education* 18(3): 269–82.

—— (1993b) 'Some problems in identifying racial/ethnic equality or inequality in schools', *British Journal of Sociology* 44(3): 519–35.

—— (1993c) 'Equal treatment and cultural difference in multi-ethnic schools: A critique of teacher ethnocentrism theory', *International Studies in the Sociology of Education* 2(1): 89–103.

—— (1993d) ' "Methodological purism" or "a defence against hype"? Critical readership in research on "race" and education', *New Community* 19(3): 547–52.

—— (1992) 'What are Connolly's rules? A reply to Paul Connolly', *British Educational Research Journal* 18(2): 149–54.

—— (1991) 'Cases still not proven: A reply to Cecile Wright', *British Educational Research Journal* 17(2): 165–70.

—— (1990a) *Policy and Practice in Multicultural and Anti-racist Education*, London: Routledge.

—— (1990b) 'Cases not proven: An evaluation of two studies of teacher racism', *British Educational Research Journal* 16(4): 335–48.

—— (1989) *Policy and Practice in Multicultural and Anti-racist Education*, unpublished Ph.D. thesis, Open University.

Foster, P., Gomm, R. and Hammersley, M. (1996) *Constructing Educational Research: An Assessment of Research on School Processes*, London: Falmer.

Foucault, M. (1977) 'Interview with Michel Foucault: Truth and power', English translation in C. Gordon (ed.) *Power/Knowledge*, New York: Pantheon Books.

Foucault, M. and Deleuze, G. (1972) 'Intellectuals and power', English translation in D.F. Bouchard (ed.) (1977) *M. Foucault: Language, Counter-Memory, Practice*, Oxford: Blackwell.

Freeman, D. (1983) *Margaret Mead and Samoa: The Making and Unmaking of an Anthropological Myth*, Cambridge, MA: Harvard University Press.

Galliher, J.F. (1995) 'Chicago's two worlds of deviance research: Whose side are they on?', in G.A. Fine (ed.) *A Second Chicago School? The Development of Postwar American Sociology*, Chicago, IL: University of Chicago Press.

Galston, W. (1991) *Liberal Purposes: Goods, Virtues, and Diversity in the Liberal State*, Cambridge: Cambridge University Press.

Gay, P. (1963) *The Party of Humanity*, London: Weidenfeld & Nicolson.

Geertz, C. (1964) 'Ideology as a cultural system', in D.E. Apter (ed.) *Ideology and Discontent*, New York: Free Press.

Gellner, E. (1974) *The Legitimation of Belief*, Cambridge: Cambridge University Press.

Gerth, H.H. and Mills, C.W. (eds) (1948) *From Max Weber: Essays in Sociology*, London: Routledge & Kegan Paul.

Gibbons, M., Limoges, C., Nowotny, H., Schwartzman, S., Scott, P. and Trow, M. (1994) *The New Production of Knowledge*, London: Sage.

Gilbert, A. (1981) *Marx's Politics*, Oxford: Martin Robertson.

Gillam, R. (1977/8) 'Richard Hofstadter, C. Wright Mills and the critical ideal', *The American Scholar*, Winter, pp. 69–85.

Gillborn, D. (1998) 'Racism and the politics of qualitative research: Learning from controversy and critique', in P. Connolly and B. Troyna (eds) *Researching Racism in Education: Policy, Theory and Practice*, Buckingham: Open University Press.

—— (1995) *Racism and Antiracism in Real Schools, Buckingham*, Buckingham: Open University Press.

—— (1993) 'Racism and the sociological imagination', paper presented at the British Sociological Association Annual Conference, University of Essex.

Gillborn, D. and Drew, D. (1993) 'The politics of research: Some observations on "methodological purity"', *New Community* 19(2): 354–60.

—— (1992) '"Race", class and school effects', *New Community* 18(4): 551–65.

Gillborn, D. and Gipps, C. (1996) *Recent Research on the Achievements of Ethnic Minority Pupils* (London, Office for Standards in Education, London: HMSO).

Gillies, D. (1993) *Philosophy of Science in the Twentieth Century*, Oxford: Blackwell.

Gitlin, A. (ed.) (1994) *Power and Method: Political Activism in Educational Research*, New York: Routledge.

Gitlin, A. and Russell, R. (1994) 'Alternative methodologies and the research context', in A. Gitlin (ed.) *Power and Method: Political Activism in Educational Research*, New York: Routledge.

Gitlin, A., Siegel, M. and Boru, K. (1989) 'The politics of method: From leftist ethnography to educative research', *International Journal of Qualitative Studies in Education* 2(3): 237–53.

Glaser, B. and Strauss, A. (1967) *The Discovery of Grounded Theory*, Chicago, IL: Aldine.

Glass, D. (1950) 'The application of social research', *British Journal of Sociology* 1: 17–30.

Goffman, E. (1961) *Asylums*, Garden City, NY: Anchor.

Goldsen, R.K. (1964) 'Mills and the profession of sociology', in I. L. Horowitz (ed.)*The New Sociology: Essays in Social Science and Social Theory in Honor of C. Wright Mills*, New York: Oxford University Press.

Goldthorpe, J.H. (1964) 'Social stratification in industrial society', in P. Halmos (ed.) *The Development of Industrial Society*, Sociological Review Monograph No. 8, University of Keele.

Gomm, R. (1995) 'Strong claims, weak evidence: A response to Troyna's "Ethnicity and the organisation of learning"', *Educational Research* 37(1): 79–86.

—— (1993) 'Figuring out ethnic equity', *British Educational Research Journal* 19(2): 149–65.

—— (1976) 'Discovering anthropology', *Cambridge Anthropology* 3(1): 61–70.

Goode, E. and Ben Yehuda, N. (1994) *Moral Panics: The Social Construction of Deviance*, Oxford: Blackwell.

Gouldner, A.W. (1973a) *For Sociology*, Harmondsworth: Penguin.

—— (1973b) Foreword to I. Taylor, P. Walton and J. Young (1973) *The New Criminology: For a Social Theory of Deviance*, London: Routledge & Kegan Paul.

—— (1970) *The Coming Crisis of Western Sociology*, New York: Basic Books.

—— (1968) 'The sociologist as partisan', *American Sociologist*, May, pp. 103–16.

—— (1967) *Enter Plato: Classical Greece and the Origins of Social Theory*, London: Routledge & Kegan Paul.

—— (1965) 'Explorations in applied social science', in A.W. Gouldner and S.M. Miller (eds) *Applied Sociology*, New York: Free Press.

—— (1962) 'Anti-minotaur: The myth of a value-free sociology', *Social Problems* 9: 199–213.

—— (1954) *Patterns of Industrial Bureaucracy*, Glencoe, IL: Free Press.

Grant, J. (1987) 'I feel therefore I am: A critique of female experience as a basis for feminist epistemology', *Women and Politics* 7(3): 99–114.

Gray, J. (1995) *Berlin*, London: Fontana.

Grice, P. (1989) *Studies in the Way of Words*, Cambridge, MA: Harvard University Press.

Griffiths, M. (1998) *Educational Research for Social Justice: Getting off the Fence*, Buckingham: Open University Press.

Guba, E. (1992) 'Relativism', *Curriculum Inquiry* 22(1): 17–23.

Haack, S. (1993) 'Science "from a feminist perspective"', *Philosophy* 67: 5–18.

Habermas, J. (1987) *The Philosophical Discourse of Modernity*, Cambridge: Polity Press (first published in German in 1985.)

—— (1982) 'A reply to my critics', in J.B. Thompson and D. Held (eds) *Habermas: Critical Debates*, London: Macmillan.

Halfpenny, P (1983) 'A refutation of historical materialism?', *Social Science Information* 22(1): 61–87.

Hamilton, P. (1974) *Knowledge and Social Structure*, London: Routledge & Kegan Paul.

Hammersley, M. (1999a) 'Not bricolage but boatbuilding', *Journal of Contemporary Ethnography* 28(6).

—— (1999b) 'Varieties of research: A typology', unpublished.

—— (1998a) 'Partisanship and credibility: The case of anti-racist educational research', in P. Connolly and B. Troyna (eds) *Researching "Race" in Educational Settings*, Buckingham: Open University Press.

—— (1998b) 'Get real! A defence of realism', in P. Hodkinson (ed.) *The Nature of Educational Research: Realism, Relativism or Postmodernism?*, Manchester: Manchester Metropolitan University.

—— (1998c) 'Why research into practice does not go: Some questions about the enlightenment model', unpublished.

—— (1998d) 'The profession of a "methodological purist"?', in G. Walford (ed.) *Doing Research about Education*, London: Falmer.

—— (1998e) 'How not to engage in academic discussion: A commentary on Gillborn's "Racism and Research"', unpublished.

—— (1998f) *Reading Ethnographic Research: A Critical Guide*, second edition, London: Longman.

—— (1997) 'Educational inequalities', Block 5, Unit 1, Open University Course EU208 *Exploring Educational Issues*, Milton Keynes: Open University.

—— (1995a) *The Politics of Social Research*, London: Sage.

—— (1995b) 'Beyond reason? A response to Barry Troyna', unpublished.

—— (1993) 'On methodological purism', *British Educational Research Journal* 19(4): 339–41.

—— (1992a) *What's Wrong with Ethnography?*, London: Routledge.

—— (1992b) 'A response to Barry Troyna's "Children, 'race' and racism: the limitations of research and policy"', *British Journal of Educational Studies* 40(2): 174–7.

—— (1989) *The Dilemma of Qualitative Method*, London: Routledge.

Hammersley, M. and Atkinson, P. (1995) *Ethnography: Principles in Practice*, second edition, London: Routledge.

Hammersley, M. and Gomm, R. (1997a) 'A response to Romm', *Sociological Research Online* 2(4). Available at: http://www.socresonline.org.uk/socresonline/2/4/7.html.

—— (1997b) 'A response to Temple on bias and feminism', unpublished.

—— (1993) 'A response to Gillborn and Drew on "race", class and school effects', *New Community* 19(2): 348–53.

Hampson, C. (1968) *The Enlightenment*, Harmondsworth: Penguin.

Hanson, N.R. (1958) *Patterns of Discovery*, Cambridge: Cambridge University Press.

Harding, S. (1992) 'After the neutrality ideal: Science, politics and "strong objectivity"', *Social Research* 59(3): 568–87.

—— (ed.) (1987) *Feminism and Methodology*, Bloomington, IN: Indiana University Press.

—— (1986) *The Science Question in Feminism*, Milton Keynes: Open University Press.

—— (1983) 'Why has the sex/gender system become visible only now?', in S. Harding and M.B. Hintikka (eds) *Discovering Reality: Feminist Perspectives on Epistemology, Metaphysics, Methodology and Philosophy of Science*, Dordrecht: Reidel.

Harding, S. and Hintikka, M.B. (eds) (1983) *Discovering Reality: Feminist Perspectives on Epistemology, Metaphysics, Methodology and Philosophy of Science*, Dordrecht: Reidel.

Hargreaves, D.H. (1996) 'Teaching as a research-based profession: Possibilities and prospects', Teacher Training Agency Annual Lecture 1996.

Harrison, M. (1985) *TV News: Whose Bias?*, Hermitage, Berks: Policy Journals.

Hartsock, N. (1983) 'The feminist standpoint', in S. Harding and M.B. Hintikka (eds) *Discovering Reality: Feminist Perspectives on Epistemology, Metaphysics, Methodology and Philosophy of Science*, Dordrecht: Reidel.

Hartung, F. (1952) 'Problems of the sociology of knowledge', *Philosophy of Science* XIX: 17–32. Reprinted in J.E. Curtis and J.W. Petras (eds) (1970) *The Sociology of Knowledge: A Reader*, London: Duckworth.

Harvey, L. (1987) *Myths of the Chicago School*, Aldershot: Gower.

Hawkesworth, M.E. (1989) 'Knowers, knowing, known: Feminist theory and claims of truth', *Signs* 14(3): 533–57.

Hazard, P. (1964) *The European Mind 1680–1715*, Harmondsworth: Penguin (first published in French in 1935).

Hegel, G.W.F. (1977) *Phenomenology of Spirit*, Oxford: Oxford University Press (first published in German in 1807).

Hekman, S. (1986) *Hermeneutics and the Sociology of Knowledge*, Cambridge: Polity.

Helm, P. (1971) 'Manifest and latent functions', *Philosophical Quarterly* 21: 51–60.

Hennis, W. (1994) 'The meaning of "Wertfreiheit": On the background and motives of Max Weber's "postulate"', *Sociological Theory* 12(2): 113–25.

—— (1988) *Max Weber: Essays in Reconstruction*, London: Allen & Unwin.

—— (1987) 'A science of man: Max Weber and the political economy of the German Historical School', in W.J. Mommsen, and J. Osterhammel (eds) *Max Weber and his Contemporaries*, London: Allen & Unwin.

Herskovits, M. (1972) *Cultural Relativism: Perspectives in Cultural Pluralism*, New York: Random House.

Hoare, Q. and Nowell Smith, G. (eds) (1971) *Selections from the Prison Notebooks of Antonio Gramsci*, London: Lawrence & Wishart.

Holstein, J.A. and Miller, G. (eds) (1993) *Reconsidering Social Constructionism: Debates in Social Problems Theory*, New York: Aldine de Gruyter.

Horowitz, I.L. (1983) *C. Wright Mills: An American Utopian*, New York: Free Press.

—— (ed.) (1964) *The New Sociology: Essays in Social Science and Social Theory in Honor of C. Wright Mills*, New York: Oxford University Press.

—— (1963) 'An introduction to C. Wright Mills', in C.W. Mills, *Power, Politics and People: The Collected Essays of C. Wright Mills*, ed. I.L. Horowitz, New York: Oxford University Press.

Howe, I. (1966) 'On the career and example of C. Wright Mills', in *Steady Work: Essays in the Politics of Democratic Radicalism*, New York: Harcourt, Brace & World.

Hughes, E.C. (1971) 'Sociologists and the public', in E.C. Hughes, *The Sociological Eye*, Chicago, IL: Aldine-Atherton.

Hughes, H.M. (1961) *The Fantastic Lodge*, Greenwich, CT: Fawcett.

Hughes, H.S. (1959) *Consciousness and Society*, London: MacGibbon & Kee.

Humphries, B. and Truman, C. (eds) (1994) *Re-thinking Social Research: Anti-discriminatory Approaches in Research Methodology*, Aldershot: Avebury.

Huntingdon, S.P. (1996) *The Clash of Civilisations*, New York: Simon & Schuster.

Ibarra, P.R. and Kitsuse, J.I. (1993) 'Vernacular constituents of moral discourse: An interactionist proposal for the study of social problems', in J.A. Holstein and G. Miller (eds) *Reconsidering Social Constructionism*, New York: Aldine de Gruyter.

James, W. (1912) *Essays on Radical Empiricism*, New York: Longmans Green.

Jay, M. (1973) *The Dialectical Imagination*, Berkeley: University of California Press.

Jayaratne, T. Epstein (1983) 'The value of quantitative methodology for feminist research', in G. Bowles and R. Duelli Klein (eds) *Theories of Women's Studies*, London: Routledge & Kegan Paul.

Jennings, J. (1997) 'Of treason, blindness and silence: Dilemmas of the intellectual in modern France', in J. Jennings and A. Kemp-Welch (eds) *Intellectuals in Politics: From the Dreyfus Affair to Salman Rushdie*, London: Routledge.

Johnson, H.G. (1968) 'International trade: Theory', in D. Sills (ed.) *International Encyclopedia of the Social Sciences*, London: Macmillan.

Johnson, T. J. (1972) *Professions and Power*, London: Macmillan.

Joll, J. (1977) *Gramsci*, London: Fontana/Collins.

Kamin, L. (1977) *The Science and Politics of I.Q.*, Harmondsworth: Penguin.

Kaufmann, F. (1949) 'Ethical neutrality', *Social Research* 16: 344–52.

Kemmis, S. (1988) 'Action research', in J.P. Keeves (ed.) *Educational Research Methodology and Measurement: An International Handbook*, Oxford: Pergamon.

Kennedy, P. (1993) *Preparing for the Twenty First Century*, New York: HarperCollins.

Khilnani, S. (1993) *Arguing Revolution: The Intellectual Left in Postwar France*, New Haven, CT: Yale University Press.

Kidder, L. and Judd, C.M. (1986) *Research Methods in Social Relation*, fifth edition, New York: CBS Publishing.

Kirkham, R.L. (1992) *Theories of Truth*, Cambridge, MA: MIT Press.

Kisiel, T. (1971) 'Introduction', in W. Marx, *Heidegger and the Tradition*, Evanston, IL: Northwestern University Press.

Kitsuse, J.I. (1962) 'Societal reaction to deviant behavior: Problems of theory and method', *Social Problems* 9: 247–56.

Kitsuse, J.I. and Spector, M. (1973) 'Toward a sociology of social problems', *Social Problems* 20: 407–19.

Kogan, M. (1971) *The Politics of Education*, Harmondsworth: Penguin.

Kolakowski, L. (1978) *Main Currents in Marxism*, vol. 1, Oxford: Oxford University Press.

Krieger, L. (1957) *The German Idea of Freedom*, Chicago, IL: University of Chicago Press.

Kristeva, J. (1977) 'A new type of intellectual: The dissident', *Tel Quel* 74: 3–8. Translation in T. Moi (ed.) (1986) *The Kristeva Reader*, Oxford: Blackwell.

Kuhn, T.S. (1970) *The Structure of Scientific Revolutions*, second edition, Chicago, IL: University of Chicago Press.

Kvale, S. (ed.) (1989) *Validity Issues in Qualitative Research*, Stockholm: Studentlitteratur.

Larmore, C. (1996) *The Morality of Modernity*, Cambridge: Cambridge University Press.

—— (1987) *Patterns of Moral Complexity*, Cambridge: Cambridge University Press.

Lather, P. (1993) 'Fertile obsession: Validity after poststructuralism', *Sociological Quarterly* 34(4): 673–93.

—— (1986a) 'Issues of validity in openly ideological research', *Interchange* 17(4): 63–84.

—— (1986b) 'Research as praxis', *Harvard Educational Review* 56(3): 257–77.

Latour, B. (1987) *Science in Action*, Buckingham: Open University Press.

Law, J. and Lodge, P. (1984) *Science for Social Scientists*, London: Macmillan.

Lemert, E. (1974) 'Beyond Mead: the societal reaction to deviance', *Social Problems* 21(4): 457–68.

—— (1967) *Human Deviance, Social Problems, and Social Control*, Englewood Cliffs, NJ: Prentice-Hall.

Lenzo, K. (1995) 'Validity and self-reflexivity meet poststructualism: Scientific ethos and the transgressive self', *Educational Researcher* 24(4), May, pp. 17–23.

Levine, J.H. (1993) *Exceptions are the Rule: An Inquiry into Methods in the Social Sciences*, Boulder, CO: Westview Press.

Lichtheim, G. (1970) *Lukacs*, London: Fontana.

—— (1967) *The Concept of Ideology and Other Essays*, New York: Vintage.

—— (1966) *Marxism in Modern France*, New York: Columbia University Press.

Lieberson, S. (1985) *Making it Count: The Improvement of Social Research and Theory*, Berkeley: University of California Press.

Lincoln, Y.S. (1990) 'Toward a categorical imperative for qualitative research', in E. Eisner and A. Peshkin (eds) *Qualitative Inquiry in Education*, New York: Teachers' College Press.

Lindenfeld, D.F. (1997) *The Practical Imagination: The German Sciences of State in the Nineteenth Century*, Chicago, IL: University of Chicago Press.

Lipset, S.M. (1960) *Political Man*, London: Heinemann

Lorber, J. (1967) 'Deviance as performance: The case of illness', *Social Problems* 14: 302–10.

Löwith, K. (1960) *Max Weber and Karl Marx* (English translation 1982), London: Allen & Unwin.

Lubasz, H. (1969) 'Marx's conception of the revolutionary proletariat', *Praxis* 5(1–2): 288–90.

Lukes, S. (1982) 'Of gods and demons: Habermas and practical reason', in J.B. Thompson and D. Held (eds) *Habermas: Critical Debates*, London: Macmillan.

—— (1973) *Emile Durkheim*, London: Allen Lane.

Lyotard, J-F. (1993) *Political Writings*, London: UCL Press.

—— (1988) *The Differend: Phrases in Dispute*, Manchester: Manchester University Press (first published in French in 1981).

Mac an Ghaill, M. (1991) '*Young, Gifted and Black*: Methodological reflections of a teacher/researcher', in G. Walford (ed.) *Doing Educational Research*, London: Routledge & Kegan Paul.

—— (1988) *Young, Gifted and Black*, Milton Keynes: Open University Press.

McCarthy, T. (1978) *Marx and the Proletariat*, Westport, CT: Greenwood Press.

Macdonald, D. (1974) *Discriminations*, New York: Grossman.

McHugh, P. (1970) 'A commonsense conception of deviance', in J.D. Douglas (ed.) (1970) *Deviance and Respectability*, New York: Basic Books.

McHugh, P., Raffel, S., Foss, D. and Blum, A. (1974) *On the Beginning of Social Inquiry*, London: Routledge & Kegan Paul.

MacIntyre, A. (1990) *Three Rival Versions of Moral Enquiry: Encyclopaedia, Genealogy, Tradition*, London: Duckworth.

—— (1971) 'The end of ideology and the end of the end of ideology', in A. MacIntyre, *Against the Self-Images of the Age*, London: Duckworth.

Mackintosh, N.J. (ed.) (1995) *Cyril Burt: Fraud or Framed*, Oxford: Oxford University Press.

McLellan, D. (1973) *Karl Marx: His Life and Thought*, London: Macmillan.

Marcus, G. (1994) 'What comes (just) after "post"?', in N.K. Denzin and Y.S. Lincoln (eds) *Handbook of Qualitative Research*, Thousand Oaks, CA: Sage.

Marshall, T.H. (1963) *Sociology at the Crossroads and Other Essays*, London: Longmans.

Martindale, D (1975) *Prominent Sociologists since World War II*, Columbus, OH: Merrill.

Matthews, E.C. (1996) *Twentieth Century French Philosophy*, Oxford: Oxford University Press.

Matza, D. (1969) *Becoming Deviant*, Englewood Cliffs, NJ: Prentice-Hall.

—— (1964) *Delinquency and Drift*, New York: Wiley.

Mead, M. (1928) *Coming of Age in Samoa*, New York: Morrow, 1961.

Merleau-Ponty, M. (1973) *Adventures of the Dialectic*, Evanston, IL: Northwestern University Press.

Merrington, J. (1977) 'Theory and practice in Gramsci's Marxism', in *New Left Review* (ed.) *Western Marxism: A Critical Reader*, London: New Left Review.

Merton, R.K. (1982) 'Genesis and growth of a friendship', *Theory and Society* 11(6): 915–38.

—— (1973) *The Sociology of Science*, Chicago, IL: University of Chicago Press.

—— (1968) *Social Theory and Social Structure*, New York: Free Press.

Michelfelder, D.P. and Palmer, R.E. (eds) (1989) *Dialogue and Deconstruction: The Gadamer-Derrida Encounter*, Albany: State University of New York Press.

Mies, M. (1991) 'Women's research or feminist research? The debate surrounding feminist science and methodology', in M.M. Fonow and J.A. Cook (eds) *Beyond Methodology: Feminist Scholarship as Lived Research*, Bloomington, IN: Indiana University Press.

—— (1983) 'Towards a methodology for feminist research', in G. Bowles and R. Duelli Klein (eds) *Theories of Women's Studies*, London: Routledge & Kegan Paul.

Miliband, R. (1969) *The State in Capitalist Society*, London: Weidenfeld & Nicolson.

Miller, J. (1986) 'Democracy and the intellectual: C. Wright Mills reconsidered', *Salmagundi* 70–1: 82–101.

Mills, C.W. (1965) *Sociology and Pragmatism: The Higher Learning in America*, New York: Oxford University Press.

—— (1963) *Power, Politics and People: The Collected Essays of C. Wright Mills*, ed. I.L. Horowitz, New York: Oxford University Press.

—— (1960a) (ed.) *Images of Man: The Classic Tradition in Sociological Thinking*, New York: George Braziller.

—— (1960b) *Listen Yankee: The Revolution in Cuba*, New York: McGraw Hill.

—— (1960c) 'Letter to the New Left', *New Left Review* 5, September–October.

—— (1959a) 'On intellectual craftsmanship', in L. Gross (ed.) *Symposium on Sociological Theory*, Evanston, IL: Peterson and Co.

—— (1959b) *The Sociological Imagination*, New York: Oxford University Press.

—— (1958) *The Causes of World War Three*, New York: Simon & Schuster.

—— (1956) *The Power Elite*, New York: Oxford.

—— (1955) 'On knowledge and power', *Dissent* 2(3): 201–12.

—— (1951) *White Collar: The American Middle Classes*, New York: Oxford University Press.

—— (1948a) *The New Men of Power: America's Labor Leaders*, New York: Harcourt, Brace & Co.

—— (1948b) 'Edward Alexander Westermarck and the application of ethnographic methods to marriage and morals', in H.E. Barnes (ed.) *An Introduction to the History of Sociology*, Chicago, IL: University of Chicago Press.

—— (1944) 'The social role of the intellectual', *Politics* 1(3). Reprinted in I.L. Horowitz (ed.) *Power, Politics and People: The Collected Essays of C. Wright Mills*, New York: Oxford University Press.

Mishler, E. (1990) 'Validation in inquiry-guided research', *Harvard Education Review* 60(4): 415–42.

Moerman, M. (1968) 'Being Lue: Uses and abuses of ethnic identification', in J. Helm (ed.) *Essays on the Problem of the Tribe*, Seattle: University of Washington Press.

Mommsen, W.J. (1989) *The Political and Social Theory of Max Weber*, Cambridge: Polity Press.

—— (1984) *Max Weber and German Politics 1890–1920*, Chicago, IL: University of Chicago Press (first published in German in 1959; second edition 1974).

Moore, M., Beazely, S. and Maelzer, J. (1998) *Researching Disability Issues*, Buckingham: Open University Press.

Nehamas, A. (1985) *Nietzsche: Life as Literature*, Cambridge, MA: Harvard University Press.

Nietzsche, F. (1874) 'On the uses and disadvantages of history for life', in *Untimely Meditations*, Cambridge: Cambridge University Press, 1993.

Norris, N. (1995) 'Contracts, control and evaluation', *Journal of Education Policy* 10(3): 271–85.

Oakes, G. (1988) *Weber and Rickert: Concept Formation in the Cultural Sciences*, Cambridge, MA: MIT Press.

Oakes, M. (1986) *Statistical Inference: A Commentary for the Social and Behavioural Sciences*, Chichester: Wiley.

Okrent, M. (1993) 'The truth, the whole truth, and nothing but the truth', *Inquiry* 36(4): 381–404.

Oliver, M. (1992) 'Changing the social relations of research production?', *Disability, Handicap and Society* 7(2): 101–14.

O'Malley, J. (1994) *Marx: Early Political Writings*, Cambridge: Cambridge University Press.

Oppenheim, A.N. (1966) *Questionnaire Design and Attitude Measurement*, London: Heinemann.

Paechter, C. (1996) 'Power, knowledge and the confessional in qualitative research', *Discourse: studies in the politics of education* 17(1): 75–84.

Paine, R. (ed.) (1985) *Advocacy and Anthropology: First Encounters*, St John's Institute of Social and Economic Research: Memorial University of Newfoundland.

Parsons, T. (1967) *Sociological Theory and Modern Society*, New York: Free Press.

—— (1959) 'An approach to the sociology of knowledge', from *Transactions of the Fourth World Congress of Sociology at Stresa, Italy*, vol. IV, September 1959. Reprinted in T. Parsons (1967) *Sociological Theory and Modern Society*, New York: Free Press.

Patai, D. (1994) 'When method becomes power', in A. Gitlin (ed.) (1994) *Power and Method: Political Activism in Educational Research*, New York: Routledge.

Patai, D. and Koertge, N. (1994) *Professing Feminism: Cautionary Tales from the Strange World of Women's Studies*, New York: Basic Books.

Pateman, T. (1981) 'Linguistics as a branch of critical theory', *University of East Anglia Papers in Linguistics* 14/15: 1–29.

Pawson, R. (1989) *A Measure for Measures: A Manifesto for Empirical Sociology*, London: Routledge.

Pettigrew, M. (1994) 'Coming to terms with research: The contract business', in D. Halpin and B. Troyna (eds) *Researching Education Policy: Ethical and Methodological Issues*, London: Falmer.

Phillips, D.C. (1990) 'Subjectivity and objectivity: An objective inquiry', in E. Eisner and A. Peshkin (eds) *Qualitative Inquiry: The Continuing Debate*, New York: Teachers' College Press.

Pippin, R.B. (1991) *Modernism as a Philosophical Problem*, Oxford: Blackwell.

Polanyi, M. (1958) *Personal Knowledge*, London: Routledge & Kegan Paul.

Pollner, M. (1974) 'Sociological and common-sense models of the labelling process', in R. Turner (ed.) *Ethnomethodology*, Harmondsworth: Penguin.

Polsky, N. (1967) 'Research method, morality and criminality', in *Hustlers, Beats and Others*, Chicago, IL: Aldine.

Popkin, R.H. (1979) *The History of Scepticism from Erasmus to Spinoza*, Berkeley: University of California Press.

Popper, K. R. (1976) 'The logic of the sciences', in T.W. Adorno, H. Albert, R. Dahrendorf, J. Habermas, H. Pilot and K.R. Popper, *The Positivist Dispute in German Sociology*, London: Heinemann.

—— (1966) *The Open Society and its Enemies*, vol. II, London: Routledge & Kegan Paul.

—— (1959) *The Logic of Scientific Discovery*, London: Hutchinson.

Porter, R. (1997) *The Greatest Benefit to Mankind: A Medical History of Humanity from Antiquity to the Present*, London, HarperCollins.

Press, H. (1978) *C. Wright Mills*, Boston, MA: Twayne.

Proctor, R.N. (1991) *Value-Free Science?*, Cambridge, MA: Harvard University Press.

Prokopczuk, C. (1980) *Truth and Reality in Marx and Hegel*, Amherst, MA: University of Massachusetts Press.

Punch, M. (1994) 'Politics and ethics in qualitative research', in N.K. Denzin and Y.S. Lincoln (eds) *Handbook of Qualitative Research*, Thousand Oaks, CA: Sage.

Rabinbach, A. (1994) 'Heidegger's *Letter on Humanism* as text and event', *New German Critique* 62: 3–38.

Ragin, C. (1987) *The Comparative Method: Moving Beyond Qualitative and Quantitative Strategies*, Berkeley: University of California Press.

Rains, P. (1975) 'Imputations of deviance: A retrospective essay on the labeling perspective', *Social Problems* 23: 1–11.

Ray, M.B. (1961) 'Abstinence cycles and heroin addicts', *Social Problems* 9(2): 132–40.

Reader, K. (1995) *Regis Debray: A Critical Introduction*, London: Pluto Press.

Ricoeur, P. (1970) *Freud and Philosophy: An Essay on Interpretation*, New Haven, CT: Yale University Press.

Riley, G. (1974a) 'Partisanship and objectivity in the social sciences', in G. Riley (ed.) *Values, Objectivity and the Social Sciences*, Reading, MA: Addison-Wesley.

—— (1974b) 'Comments on Howard Becker's "Reply"', in G. Riley (ed.) *Objectivity and the Social Sciences*, Reading, MA: Addison-Wesley.

Ringer, F. (1969) *The Decline of the German Mandarins*, Cambridge, MA: Harvard University Press.

Rock, P. (1979) *The Making of Symbolic Interactionism*, London: Macmillan.

Roman, L.G. and Apple, M.W. (1989) 'Is naturalism a move away from positivism? Materialist and feminist approaches to subjectivity in ethnographic research', in E. Eisner and A. Peshkin (eds) *Qualitative Inquiry: The Continuing Debate*, New York: Teachers' College Press.

Romm, N. (1997) 'Becoming more accountable: A comment on Hammersley and Gomm', *Sociological Research Online* 2(3). Available at: http://www.socresonline.org.uk/socresonline/2/3/2.html.

Rorty, R. (1991) 'Introduction: Antirepresentationalism, ethnocentrism and liberalism', in *Objectivism, Relativism and Truth*, Cambridge: Cambridge University Press.

Rosenthal, R. (1976) *Expectation Effects in Behavioral Research*, New York: Wiley.

Rosenthal, R. and Rosnow, R. (eds) (1969) *Artifact in Behavioral Research*, New York: Academic Press.

Roth, G. (1993) 'Between cosmopolitanism and ethnocentrism: Max Weber in the "nineties"', *Telos* 96: 148–62.

Roth, M. (1988) *Knowing and History: Appropriations of Hegel in Twentieth Century France*, Ithaca, NY: Cornell University Press.

Rowe, J.H. (1965) 'The renaissance foundations of anthropology', *American Anthropologist* 67: 1–20.

Rule, J.B. (1978) *Insight and Social Betterment*, New York: Oxford University Press.

Runciman, W.G. (1963) 'Karl Marx and Max Weber', in *Social Science and Political Theory*, Cambridge: Cambridge University Press.

Ryan, A. (1995) *John Dewey and the High Tide of American Liberalism*, New York: W.W. Norton.

Sandel, M. (ed.) (1984) *Liberalism and its Critics*, New York: New York University Press.

Sartre, J-P. (1957) *Existentialism and Humanism*, London: Methuen (first published in French in 1946).

Schalk, D.L. (1979) *The Spectrum of Political Engagement*, Princeton, NJ: Princeton University Press.

Schuman, H. (1982) 'Artifacts are in the mind of the beholder', *American Sociologist* 17(1): 21–8.

Schur, E.M. (1973) *Radical Non-Intervention: Rethinking the Delinquency Problem*, Englewood Cliffs, NJ: Prentice-Hall.

Scimecca, J. A. (1977) *The Sociological Theory of C. Wright Mills*, Port Washington, NY: Kennikat Press.

Scott, A. (1995) 'Value freedom and intellectual autonomy', *History of the Human Sciences* 8(3): 69–88.

Shapiro, W. (1978) 'The Nietzschean Roots of Max Weber's Social Science', unpublished Ph.D. thesis, Cornell University.

Sharlin, A.N. (1974) 'Max Weber and the origins of value-free social science', *Archiv Europ Sociolog* XV: 337–53.

Sharrock, W.W. (1974) 'On owning knowledge', in R. Turner (ed.) *Ethnomethodology*, Harmondsworth: Penguin.

Sharrock, W.W. and Anderson, D.C. (1981) 'Language, thought and reality, again', *Sociology* 15(2): 287–93.

Shils, E. (1980) 'Social inquiry and the autonomy of the private sphere', in E. Shils, *The Calling of Sociology*, Chicago, IL: University of Chicago Press.

—— (1960) 'Imaginary sociology: Review of C. Wright Mills' "The Sociological Imagination"', *Encounter* 14: 77–81.

—— (1955) 'The end of ideology', *Encounter* 5: 52–8.

Silverman, D. (1985) *Qualitative Methodology and Sociology*, Aldershot: Gower.

Simirenko, A. (ed.) (1967) *Soviet Sociology*, London: Routledge & Kegan Paul.

Simon, J. (1975) 'Sociology, "new directions", and comprehensive schooling', *Forum: For the Discussion of New Trends in Education* 17(1): 8–14.

Simon, W. (1963) *European Positivism in the Nineteenth Century*, Ithaca, NY: Cornell University Press.

Siraj-Blatchford, I. (1994) *Praxis Makes Perfect: Critical Educational Research for Social Justice*, Ticknall, Derby: Education Now Books.

Skinner, Q. (1981) *Machiavelli*, Oxford: Oxford University Press.

Sluga, H. (1993) *Heidegger's Crisis: Philosophy and Politics in Nazi Germany*, Cambridge, MA: Harvard University Press.

Smith, D.E. (1987) *The Everyday World as Problematic: A Feminist Sociology*, Milton Keynes: Open University Press.

—— (1974) 'Women's perspective as a radical critique of sociology', *Sociological Inquiry* 44: 7–13.

Smith, J.K. (1989) *The Nature of Social and Educational Inquiry*, Norwood, NJ: Ablex.

Solomos, J. and Back, L. (1995) *Race, Politics and Social Change*, London: Routledge.

Spector, M. (1976) 'Labeling theory in Social Problems: A young journal launches a new theory', *Social Problems* 24: 69–75.

Spector, M. and Kitsuse, J.I. (1977) *Constructing Social Problems*, Menlo Park, CA: Cummings.

Spitzer, S.P. and Denzin, N.K. (ed.) (1968) *The Mental Patient*, New York: McGraw Hill.

Stammer, O. (ed.) (1971) *Max Weber and Sociology Today*, Oxford: Blackwell.

Stanley, L. and Wise, S. (1983) *Breaking Out: Feminist Consciousness and Feminist Research*, London: Routledge & Kegan Paul.

Stavenhagen, R. (1971) 'Decolonializing applied social sciences', *Human Organization* 30(4): 333–44.

Stenhouse, L. (1975) *An Introduction to Curriculum Research and Development*, London: Heinemann.

Stojanovic, S. (1973) *Between Ideals and Reality: A Critique of Socialism and its Future*, New York: Oxford University Press (first published in Polish in 1969).

Strauss, A.L. (1987) *Qualitative Analysis for Social Scientists*, Cambridge: Cambridge University Press.

Strauss, L. (1975) 'The three waves of modernity', in H. Gildin (ed.) *Political Philosophy: Six Essays by Leo Strauss*, Indianapolis, IN: Bobbs-Merrill.

Suppe, F. (ed.) (1954) *The Structure of Scientific Theories*. Chicago: University of Illinois Press.

Sykes, G.M. and Matza, D. (1957) 'Techniques of neutralization: A theory of delin-quency', *American Sociological Review* 22: 664–70.

Szasz, T. (1971) *The Manufacture of Madness*, London: Routledge & Kegan Paul.

Taylor, I. and Walton, P. (1972) 'Values in deviancy theory and society', *British Journal of Sociology* 21: 362–74.

Taylor, I., Walton, P. and Young, J. (1973) *The New Criminology: For a Social Theory of Deviance*, London: Routledge & Kegan Paul.

Taylor, K. (1975) *Henri Saint-Simon (1760–1825): Selected Writings on Science, Industry and Social Organisation*, London: Croom Helm.

Temple, B. (1997) ' "Collegial accountability" and bias: The solution or the problem?', *Sociological Research Online* 2(4). Available at: http://www.socresonline.org.uk/socresonline/2/4/8.html.

Tierney, W.G. (1994) 'On method and hope', in A. Gitlin (ed.) (1994) *Power and Method: Political Activism in Educational Research*, New York: Routledge.

Toulmin, S. (1953) *The Philosophy of Science*, London: Hutchinson.

Tribe, K. (1988) 'Introduction', in W. Hennis, *Max Weber: Essays in Reconstruction*, London: Allen & Unwin.

Triplett, T. (1987) 'Rorty's critique of foundationalism', *Philosophical Studies* 52: 115–29.

Troyna, B. (1995) 'Beyond reasonable doubt? Researching 'race' in educational settings', *Oxford Review of Education* 21(4): 395–408.

—— (1994) 'Reforms, research and being reflexive about being reflective', in D. Halpin and B. Troyna (eds) *Researching Education Policy*, London: Falmer.

—— (1993) 'Underachiever or misunderstood? A reply to Roger Gomm', *British Educational Research Journal* 19(2): 167–74.

—— (1991) 'Children, "race" and racism: The limitations of research and policy', *British Journal of Educational Studies* 39(4): 425–36.

Troyna, B. and Carrington, B. (1989) 'Whose side are we on? Ethical dilemmas in research on "race" and education', in R.G. Burgess (ed.) *Ethics in Educational Research*, Lewes: Falmer.

Tumin, M. (1965) 'The functional approach to social problems', *Social Problems* 12: 379–88.

Turner, S.P. and Factor, R. (1984) *Max Weber and the Dispute over Reason and Value: A Study in Philosophy, Ethics and Politics*, London: Routledge & Kegan Paul.

Uebel, T.E. (1996) 'Conventions in the *Aufbau*', *British Journal of History of Philosophy* 4(2): 381–97.

Verhoeven, J. (1993) 'An interview with Erving Goffman, 1980', *Research in Language and Social Interaction* 26(3): 317–48.

Vincent, C. (1998) 'Barry Troyna: A dissenting voice', in P. Sikes and F. Rizvi (eds) *Researching Race and Social Justice in Education: Essays in Honour of Barry Troyna*, Stoke on Trent: Trentham Books.

Walzer, M. (1983) 'The politics of Michel Foucault', *Dissent*, fall, pp. 481–90.

Warnke, G. (1987) *Gadamer: Hermeneutics, Tradition and Reason*, Cambridge: Polity Press.

—— (1984) 'Hermeneutics and the social sciences: A Gadamerian critique of Rorty', *Inquiry* 28: 339–57.

Weber, M. (1980) 'The national state and economic policy (Freiburg address)', *Economy and Society* 9(4): 420–49. Address given in 1895.

—— (1949) *The Methodology of the Social Sciences*, New York: Free Press.

—— (1948) 'Science as a vocation', in H.H. Gerth and C.W. Mills (eds) *From Max Weber*, London: Routledge (first published in German in 1919).

White, A.R. (1970) *Truth*, London: Macmillan.

Whiteside, K.H. (1988) *Merleau-Ponty and the Foundations of an Existential Politics*, Princeton, NJ: Princeton University Press.

Whitty, G. (1977) 'Sociology and the problem of radical educational change: Notes towards a reconceptualisation of the "new" sociology of education', in M.F.D. Young and G. Whitty (eds) *Society, State, and Schooling*, Ringmer: Falmer Press.

Williams, M. (1995) 'Contextualism', in R. Audi (ed.) *The Cambridge Dictionary of Philosophy*, Cambridge, Cambridge University Press.

—— (1991) *Unnatural Doubts: Epistemological Realism and the Basis of Scepticism*, Oxford: Blackwell.

—— (1976) *Keywords: A Vocabulary of Culture and Society*, London: Fontana.

Wilson, E. (1931) *Axel's Castle*, New York: Scribner (London: Fontana, 1961).

Wittgenstein, L. (1969) *On Certainty*, Oxford: Blackwell.

Wolcott, H. F. (1990) 'On seeking – and rejecting – validity in qualitative research', in E.W. Eisner and A. Peshkin (eds) *Qualitative Inquiry in Education: The Continuing Debate*, New York: Teachers' College Press.

Wood, A. (1991) 'Marx against morality', in P. Singer (ed.) *A Companion to Ethics*, Oxford: Blackwell.

Woolgar, S. (1988) *Science: The Very Idea*, London: Routledge.

Woolgar, S. and Pawluch, D. (1985) 'Ontological gerrymandering: The anatomy of social problems' explanations', *Social Problems* 32(3): 314–27.

Wright, C. (1991) 'Comments in reply to the article by P. Foster', *British Educational Research Journal* 16(4): 351–5.

Young, J. (1970) 'The zoo-keepers of deviance', *Catalyst* 5: 38–46.

Young, M.F.D. (1973) 'Taking sides against the probable: Problems of relativism and commitment in teaching and the sociology of knowledge', *Educational Review* 25: 210–22.

Zarb, G. (1992) 'On the road to Damascus: First steps towards changing the relations of disability research production', *Disability, Handicap and Society* 7(2): 125–38.

Index